Some Main Things
Essays on Contemporary American Poetry

SOME MAIN THINGS
Essays on Contemporary American Poetry

Chard deNiord

MADHAT PRESS
CHESHIRE, MASSACHUSETTS

MadHat Press
MadHat Incorporated
PO Box 422, Cheshire, MA 01225

Copyright © 2025 Chard deNiord
All rights reserved

The Library of Congress has assigned
this edition a Control Number of
2025946109

ISBN 978-1-968422-05-9 (paperback)

Cover image: *Foster the Light* by Liz Hawkes deNiord
Book design by MadHat Press

www.madhat-press.com

First Printing
Printed in the United States of America

for Liz Hawkes deNiord, without whose patience, encouragement, and wise advice I would never have completed this book

*I am a man who, sauntering along without fully stopping, turns
   a casual look upon you and then averts his face,
Leaving it to you to prove and define it,
Expecting the main things from you.*

—Walt Whitman, "Poets to Come"

Table of Contents

Foreword	xiii
Preface	xvii
Can Poetry Save America?	3
The Place Where You Lie: James Wright's "To the Muse"	13
"But They Have Dwindled": Wordsworth's "Resolution and Independence" as a Modern-Day Cautionary Tale	19
He Who Remembers His Shoes: Charles Simic	25
On Poetry: Looking out From a Poem's Second-Story Window	35
For Each Ecstatic Moment: Impossibility, Unknowing and the Lyric	39
Suspense, Suspension, and the Sublime in the Poetry of Robert Frost	57
That Odor, That Other: On Louise Glück's "Mock Orange" and Beyond	71
The Nature of Voice	79
The Other	91
A Tribute to the Current	95
Sad Friend	103
The Teasing Corner of Oblivion: On the Career and Poetry of Ruth Stone	111
Swimming in the Drowned River of Contemporary American Poetry	117
Like a Book at Evening Beautiful but Untrue, Like a Book on Rising Beautiful and True	123
The Tradition of Resistance and Independence in Contemporary Poetry	133
Getting It Right	141
Silence Amidst the Crowd: Philip Levine's "The Simple Truth" and "Call It Music"	151
The Poetic "Engine" in Flannery O'Connor's Fiction	161
The Sublime Irony of Nothing and the Divine Imagination	169
"Back to My Ohio": The Life and Poetry of James Wright	185
Blurred Lines: Some Thoughts on Hybrid, Liminal, and Prose Poetry	195
Lone Strikers: Some Thoughts on the Legacy of Poetry in Vermont	211
What Do You Think?: Some Thoughts on Reading and Teaching Poetry	215
Acknowledgments	223
Works Cited	225
About the Author	233

Foreword

Chard deNiord has compiled a lifetime of dazzling insights into the foundation and practice of contemporary poetry. This book is an erudite initiation for the student, a guide for the perplexed, and a mystery voyage for the practiced reader.

DeNiord's prose is charged with what poems aspire to: "negative capability," the ability to remain radically open to a world which will never know us. These essays thrill to the joy of exploration rather than the thud of judgment. Henri Michaux said that "the will is the death of art," and we all know critical prose that demonstrates its own expertise while leaving its subjects flattened, emptied of the unsayable. DeNiord stands with Walt Whitman, who wrote, "Not to-day is to justify me and answer for what I am." These essays burn with the fierce life and questioning itch of their subjects.

American poetry is born under a fire sign: the flame of transcendence. "Every thought is also a prison; every heaven is also a prison. Therefore we love the poet," Ralph Waldo Emerson wrote. In the early years of the republic, Emerson wanted not just beauty but liberation—the poet "unlocks our chains, and admits us to a new scene." Liberation from the nightmare past of one-man rule and authoritarianism, no doubt, but also from the dead weight of the past on the psyche, from internalized hierarchies, from the determinisms that seduce us to live our lives imprisoned in self-reinforcing monologues.

It's no light thing to work in a tradition which is also an anti-tradition. Our spiritual parents, Walt Whitman and Emily Dickinson, were both iconoclasts, more by nature than design. They walked fearlessly with no guides. Their goals were utterly different. Without a master narrative, American poetry became, in Louis Simpson's words, "a shark that can digest a shoe"—able to absorb influences like haiku, the ghazal, the blues, pop culture, and remain true to itself: because its identity is volatile. Eclecticism is powerful. A generation ago, the poet Larry Levis described the Mexican workers on his father's farm singing their enigmatic songs "Amapola," "Jalisco," "No Te Rajes." Now we have poets like Rigoberto González and Eduardo Correale who can give us the Chicano experience from the inside, in contemporary verse. Joy Harjo can show us our own landscape from the vantage point of "a conquered people."

How do you negotiate a tradition that goes deep, survives the winter of public disrespect, and yet negates itself to renew itself, generation after generation? DeNiord's lens is parallax and his focus is sharp. He's interested in the daily practice and bedrock ethics of the artist rather than the theoretical aura. Always he engages in intimate dialogue with the text, the syntax, even the breath. We get the taste of the source, the vulnerability and uniqueness of the human voice.

Poetry is elusive. You'll find some beautifully eclectic intuitions of its essence throughout these essays: Lucille Clifton says, "I'm a carpenter, and I follow the carpenter's rule." Wallace Stephens anticipates "the intensest rendezvous." Donald Hall claims, "Poetry is a device for saying something and taking it back at the same time." Emily Dickinson writes, "Nothing is the force / that renovates the World." Robert Frost says, "Poetry is a way of taking life by the throat." Robert Bly asks the poet to let "the wolf into the house." Keats writes that "the poet has no identity ... the identity of everyone in the room begins to press on me that I am in very little time annihilated." William Blake asserts that wisdom emanates from Hell.

Ruth Stone remembers that, even as a child, she would hear a poem coming toward her from "across the universe." An elder in Plato's Phaedo dialogue confides, "I composed these poems ... because I wanted to test the meaning of certain dreams I had." Samuel Johnson claims that the poet must "disregard present laws and opinions, and rise to general and transcendent truths." Louise Glück says that "authenticity, in the poem, is not produced by sincerity." Nazim Hikmet advises, "you must live with great seriousness / like a squirrel, for example." William Stafford writes that "there is a spry little animal / the color of ink that wiggles through / perils and comforts, but never stays, / and while you whistle it along new paths / it always makes an inspired escape." A personal favorite is Jack Gilbert's remark: "I don't trust myself.... I don't want to become that person, that performer, that figure who can intoxicate his audience."

These aren't just aphorisms. DeNiord takes you under the surface and shows you how these credos and aspirations play out in the actual lives of the practitioners. A poet himself, deNiord can give you insight into the texture of poetic life, not just the epiphanies. In evocations of Ruth Stone's struggles, or Robert Lowell's difficult relationship with Elizabeth Bishop, you'll find an understanding of the challenge of living according to standards you alone set for yourself, standards that may be meaningless to your peers and family, while still allowing yourself to experience the relatedness from which poems spring.

Then there's deNiord's own eloquence. His response to D. H. Lawrence's "Bavarian Gentians" has the mythic zing of the original text, guiding the reader down slippery steps to the psyche. DeNiord can respond to a text like a virtuoso interpreting a score, rather than a cryptographer cracking a code. Witness the passages of sustained prose lyricism that are deNiord's alone. Vision flights like "The Sublime Irony of Nothing and the Divine Imagination" or "Electric Poetics" are as volatile as poems, mining metaphor and the power of the unspoken to transcend their own premises.

Poetry is a naked art. It requires only a pencil stub and the back of a utility bill. Or a twig for scratching in the dust. It's solitary, riddled with silences—between lines, between stanzas. DeNiord writes, "Like Eros, it was born poor and has remained so to keep its blessing." Poetry stands helpless before the final questions and may take on their power. Why do we love and destroy? How can we understand the night sky and still be tongue-tied before death?

This book is inscribed with that power, that mystery.

—D. Nurkse

Preface

This collection of essays represents four decades of thinking and writing about the poetry of eleven eminent American poets who have played influential roles in my own development as a poet and teacher during my career as a high school, college, and graduate school teacher. Their poetry drew me first to what W. H. Auden called great poetry's enduring hallmark, namely "memorable speech." I wasn't always conscious of how their influence, advice, and company were informing my poetry until I started writing these essays and reviews. While essay-writing has taken valuable time away from my creative writing, it has contributed invaluably to my "self-delighting, self-appeasing, self-affrighting" (John Keats) study of poetry in general from my high school days when I became particularly fascinated with the poetry of Catullus, Horace, and Robert Frost, whose classical lyrical economy inspired me to write my own poems. Why I turned in college and graduate school to writing essays remains a mystery as I didn't at first excel at writing them.

Writing these essays has provided a literary echo chamber in which I've overheard myself far more objectively and clearly than if I hadn't thought and written about them, creating, as Philip Larkin writes in his poem "Talking In Bed," "a unique distance from isolation." I am deeply grateful for this distance when I achieve it, despite the often agonizing process of finding "the right words in the right order."

I cannot thank enough those who have mentored and encouraged me over the years to keep writing, particularly Edwin Custer, Gerald Stern, Marvin Bell, Jorie Graham, Ed Ochester, Jack Gilbert, Maxine Kumin, Linda Gregg, Thomas Lux, Philip Levine, my New Haven neighbor Harold Bloom, Bruce Smith, and most of all my wife, Liz Hawkes deNiord, who has endured my long writing absences over the years with grace and saintly patience.

Some Main Things

Can Poetry Save America?

Czeslaw Miłosz, the Polish poet and Nobel laureate who became a US citizen in 1970, published a poem titled "Dedication" in 1946 in which he wrote, "What is poetry which does not save / Nations or people? / A connivance with official lies." In acknowledging poetry as an art with the power to save nations, Miłosz contradicts the claim that fellow poet W. H. Auden, a dual citizen of the United States and England and a cultural spokesman of his age, made in his 1938 elegy for W. B. Yeats—namely, that "poetry makes nothing happen." Poets are famous for contradicting themselves, but their contradictions often contain paradoxes born of the rich complexities of human experience, or as Walt Whitman claimed, "multitudes." The best poets in every nation divine the double nature of truth in memorable language, capturing the alloyed relations between joy and sorrow, victory and defeat, power and helplessness. I think Miłosz and Auden would, given the legacy of poetry's political efficacy and witness throughout history, most likely agree more than disagree about poetry's double nature as a redemptive and elegiac literary force.

History supports both Miłosz's and Auden's claims, for it is true that poetry has failed to prevent wars and atrocities, but it's also true that poetry has served as a vital witness to oppression in its truth-telling in both fictive and literal ways. In the political darkness of the 1930s no poetry halted Hitler's racist war machine. Even if one acknowledges Miłosz's belief in poetry's inherent power to save nations, such a statement seems preposterous as a political claim. So, why do poets and lovers of poetry continue to quote Miłosz's famous line about poetry's nation-saving ability? What exactly are poetry's nation-saving powers? Miłosz fails to mention any of them specifically in his poem "Dedication."

Poetry is a transformational language with the capacity to issue passports to its readers for entering transcendent realms of awareness; where strange associations make striking new sense, where unlike things coalesce in figurative magic; where minuscule details turn into immense particulars; where "language means more and sounds better" (Charles Wright), where language finds form and verbal music, where language ends and silence begins, where the sayable defers to the unsayable. It's no coincidence that the language in two definitive American documents—the Declaration of Independence and the Gettysburg Address—flows with a verbal economy that expresses truths Thomas Jefferson called "self-evident." These two prose poems fly under the radar of poetry as manifesto and speech-writing respectively, but it shouldn't be that difficult or strange for Americans to read similarly essential language as complements to these two documents. Walt Whitman's "Song of Myself," Anna Akhmatova's "Requiem," Wallace Stevens's "The Final Soliloquy of the Interior Paramour," Galway Kinnell's "The Avenue Bearing the Initial of Christ into the New World," Paul Celan's "Death Fugue," Nazim Hikmet's "On Living," Miklos Radnoti's "Letter to My Wife," the anonymously composed Gilgamesh, Adrienne Rich's "Atlas of a Difficult World," Adam Zagajewski's "Try to Praise the Mutilated World," Philip Levine's "The Mercy," Carolyn Forché's "The Boatman," Vijay Seshadri's "Trailing Clouds of Glory," David Tomas Martinez's "The Only Mexican," Natasha Trethewey's "The Age of Reason," Wislawa Szymborska's "Hunger Camp at Jasko," and Mahmoud Darwish's "In Jerusalem" merely begin a list of poems that could serve as primers for a much longer list of potentially nation-saving verses.

The first thing democracy requires is also the first thing poetry requires, which is imagination. Without it, it is impossible to envision a state or country where the genius of its people thrives in both personal and political freedom. Like democracy, poetry is an ongoing experiment that tests its readers ability to "get the meanings of poems" which convey "the main things" (Walt Whitman) in every new age. One of the main things, if not the main thing, that gets lost in demagoguery is a citizen's recognition of the other as one's self. "The most sublime act is to set another before you," wrote William Blake in *The Marriage of Heaven and Hell*. The poet finds a way via a transpersonal speaker to cross over from self to neighbor, self to stranger. In her poem "In the Waiting Room," Elizabeth Bishop wrote in the voice of her six-year-old self: "But I felt: you are an *I*, you are an *Elizabeth*, / you are one of *them*. / *Why* should you be one, too?" And so are we all "one of them, too," but only if we exercise our imagination in acts that are both artistic and social, intellectual and compassionate, discerning and fearless. Such spiritual transport is human and thereby nation-saving business.

Poetry as well as fiction serves as a literary vehicle for transporting its readers across the transom of self to other where one discovers that she is "one [of them], too." The poet Mary Szybist captured this transformative quality of "the other" that is necessary for what John Keats called "soul-making" in her acceptance speech at the National Book Awards ceremony in 2013:

> Sometimes, when I find myself in a dark place, I lose all taste for poetry. If it cannot do what I want it to do, if it cannot restore those I have lost, then why bother with it at all? There's plenty that poetry cannot do, but the miracle, of course, is how much it can do, how much it *does* do. So often I think I know myself, only to discover in a poem a difference, an otherness that resonates, where I find myself, as Wallace Stevens once put it, "more truly and more strange." It is what some describe as soul-making. I count myself among them. I think often of the words of Paul Connolly, who said, "I believe it is not arguing well, but speaking differently that changes a culture." Poetry is the place where speaking differently is the most prevalent. Speaking differently is what I aspire to....

Inherent in the transpersonal act of "speaking differently" as a poet lies the same intellectual challenge of imagining the lives and work of others, which is the social calculus of democracy. Walt Whitman celebrates this as his first order of democratic business as a poet. He views this poetic challenge as a necessary intellectual exercise in the second canto of his sublime manifesto, "Song of Myself," where he poses these questions to his reader:

> Have you practiced so long to learn to read?
> Have you felt so proud to get at the meaning of poems?

In questioning his fellow citizens about their capacity to possess the intellectual readiness for reading poetry, he invites them to "practice" learning to read, rather than merely exhorting them to do so. He knew that the only way for a person to establish a proud sense of intellectual and emotional ownership of the corrective truth that poetry conveys is for them to "get" poetry's meaning on their own, to possess it proudly as both an intellectual and affective gift.

As a disseminator of poetic meanings in the landscape of American life, Whitman started simply with "songs" that celebrated the sundry voices of his fellow citizens:

> The varied carols I hear,
> Those of mechanics, each one singing his as it should be blithe
>   and strong,
> The carpenter singing his as he measures his plank or beam,
> The mason singing his as he makes ready for work, or leaves off
>   work,
> The boatman singing what belongs to him in his boat, the deck-
>   hand singing   on the steamboat deck
> ...
> The delicious singing of the mother, or of the young wife at work,
>   or of the   girl sewing or washing,
> Each singing what belongs to him or her and to none else ...

This music of immense particulars annealed what Whitman believed was an indefatigable human metal that comprises the undergirding of the nation's democratic principles. The corporate genius of America's body politic renewed itself, he maintained, with nonlegislative principles that were inherently sublime if fragile, prompting him to draft his own secular beatitudes:

> Love the earth and sun and the animals, despise riches, give alms to everyone that asks, stand up for the stupid and crazy, devote your

income and labor to others, hate tyrants, argue not concerning God, have patience and indulgence toward the people, take off your hat to nothing known or unknown, or to any man or number of men—go freely with powerful uneducated persons, and with the young, and with the mothers of families—re-examine all you have been told in school or church or in any book, and dismiss whatever insults your own soul; and your very flesh shall be a great poem, and have the richest fluency, not only in its words, but in the silent lines of its lips and face, and between the lashes of your eyes, and in every motion and joint of your body.

The poetic nation-saving medicine that Miłosz proposes originates from a creative assertion of freedom that militates against demagoguery, an act for which myriad poets have died and suffered. Carolyn Forché's anthology *Against Forgetting: Twentieth-Century Poetry of Witness* is full of such poets whose work shames chicanery, elegizes martyrs, bears witness to injustice, speaks truth to power, makes new.

But poets don't write with the self-conscious intent to save nations. They write to write, usually after being "hurt into poetry," as Auden said Yeats was by "mad Ireland." The best muse is always less political than poetical, but occasionally both, as in the cases of Walt Whitman, W. H. Auden, Czeslaw Miłosz—poets who are gifted as both poets and prophets. As with Esteban, the handsome dead giant in Gabriel García Márquez's parable, "The Handsomest Drowned Man in the World," beauty possesses the power to change people and, in that act of changing, save them as well. In Márquez's story, the townspeople don't recognize Esteban at first as beautiful; in fact, they call him a "big boob" since they imagine him breaking chairs and hitting his head on door beams. But soon they come to appreciate his good looks and fall in love with him, exactly as new readers of poetry do in the figurative sense. Márquez captures the magic of poetry in the ironic but passive effect that Esteban has on the townspeople's imagination. He describes it this way in a paragraph that could be a prose poem at the end of the story following Esteban's funeral:

> They knew everything would be different from then on, that their houses would have wider doors, higher ceilings, and stronger

floors so that Esteban's memory could go everywhere without bumping into beams and so that no one in the future would dare whisper the big boob finally died, too bad, the handsome fool has finally died, because they were going to paint their house fronts gay colors to make Esteban's memory eternal and they were going to break their backs digging for springs among the stones and planting flowers on the cliffs so that in future years at dawn the passengers on great liners would awaken, suffocated by the smell of gardens on the high seas, and the captain would have to come down from the bridge in his dress uniform, with his astrolabe, his pole star, and his row of war medals and, pointing to the promontory of roses on the horizon, he would say in fourteen languages, look there, where the wind is so peaceful now that it's gone to sleep beneath the beds, over there, where the sun's so bright that the sunflowers don't know which way to turn, yes, over there, that's Esteban's village.[1]

Poetry is that body which lies beautiful but hidden in the open before the reader, the village, the nation, appearing strange and even off-putting at first. It's Walt Whitman's muscular "meter-making arguments," Emily Dickinson's runic riddles, Robert Frost's terrifying georgics, Sylvia Plath's haunting mythologies, John Ashbery's hypnotic disquisitions, Allen Ginsberg's candid love poems to America. If the body lies unattended—ungroomed—its beauty remains inert, the town untransformed. A nation must "weigh and consider" its poetry in order to be saved, to venture speaking "differently" as Mary Szybist has challenged herself to do as a poet. The new language of the country— what James Wright called "the new imagination" in a letter to his friend Robert Bly—lies in the midst of the crowd as good medicine for demagoguery. And yet, as the philosopher Martha Nussbaum has pointed out about the poet, particularly the poet of praise, in her book *The Fragility of Goodness*, "the peculiar beauty of human excellence is its vulnerability" like the "tenderness of a plant." The same can be said of democracy itself as a civic reification of "goodness," since it is formed, engineered, and balanced as a political act of faith by the "fragile plant" of the citizenry.

---

1. Translated by Gregory Rabassa and J. S. Bernstein.

Sixteen years after Whitman celebrated what he called "these United States" as "the greatest poem," he had a change of mind following the Civil War and the assassination of Abraham Lincoln; his "patriotism" had changed from euphoric praise to deep disappointment during the regressive administration of Andrew Johnson, compelling him to write in *Specimen Days*:

> I say we had best look our times and lands searchingly in the face, like a physician diagnosing some deep disease. Never was there, perhaps, more hollowness at heart than at present, and here in the United States. Genuine belief seems to have left us. The underlying principles of the States are not honestly believ'd in, (for all this hectic glow, and these melo-dramatic screamings,) nor is humanity itself believ'd in. What penetrating eye does not everywhere see through the mask? The spectacle is appalling. We live in an atmosphere of hypocrisy throughout.

Whitman felt that his and Lincoln's "meter-making arguments" had made "nothing happen," which raises the question: If poets are in fact the "unacknowledged legislators of the world," as Percy Shelley had claimed, then just how was a country or a people to go about enacting its poets' "laws" in order to safeguard against the very kind of hypocrisy that Whitman laments in his diatribe above? What political instrument lies at poets' disposal for implementing their principles? The answer to this is, as it has always been, deceptively simple, singular, and unchanging: the pen. Simply continuing to write, and thereby witnessing to the reality of the age in language that, as the poet C. D. Wright noted, "sounds better and means more."

William Carlos Williams's caveat—"It is difficult / to get the news from poems / yet men die miserably every day / for lack / of what is found there"— continues to resound as strongly as it did in 1955 when he wrote "Asphodel, That Greeny Flower," in which this line appears.

At the time of this writing, an unprecedented number of lies emanates from the White House on a daily basis (more than 3,000 lies in 466 days, according to CNN Politic), and Congress, along with presidential advisors, appears feckless in its attempts to prevent President Trump from reversing environmental safeguards, committing human rights violations against immigrant families, slinging profane invectives at developing countries, initiating hostile economic policies toward the American allies Canada, the United Kingdom, Germany, and Mexico, indulging in daily Twitter rampages, making vile misogynistic and racist remarks, complimenting such demagogues as Vladimir Putin, Rodrigo Duterte, and Kim Jong Un while in the same breath traducing fellow Americans John McCain, Barack Obama, and fallen soldier Humayun Saqib Muazzam Khan, and refusing to recant his claim of moral equivalency between white supremacists and anti-racists protesters. It is clear that the country has entered a moral crisis that's testing its very credibility as a functional democracy. Such contemporary American poets as Yusef Komunyakaa, Philip Levine, Claudia Rankine, Natasha Trethewey, Bruce Smith, Erin Belieu, Robert Hass, Patricia Smith, Carolyn Forché, Ishmael Reed, Sam Hamill, Anne Waldman, and Martín Espada, to mention only a few, have witnessed boldly to the despotic behavior of the president—behavior that presupposes the public's gullibility.

"Life without poetry is, in effect, life without sanction," Wallace Stevens claimed. In its truth-telling, poetry witnesses against perfidy, oppression, and demagoguery, whether its subject is flowers, salamanders, or politics. Implicit in Miłosz's claim for poetry as a nation-saving art form is the caveat that most poets who write poetry as antidotes to "official lies" won't live long enough to see their nations saved by their verses. In fact, many will die forgotten and will suffer what the late Irish poet Matthew Sweeney referred to shortly before he died as "posthumous oblivion." So, the mere act of writing must be enough in any poet's hope to extend poetry's legacy as a literary force that "sanctions life." The precepts of democracy itself are founded on the human right of citizens to exercise not only their right to vote but a daring belief in the citizenry's collective wisdom to reify what Aristotle called "the common good." Each new generation of poets, in their mostly unelected roles as witnesses, strives to reimagine the sheer experience of being alive in their particular epoch. Too many great poets like Osip Mandelstam, Nazim Hikmet, Dante Alighieri, Boris Pasternak, Paul Celan, and Joseph Brodsky have been censored, banished, imprisoned or executed during their lifetimes for doing this. How, then, to respond today to Auden's claim with some evidence that his denouncement of poetry's efficacy is at least alloyed paradoxically to the opposite claim that Miłosz made for it?

Zbigniew Herbert, Miłosz's countryman and fellow poet, captured the selfless artistic enterprise of writing the kind of poetry that Miłosz praised as nation-saving in his poem "The Envoy of Mr. Cogito":

> Go where those others went to the dark boundary
> for the golden fleece of nothingness your last prize
>
> go upright among those who are on their knees
> among those with their backs turned and those toppled in the dust
>
> you were saved not in order to live
> you have little time you must give testimony
>
> be courageous when the mind deceives you be courageous
> in the final account only this is important ...[2]

Can poetry save America? "I wanted good poetry without knowing it," Miłosz goes on to write in "Dedication" following his bold, rhetorical question about the corrective nature of poetry: "That I discovered, late, its salutary aim, / In this and only this I find salvation." Like the townspeople in Márquez's story, even the most sensitive and artistic citizens seem to discover the "salutary aim" of poetry late, often too late.

A beautiful body lies on its catafalque before the eyes of the country. What new window sills, doorways, and ceilings will it inspire Americans to build? What new colors to cover the walls? What courage to discard the detritus that has gathered in its attic, cellar, and White House? "Be faithful," Herbert abjures his reader in the last line of Mr. Cogito's envoy. "Go."

2018

---

2. Translated by Bogdana and John Carpenter.

The Place Where You Lie: James Wright's "To the Muse"

In thinking about the appeal of enduring love lyrics, I return over and over to the striking contemporary poem "To the Muse" by James Wright, which curiously, given Wright's sustained popularity and critical attention since his death in 1980, has not, to my knowledge, received the kind of close reading it deserves since its publication in *Shall We Gather at the River* in 1968. In his address to his beloved, the speaker gives voice to a host of extreme emotions and thoughts that range from human unknowing to a progressively changing yet freshly present agony to unbridled intimacy to an unrestrained protest against the sheer impossibility of life, to an ultimately illuminating madness. Is there another contemporary love poem that explores the grieving lover's bardo state with such economy, intensity, and *sprezzatura*?

To the Muse

It is all right. All they do
Is go in by dividing
One rib from another. I wouldn't
Lie to you. It hurts
Like nothing I know. All they do
Is burn their way in with a wire.
It forks in and out a little like the tongue
Of that frightened garter snake we caught
At Cloverfield, you and me, Jenny
So long ago.

I would lie to you
If I could.
But the only way I can get you to come up
Out of the suckhole, the south face
Of the Powhatan pit, is to tell you
What you know:

You come up after dark, you poise alone
With me on the shore.
I lead you back to this world.

Three lady doctors in Wheeling open
Their offices at night.
I don't have to call them, they are always there.
But they only have to put the knife once
Under your breast.
Then they hang their contraption.
And you bear it.

It's awkward a while. Still, it lets you
Walk about on tiptoe if you don't
Jiggle the needle.
It might stab your heart, you see.
The blade hangs in your lung and the tube
Keeps it draining.
That way they only have to stab you
Once. Oh Jenny.

I wish to God I had made this world, this scurvy
And disastrous place. I
Didn't, I can't bear it
Either, I don't blame you, sleeping down there
Face down in the unbelievable silk of spring,
Muse of black sand,
Alone.

I don't blame you, I know
The place where you lie.
I admit everything. But look at me.

> How can I live without you?
> Come up to me, love,
> Out of the river, or I will
> Come down to you.

Wright echoes the anonymous classic ballad "The Unquiet Grave" in this poem, melding his grief with his love. Just as the speaker in "The Unquiet Grave" refuses to accept the death of his beloved, proclaiming, "I'll do as much for my true-love, / As any young man may; / I'll sit and mourn all at the grave / For a twelvemonth and a day," Wright's speaker also maintains his vigil at Jenny's cenotaph. In both these poems, death holds the beloved hostage in the underworld. But unlike the admonishing voice of the beloved in "The Unquiet Grave," Jenny remains silent and "alone," leaving the poem's speaker utterly disconsolate, with only himself to rely on for an answer, which he poses in the form of a question: "How can I live without you?" Wright has rubbed directly against the limit of his human understanding here, which is also the boundary of the lyric. He is intent on getting down the expression of his most immediate feelings in the wake of Jenny's drowning. No Wordsworthian strategy of recalling emotion later in tranquility here; rather raw, unbridled love and grief infusing Wright with the inherent poetic expression of an Orphic speaker intent on leading his beloved "back to this world." But unlike Orpheus, he utters an ultimatum that reveals the madness of his grief: "Come up to me, love, / Out of the river, or I will / Come down to you." Precedents for such romantic suicide occur in every age as testimonies to the extreme measures lovers are willing to undertake, viewing death as an afterlife free from "this scurvy and disastrous place" and the impossibility of "this world."

This poem, however, is less about suicidality than survival through poetry. Wright's muse does "come up" to the speaker in the poem, just as he goes down to her, knowing "the place" where she lies. She inspires an Orphic music in him that decries this world, where contingency conspires with circumstance to wreak havoc on love. The enjambments throughout the poem evince the fractious, run-on nature of the speaker's voice. Breakage and violence instill his keening with heartbreaking tones, conveying both the velocity and urgency of his futile address to

Jenny. This poem depends almost solely on voice for its evocation, so the speaker's convulsive voice dictates the short, lines that pivot on pregnant adverbs, verbs, and nouns. The power of the poem lies in the uneven breaths of the narrator's love and grief. In both form and content, the poem testifies at every turn to the heroic power of witnessing over death; the chthonic details in stanza six, "the unbelievable silk of spring" and "the black sand," are the subterranean stuff that the speaker knows and names. Like Orpheus, the speaker has been to the underworld and spoken to Hades. He "admits everything." And like Orpheus, he attempts to lead his dead beloved out of the Powhatan pit "back to this world." Wright's landscape, therefore, is both real and mythological here. The Powhatan pit is the "suckhole" where Jenny died, as well as the underworld out of which she emerges to "poise alone / With me on the shore."

But what to do with Jenny once she has been led back? Wright creates a torturous, visceral conceit for this resurrected suicide (we surmise she is a suicide from the speaker's forgiving line, "I don't blame you," in the last stanza) rather than "disappearing" her *à la* Eurydice. The speaker escorts his love to the night office of the "three lady doctors in Wheeling" who "are always there." What happens to her there is hideous and mysterious. She is tortured at the hands of the lady doctors, who resemble the three fates.

> It's awkward a while. Still, it lets you
> Walk about on tiptoe if you don't
> Jiggle the needle.
> It might stab your heart, you see.
> The blade hangs in your lung and the tube
> Keeps it draining.
> That way they only have to stab you
> Once.

But no soothsaying takes place in the lady doctors' office. Jenny is less an oracle than a forbidden returnee from the underworld. Inanna removes her clothes and enters a bardo state in order to meet with her sister Erishkegal in hell. Osiris lives inside a pillar as the result of Isis's brother, Seth, entombing him there. Persephone resides for six months in hell with Hades after eating his pomegranate seeds.

Eurydice disappears in the cave entrance at Erebus. In his own private myth in "To the Muse," Wright subjects the lost beloved, Jenny, to the ghastly machinations of the three lady doctors in Wheeling, an array of anomalous surgeries and "treatments" that no doctor would even recognize. The "contraption" in which Jenny must "tiptoe" around in in order to prevent the needle from stabbing her heart is a weird, nonsensical device that Wright purposefully avoids identifying lest he ruin the hierophantic mystery of his own myth. The three priestesses, who masquerade as dominatrix-like doctors in Wheeling, West Virginia, safeguard life's impossibility for the grievous speaker by imprisoning her in an office straight out of a David Lynch film.

Jenny exists in two realms at once, as a resurrected but suspended body locked in a torture "contraption" at the threshold, and a dead girlfriend in the Powhatan suckhole, creating the conceit of her resurrection as a palpable vision of his grief. She is a delicately balanced, booby-trapped cipher who speaks under great duress, with a "blade" pressed against her heart. (What a poignantly accurate description of Wright's own psyche as conveyed again and again in his deeply emotional poems that chronicle the "intensest rendezvous.") Death is the impossibility in the poem—the inconceivable reality of the loss of the beloved—that also renders life impossible for the speaker. Without her, he feels utterly abandoned in "this world" that he has no control over, whose inexorable forces abrogate his deepest needs with chilling disregard.

And yet ironically, it is only in this very world, "this scurvy and disastrous place," that the Orphic singer can sing, expressing the pathos that emanates directly from his experience of life's impossibility and unknowing. Indeed, the image of Jenny suspended in the lady doctors' anomalous contraption not only works as a mythological symbol of the lost beloved's unsuccessful return to this world, but also as a vicariously evocative image that captures both abandonment and the visceral/psychic reality of grief. Jenny is the lost one, but the devastated surviving speaker is the one, not Jenny, who *feels* drained, suspended, and eviscerated.

2008

"But They Have Dwindled": Wordsworth's "Resolution and Independence" as a Modern-Day Cautionary Tale

In one of his most profound existential poems, "Resolution and Independence," William Wordsworth adds a postscript to Qoheleth's proverbial ancient mantra from Ecclesiastes—"All is vanity ... there is nothing new under the sun." The question that resounds between each line of the poem, written in 1802 when Wordsworth was thirty-two, is a cliché that poets have been doomed to find a way around since the dawn of poetry: How to go on writing after the loss of one's "summer mood"? Samuel Beckett captured Wordsworth's conundrum most succinctly in his famous statement: "I can't go on. I'll go on." In "Resolution and Independence," Wordsworth chooses a more fleshed-out, cathectic response to writer's block than did Beckett by writing an extended pastoral metaphor in the form of a dramatic narrative that begins in despair and ends on a note of ironic hope. Like Dante wandering in "a dark wood midway through the journey of [his] life" at the outset of *The Inferno*, Wordsworth's speaker, a poet also, finds himself wandering with ennui on a moor following a refreshing rainstorm that has filled the air with the "pleasant noise of waters" while "the sky rejoices in the morning's birth." Yet, despite the refreshing scenery and climate, the poet is despondent, complaining, "My old remembrances went from me wholly; / All the ways of men, so vain and melancholy." And not only the "vanity" of men, but the poet's faith as well. With no semblance even of nostalgia for his past upbeat walks on the moor or his "pleasant thought," he grieves his former "summer mood," impugning God with Job-like anger for the loss of his happiness:

> My whole life I have lived in pleasant thought,
> As if life's business were a summer mood;
> As if all needful things would come unsought
> To genial faith, still rich in genial good;
> But how can He expect that others should
> Build for him, sow for him, and at his call
> Love him, who for himself will take no heed at all?

In the midst of his aimless wandering, the poet suddenly encounters "a Man before [him] unawares: // The oldest man he seemed that ever wore grey hairs." This striking figure embodies a primordial figure, "Like a sea-beast crawled forth, that on a shelf / Of rock or sand reposeth, there to sun itself" and "not all alive nor dead." With the countenance of a mythical character, not unlike the Green Man, this man seems as oneiric as he does real:

> And the whole body of the Man did seem
> Like one whom I had met with in a dream;
> Or like a man from some far region sent,
> To give me human strength, by apt admonishment.

The poet does not yet recognize himself in the stranger—the leech gatherer—at this point in the poem, for while he needs to believe he's capable of "catching" new poems, just as the leech gatherer needs to believe in his skill at gathering leaches, he feels hopeless about the prospect of continuing to write, as well as maintaining his faith in writing in a "summer mood." The leech gatherer fails to provide any immediate hope for the poet's melancholy, as his ravaged appearance belies precisely that ironic toughness that the poet will come to discover in him soon enough:

> His body was bent double, feet and head
> Coming together in life's pilgrimage;
> As if some dire constraint of pain, or rage

> Of sickness felt by him in times long past,
> A more than human weight upon his frame had cast.

Following this introduction, the leech gatherer's struggle to continue harvesting leeches amidst their dwindling and "decay" provides a pastoral analogue to the aging poet's search for new poems. Like the leech gatherer, the poet must brave his own "dwindling" stock of poems with "cheerful" resolve if he is to overcome his fate "to begin in gladness" and "end in madness" like "the marvelous boy ... Chatterton." One could not have blamed Wordsworth for concluding his brown study on a black note, just as one could not have blamed his friend Samuel Taylor Coleridge for sentencing his Ancient Mariner to a life of endless remorse and misery. Wordsworth, like Coleridge, creates a near-impossible spiritual problem, as well as a serious thinking problem, for his protagonist to solve. Ironically, he must muddy his waters, just as the leech gatherer must stir the water of the pond in order to gather leeches:

> At length, himself unsettling, he the pond
> Stirred with his staff, and fixedly did look
> Upon the muddy water, which he conned,
> As if he had been reading in a book ...

Wordsworth's mention of "a book" provides a clue to a philosophy that influenced him profoundly—stoicism. The Wordsworth scholar Bruce Graver elucidates this in his chapter titled "Wordsworth and the Stoics" in *Rome and the Romantics*, in which he cites Cicero's *Tusculan Disputations* specifically, along with the writings of Seneca. In this philosophical light, the leech gatherer assumes the disposition of the archetypal stoic sage whose resignation to the rigors of survival is complemented by his belief in God. On the stage of the "moor," Wordsworth provides a "resolution" to the poet's despondency with a plain-spoken testimony from the leech gatherer, who the poet feels has been sent to give him "human strength, by some apt admonishment." "How is it you live, and what is it you do?" the poet asks the leech gatherer—a question that redounds as much on the poet's curiosity about his own vocation as it does on his interest in the leech gatherer's profession and survival skills. The harsh facts of the leech gatherer's life and work speak for themselves to the poet whose complaints pale in comparison to the leech gatherer's. At this point in the poem, the rural sage assumes a dummy-like quality for the poet to throw his voice into as a thinly veiled ventriloquist of his own "soul-making." It seems as though Wordsworth appears to hear in his own projected voice the very wisdom he was blocked from hearing in the "misery" he had been experiencing prior to his encounter with the leech gatherer:

> He told, that to these waters he had come
> To gather leeches, being old and poor:
> Employment hazardous and wearisome!
> And he had many hardships to endure:
> From pond to pond he roamed, from moor to moor;
> Housing, with God's good help, by choice or chance;
> And in this way he gained an honest maintenance.

Wordsworth employs what he called "recollected emotion" as a catalyst for gaining new awareness of his powers of perseverance via the poetic device of a transpersonal self—the leech gatherer. This new, stalwart awareness bears little if any resemblance to the dire emotion that initially inspired the poet and testifies to his transformative realization—"God ... be my help and stay secure"—that emerges from his dramatic resolution as a cure for his melancholy. In an epiphany that combines both stoical and religious conviction, the poet grasps the remedy for his despondency, namely, the simple will to persevere. This plain-spoken realization emerges spontaneously in the course of the poet's conversation with the leech gatherer, who exemplifies the reification of the sublime, which the third-century Greek philosopher Cassius Longinus defined memorably as "a greatness of soul, imitation, or imagery ... of art that uplifts our soul to an exalted height." The leech gatherer's simple yet noble final statement to the poet, "Yet still I persevere, and find them where I may," instills the poet with an enduring hope in a tireless muse who, like the leeches in the pond's waters, resides in the murk of his intellect and imagination.

Postscript

Although Wordsworth composes a thinly veiled Christian apology in "Resolution and Independence" for persevering in the doldrums with "God's help," his emphasis on "human strength" stands out as a strikingly secular conceit. His emphasis on human enterprise as a critical attribute for survival, and even salvation, has roots in the theology of the fourth-century English theologian Pelagius, who maintained that human effort was an essential, volitional complement for accessing God's grace—a doctrine that Saint Augustine considered heretical for its denunciation of God's utter sovereignty. By employing a credible spiritual rebuttal to the causes of writer's block, as well as the seductive *reductio ad absurdum* arguments at the heart of both Ecclesiastes and Stoicism, Wordsworth makes a romantic argument for humanity's near-miraculous legacy of survival against all odds by attributing it to mere "strength" and "maintenance."

The poem endures as much as an allegory, therefore, as it does a parable, since it works as an earthly story with both a worldly and a heavenly meaning. It also works as a powerfully prophetic poem for our present age in which climate change, a pandemic, and overpopulation present global extremities that would, no doubt, stun Wordsworth's "summer mood" with apocalyptic shock.

In his own time, with England roiled by the Industrial Revolution and disruption of the traditional agricultural economy, Wordsworth is remarkably sensitive to the fragility of the natural world, reporting through his leech gatherer the inexplicable decline of leeches:

> Once I could meet with them on every side;
> But they have dwindled long by slow decay;
> Yet still I persevere, and find them where I may.

This 220-year old report on the disappearance of leeches from moor ponds in the Lake District of England prefigures today's environmental predicament, as we witness the extinction of one species after another around the world, including recently such creatures as the Pyrenean ibyx, the passenger pigeon, the Steller's sea cow, the western black rhinoceros, the dodo, the quagga, and the Pinta Island tortoise, to mention only a few. Wordsworth's leeches symbolize these vanished creatures now, while his "leech gatherer" lives on in such modern-day Cassandras as Bill McKibben, W. S. Merwin, Elizabeth Kolbert, Rebecca Solnit, Wendell Berry, and that anonymous elderly man or woman still wandering the countryside searching for miraculous, wondrous creatures, no matter how unseemly.

2020

He Who Remembers His Shoes: Charles Simic

The "vast image" that disturbs Yeats's sight in his poem "The Second Coming" is atomized in Charles Simic's poetry into radiant matter. Whether they be spoons, ants, or a plain black cotton dress, these subjects take on character in his poetry with abiding animism. Simic perceives the world with a vision that apprehends the dynamism of small things. He is exotic for this reason, a kind of stranger in our midst who sees through the familiar into *spiritus mundi*. In "Solving the Riddle," he describes himself as a builder of a lighthouse (rather than a sailing ship) inside his wine bottle. The beacon that emanates from inside his bottle is a metaphor for the geometric illumination that occurs when one's psyche and consciousness are aligned. This light not only illuminates the visible world, those places "lit by a glass of milk," but reveals the hidden as well, the "White ants / In a white ant hill." An avatar of minutiae, his apprehension leaves him with a sense of his nameless muse. "Each one of my thoughts," he writes in "Emily's Theme," "was being ghostwritten / by anonymous authors."

Having said this, the weird menagerie of animated objects that populate Simic's poems are careful constructs, poetic boxes that are both entertaining and disturbing, often achieving a tragi-comical intensity that leaves the reader suspended between amusement and grief. Simic's mythical imagination imbues him with this parallax vision of reality's double yet seamless nature. By unveiling first impression as a rebus, he trains his poetic eye on what perhaps can only be described as the obviously invisible. "What is that little black thing I see there in the white?" he quotes Whitman in the epigraph of his poem "White." But Simic isn't just a vatic poet who discerns the darkness inside the light. His inspiration derives equally from the simple rigors of daily living. His poems consequently often sound as alarms for second awakening.

Poem

Every morning I forget how it is.
I watch the smoke mount
In great strides above the city.
I belong to no one.
Then, I remember my shoes,
How I have put them on,
How bending over to tie them up
I will look into the earth.

(from *Dismantling the Silence*, 1971)

Although he writes with an exquisite sensibility of twentieth-century alienation, Simic's psyche is archetypal, not postmodern. He wishes to make new pastoral sense by creating a contemporary landscape out of the old world, in which elderly ladies emerge from bombed-out apartment buildings during ceasefires to search for their cats. Modern in the sense that he has been a witness since World War II to the legacy of devastation in his native Serbia, Simic has, as both exile and U.S. citizen, only deepened his sense of the poet as an individual who stands heroically alone against the self-justifying "religious" tenets of nationalism.

In his "unique distance from isolation" (as Philip Larkin puts it in his poem "Talking in Bed"), he has pursued his art with the kind of purity of heart that Søren Kierkegaard defined as willing one thing. This "one thing" is a surrealistic vision of the dual nature of objects. In *Dime-Store Alchemy*, his study of the painter Joseph Cornell, Simic quotes de Chirico: "Every object has two aspects: one current one, which we see nearly always and which is seen by men in general; and the other, which is spectral and metaphysical and seen only by rare individuals in moments of clairvoyance." Nevertheless, he is neither elitist nor occult, grounding himself in ordinary life as time passes by with the conceit of history.

History

On a gray evening
Of a gray century,
I ate an apple
While no one was looking.

A small, sour apple
The color of wood fire
Which I first wiped
On my sleeve.

Then I stretched my legs
As far as they'd go,
Said to myself
Why not close my eyes now

Before the late
World News and Weather.

(from *Austerities*, 1982)

Simic knows the diachronic appeal of archetypal images in an age when the rudiments of sense have been scrutinized and questioned as never before. His runic coherence is remarkable for its success in conveying the ironic, often foreboding, life in inanimate things. With electric economy, Simic assays the world with a mythopoeic eye, coloring in negative space, singing "through the throat of an empty beer bottle." He is a Buddhist comedian, having discovered through poetry rather than catechism the inherent humor in what Walt Whitman called "the natural beauty of dumb objects." What Stephen Dobyns observed about Yannis Ritsos in his essay "Ritsos and the Metaphysical Moment" holds true for Simic's poetry as well:

The poem is anti-Aristotelian. It posits a world beyond scientific measurement. Once again we have a world of sympathetic affinities. More than a world, a universe: the very stars have quickened their breathing. Something important and mysterious has happened and this mystery communicates itself with the ripple effect of a stone dropped in a pond. The poem doesn't try to explain the mystery, it bears witness to it and to these affinities, connections, correspondences.

The antinomian surprises of Simic's imagery—a fork "right out of hell," a knife that rises and "sets in your hand"—present a refreshingly heretical rebuttal to Descartes's syllogism that equates cognition with existence. I imagine, Simic retorts, therefore I am whatever I imagine. Or, as the old witch instructs in "Make Yourself Invisible": "From now on, we were bread crumbs / In a dark forest / Where the little red birds / Had just fallen silent."

Simic has struck an originality that transports William Carlos Williams's credo, "no ideas but in things," into a narrative as well. The subjects of his poetry, things as characters, comprise the essential images on which so much depends, making claims in turn for how all things are in unlikely cahoots. What unfold consequently, in most of Simic's poems, are sudden poetic fictions in settings where the line between the phenomenal and the relational is deftly blurred. We see this beautifully accomplished in the conclusion of "Winter Evening," where the lovelorn speaker extrapolates from a single spare scene of his "love's window … on fire / With the Sunset." He allows himself to be consumed by, yet not lost in, the oceanic denouement. "Quiet as a bread crumb, / I stood and watched. / All around me birds had fallen silent. / And then the clouds moved / Their tragic robes, / And so did the night." This sympathetic awareness supplants naive hope in his poetry with metaphysical affirmation, for he has precious little faith in any happy outcome. Yet his underlying realism does not subvert his compassion. Rather, it imbues his poetry with an uncanny tension between his deep-seated pathos and his intimate knowledge of the world as a Darwinian playground. At the conclusion of his brilliant essay "The Spider's Web," he writes: "As an elegist I mourn and expect the worst. Vileness and stupidity always have a rosy future. The world is still a few evils short, but they'll come. Dark despair is the only healthy outlook if you identify yourself with flies, as I do." It is this awareness of his vulnerability that generates the power of his voice. In a poem titled "Two Riddles," he defines poetry in this way:

> Hangs by a thread—
> Whatever it is. Stripped naked.
> Shivering. Human. Mortal.
> On a thread finer than starlight.
>
> By a power of feeling.
> Hangs, impossible, unthinkable,
> Between the earth and the sky.
> I, it says, I. I.

    (from *Dismantling the Silence*)

Simic's poetic zone "beyond the dip of bell" provides a complementary view. One view apprehends the human legacy of "vileness and stupidity," while the other keeps a clear focus on the inherent peace of the world. In recounting his response to a Serbian patriot whose invitation to speak he had turned down, he makes this apology: "The true poet is never a member of any tribe. It is his refusal of his birthright that makes him a poet and an individual worth respecting, I explained." But he then refutes this assertion: "This wasn't true, of course. Many of the greatest poets have been fierce nationalists." More as an honest man, perhaps, than a lyric poet, Simic recognizes his own limitations and potential lies. This is a chicken-and-egg speculation, however, for while one senses that poetry has played a critical role in honing his honesty, it is easy to think that he would be no less a man if he weren't a poet, for his poems emanate from his humanity foremost. He is a postmodern jester in a "black cape" and "orange wraparound shades." Establishing his voice as morally audible in the wilderness of American privilege and isolation, he eschews the epic. Too often, he claims, has this genre been employed by bloodthirsty patriots who "find excuses for the butcheries of the innocent." As a lyric poet, Simic celebrates rather than mourns the epic hero's demise:

My Weariness of Epic Proportions

I like it when
Achilles
Gets killed
And even his buddy Patroclus—
And that hothead Hector—
And the whole Greek and Trojan
Jeunesse dorée
Are more or less
Expertly slaughtered
So there's finally
Peace and quiet
(The gods having momentarily
Shut up)
One can hear
A bird sing
And a daughter ask her mother
Whether she can go to the well
And of course she can
By that lovely little path
That winds through
The olive orchard

(from *Austerities*)

Simic's unnerving intelligence saves his poems from mere sentimentality. With his "darling premonition," he invites his reader into alluring pastoral scenes, such as this one: "Today we took a long walk in the forest. / There we met a couple walking / Arm and arm with eyes closed," and then he closes the poem's door on us with a gentle but resounding click. By the end of this poem, "The Forest Walk," the couple is running to return to the horrors of contemporary life.

The forest's classical foreboding has been inverted by such artificial omens as "the video store," "the ice cream truck," and, most eerily, "the plane's landing lights." Like Grimm, Simic appeals directly to the curious child in his reader for the purpose of revealing some new laconic terror about those very places we thought were most safe and familiar.

By arresting our attention with dreamlike vignettes, Simic converts his private myths into universal narratives. He dreams for us, and we let him, for he is such a good dreamer. We allow him even his nightmares. In "Club Midnight," for instance, Simic beguiles his reader with questions about the psyche itself, referring to it figuratively as a nightclub. Since we are each the "sole owner" of our psyches, we feel compelled with a kind of soulful responsibility to answer his questions about our respective "establishments." But he has trapped us. Because he knows his psyche so well, he also knows ours. We answer unhesitatingly in the affirmative when he asks in the tone of either an insouciant analyst or tired detective, "Are bearded Russian thinkers your silent partners? Do you have a doorman by the name of Dostoyevsky? Is Fu Man Chu coming tonight? Is Miss Emily Dickinson?"

Oddly, then, it's not just the strangeness of Simic's imagery that is so moving, but the illumined darkness behind the familiar. He arouses his reader from her waking sleep to remind her that she is at home on earth, and that it's a haunted house. The minutiae of daily life are personified in Simic's poems as preternatural characters. He blurs the line between symbols and real things in order to, as E. R. Dodd writes about shamans in his book *The Greeks and the Irrational*, "become a repository of a supernormal wisdom." At times we feel his landscapes transforming from conventional pastoral scenes into cartoonish tableaux where ants wear little Quaker hats, or liars have long tails and look like monkeys, or an old man who's learned to eat air floats overhead clutching his hat on a cold and windy day. These wild images nonetheless resonate with a meaning that reflects an inner reality, where the imagination dislocates and embellishes nature with incongruous yet poignant images. Simic derived much of his picaresque sensibility from the allegories of Eastern Europe, and then developed it further on his own as a young man in Chicago and New York. He has aspired since childhood to become an American poet. In achieving this he has also become an international voice.

With the same wit and self-effacing voice that resonate from his less direct poems, he writes about the tragedy of Serbia. His poem "Tragic Architecture" is particularly memorable for its disturbing prophecies couched in rhetorical reminiscence. One also gains from this poem an enormous appreciation for Simic's redoubtable authority as a witness to the events that destroyed his country:

Tragic Architecture

School, prison, trees in the wind,
I climbed your gloomy stairs.
Stood in your remotest corners
With my face to the wall.

The murderer sat in the front row.
A mad little Ophelia
Wrote today's date on the blackboard.
The executioner was my best friend.
He already wore black.
The janitor brought us mice to play with.

In that room with its red sunsets—
under its rays everyone fell silent.
It was eternity's time to speak,
So we listened
As if our hearts were made of stone.

Only the debris was left
Between the cracked, peeling walls,
And one window gone blind
Staring at the same wintry sky.
But the rest gutted,
Not even a naked light bulb left inside.

For the prisoner forgotten in the solitary,
Eyes closed like a lover,
The bad child left behind
Watching the bare winter trees
Lashed by the driving wind.

But Simic is a lyric poet first and a political witness second. He needs this titular distinction in order to write judiciously about his own tribe's "stupidity." His tribe should thank him for it, as should all other tribes, for as a lyric poet he didn't have to write about his tribe's stupidity. He is successful enough writing about anything else.

Simic remains a childlike witness to the vileness of tribes—childlike in his clear-eyed, querulous vision, though very adult in his finely tuned, lapidary irony. "The Garden of Eden parking lot / needs weeding," he writes in "The Emperor," the last poem in *Walking the Black Cat*, "And the candy store / Is now padlocked.... I saw the panhandling Jesus / And heard the wind chime in his head." This is the spectral vision that de Chirico referred to.

By resisting the ambition of the epic, Simic has set grand ideas aside and gone "inside a stone ... to make out the strange writings, the star charts / On the inner walls" ("Stone"). Like the Ancient Mariner discerning the "happy living things" after killing the albatross, Simic has felt the same kind of vicarious remorse for the sins of all of us. This grief has imbued him with metaphysical vision. What monsters he sees in the air. What praise he bestows on them.

1997

On Poetry: Looking Out from a Poem's Second-Story Window

As a poet and a reader of poetry, I never cease to be amazed by the difference difference makes. I feel this first intuitively and second consciously. A surprising connection between different things in a poem can instill it with transcendent surprise. Because poetry is often a two-story house—literal on the ground floor and figurative on the second—the act of comparing two very different things allows the poet to construct high above the ground floor. The late great poet Lucille Clifton corroborated this methodology in an interview I conducted with her a few weeks before she died in 2010. "I'm a carpenter," she announced, "and I follow the carpenter's rule." Her claim made both etymological and metaphorical sense; the word *poem* derives from the Greek word *poiesis*, which simply means "a made thing."

Difference constitutes not only an essential tool for building above the first literal floor of the poem's house, but the very building materials as well. The architecture of this two-story house may appear incongruous at first, with the figurative on top of the literal, but the more closely one examines it, the more one sees that the figurative construction of the second story depends on the joists and beams of the first story as it shifts in its ascent from the immediately familiar and actual to the strange and wildly sensible.

As a way of illustrating this poetic construction to my students, I announce to them from the attic of my small two-story house that "the heart is a radiator." After they regard me quizzically for a few moments as if I've just taken leave of my senses, I lower my retractable stairway by adding: "because it leaks, it clanks, it heats up, and it cools down." Then they are suddenly with me, peering out the dormers.

That I have indulged in difference or incongruity by so freely equating the heart to a radiator confuses and even intimidates my students initially. But then, with a little imaginative help, they feel at home on "the second floor" of higher sense, realizing that their imaginations, bizarre and dreamlike as they might be, possess a type of intelligence that connects dissimilar things in a way that their literal minds can't, and in a way that is exhilarating, enlightening, and entertaining. Without it, one is left lamenting a lack in his or her friend, or, as Robert Frost opined in his poem "Revelation," "'Tis a pity if the case require / (Or so we say) that in the end / We speak the literal to inspire / The understanding of a friend."

Gazing out the window of poetry's second floor at the infinitely complex world, one doesn't have to make an extravagant leap to what the nineteenth-century American transcendentalist Ralph Waldo Emerson called the "unifying instinct" of nature.

"By and by," he wrote in his essay "The American Scholar," "nature finds how to join two things and see in them one nature; then three, then three thousand; and so tyrannized over by its own unifying instinct, it goes on tying things together, diminishing anomalies, discovering roots running under ground whereby contrary and remote things cohere and flower out from one stem."

Walt Whitman read this and other similar insights in Emerson's writings, particularly in his essay "The Poet," and articulated for the first time in American literary history the idea of the transpersonal self, that self that crosses over from the speaker of the poem to the other. Or, as Whitman puts it himself at the opening of his great poem "Song of Myself," "… what I assume you shall assume. / Every atom that belongs to me as good belongs to you."

Similarly, about thirty-five years before Whitman published "Song of Myself," the English poet John Keats observed at the precocious age of twenty-three in a letter to his brother George that the poet must learn "to exist in uncertainty, mysteries, doubt without any irritable reaching after fact or reason." Keats might also have included the ability to connect differences as one of the criteria for what he called "negative capability."

How fascinating to discover that the poetic catalyst responsible for converting dissimilar things into powerful likenesses lies also at the heart of compassion, that human capacity for seeing oneself in something totally different. Two American poems come immediately to mind as memorable examples of such conversions. "In the Waiting Room" by Elizabeth Bishop and "Hook" by James Wright were both written around the same time, in the late 1970s.

In the first, Bishop remembers a childhood experience of waiting for her Aunt Consuelo at the dentist's office. While sitting in the waiting room, she hears her aunt cry out in pain, a sound that triggers a profound out-of-body experience in which Bishop realizes in her first startling social revelation that she "was [her] foolish aunt ... an I," as well as "one of them," too. By *them*, Bishop means the "black, naked women" she's sheepishly been gazing at in the *National Geographic* in the waiting room. She then goes on to make her first compassionate connection to others by thinking through the subterfuge of difference to the human commonalities she discovers at the conclusion of her questions about her connection to others, no matter how dissimilar they may be.

> Why should I be my aunt,
> or me, or anyone?
> What similarities—
> boots, hands, the family voice
> I felt in my throat, or even
> the *National Geographic*
> and those awful hanging breasts—
> held us all together / or made us all just one?

In "Hook," Wright encounters "a young Sioux" on a cold street corner in Minneapolis who has a hook in place of his arm as the result of "a bad time [he] had with a woman." Wright has also had a bad time with a woman. He's better off financially than the young Sioux man, but rather than give him money for the bus, Wright accepts money from him. He addresses the reader:

> Did you ever feel a man hold
> Sixty-five cents
> In a hook
> And place it
> Gently
> In your freezing hand?
>
> I took it.
> It wasn't the money I needed.
> But I took it.

Wright grasps the counterintuitive greater gift of giving by receiving in this instance and in so doing erases any superficial differences between him and the young Sioux, whose hook takes on sudden, powerful symbolism of mutual compassion in its gentle delivery, more so than any literal hand could.

These two poems not only meet W. H. Auden's criterion for poetry as "memorable speech," but tell Ezra Pound's "news that stays news" about our human capacity both to live in poetry's two-story house, and to transcend differences that seem initially impassable.

2015

For Each Ecstatic Moment: Impossibility, Unknowing, and the Lyric

In one of her most memorable epiphanies, Simone Weil proclaims that "human life is impossible." Her reasons for this deceptively religious claim serve as an eloquent apology for the lyric.

> Everything we want contradicts the conditions of the consequences attached to it, every affirmation we put forward involves a contradictory affirmation, all our feelings are mixed up with their opposites. It's because we are a contradiction.… We are beings with the faculty of knowing, willing and loving, and as soon as we turn our attention toward the objects of knowledge, will, and love, we receive evidence that there is not one which is not impossible.

It is precisely this notion of impossibility that challenges the lyric poet to witness to the tension that imbues human experience with the contradictory emotions and thoughts that appear, like atoms, to be in opposition to each other, while actually functioning in a complementary way. By stretching her strings between knowing and unknowing, the lyric poet plays a song that is paradoxical. Without uncertainty, the poet's lyre is only half strung. The strings are as good as broken, hanging detached and loose from their tuning machine. Each poet needs to discover her own unknowing and impossibility in order to string her instrument. While craft, grammar, technique and strategy can be taught, the essential unknowing of lyric poetry, which finds its way mysteriously into original syntax, emanates from the genius of the poet's voice. Emily Dickinson described this venture into unknowing as a terrifyingly solitary enterprise in her poem #633 (Franklin): "and I alone – / A Speck upon a Ball – / Went out upon Circumference – / Beyond the Dip of Bell."

The lyric poet is resigned to the inherent brokenness of her expression. In going "out upon circumference," she can never hope to complete her arc. "In the interval between reach and grasp," Anne Carson writes in *Eros the Bittersweet*, "the absent presence of desire comes alive." The poet learns how to play around the broken keys, creating a music in which the ghosts of the missing notes mingle with those that sound. The distant and close-up, the present and missing, work antiphonally in the lyric in such a way that high emotional voltage courses between absence and presence, loss and attainment, knowing and unknowing, the possible and the impossible. The strong lyric hangs in the balance, growing seemingly yet impossibly like an epiphyte. The limits of the lyric define the finite boundaries of mortality—feeling and knowing—while simultaneously aspiring toward an essential sensual and emotional awareness that transcend them.

As the essential language of emotional and sensual experience, the lyric has thrived since its earliest religious days 4,500 years ago in ancient Sumeria, evolving into new forms and aesthetics while adhering steadfastly to the same emotional and sensual content. In the introduction to his superb book *Greek Lyric Poetry*, Sherod Santos reminds us of the lyric poet's enduring connection to the legacy of lyric poetry.

> In Plato's *Phaedo*, the elder recalls: "I composed these poems … because I wanted to test the meaning of certain dreams I had." Since we are in some inevitable way a historical and cultural projection (however contested that projection may be) of the meaning the ancient poets dreamed, we might rightly assume we have something to gain by returning to the poems that were their test.

By returning to the poems that tested the dreams of our ancient and not-so-ancient forefathers and foremothers, we gain invaluable knowledge of the lyric tradition, as well as courage to proceed innovatively in our own time, with new forms and new language, but old subjects. In this essay, I will discuss four recurrent subjects of the lyric—death, pathos, ecstasy, and love—that have recurred since the first anonymous lines pressed into clay tablets, focusing on the inherent *agon* of unknowing and impossibility that has sustained the lyric's bittersweet legacy.

I have chosen five relatively modern poems that address the above subjects in concise and irreducible ways: Emily Dickinson's poem #280 (Franklin edition), in which death is the muse of everything and nothing; Hayden Carruth's "The Poet," in which pathos conjures the transpersonal self through empathy and sympathy; D. H. Lawrence's "Bavarian Gentians," in which ecstasy is the unifier of disparate things; Robert Frost's "Come In," in which alienation and exile are the impetus for transcendent resistance. These poems are examples of archetypal subjects, which I by no means intend to represent as a comprehensive overview of the boundless nature of the lyric. But like the lyric, which is essentially more about broken music—a point that Theodore Roethke celebrates in his poem "In the Evening Air"—than about completion or wholeness, this essay aspires to focus on particulars as distinct examples. Indeed, it is the lyric's "broken music" that exposes its paradox: that its charged, evocative parts add up to more than a whole. What that mysterious lyrical entity is that lies beyond the whole—the unfinished finished poem—remains ineffable, serving always as the seed for the next lyric.

Death

To begin with the most inscrutable of lyrical topics, I turn first to Emily Dickinson's poem #280 ("I felt a Funeral, in my Brain") as a lyric obsessed with impossibility, unknowing, brokenness, and what Nietzsche claimed was at the deepest level of all religious systems: cruelty. In her obsession with death, Dickinson juxtaposes everything with nothing in this poem: first, everything—which in her metaphysical mind is reason, the mortal entity that apprehends and makes sense of the world—and then nothing, or the precipitous demise of reason.

280

> I felt a Funeral, in my Brain,
> And Mourners to and fro

> Kept treading – treading – till it seemed
> That Sense was breaking through –
>
> And when they all were seated,
> A Service, like a Drum –
> Kept beating – beating – till I thought
> My mind was going numb –
>
> And then I heard them lift a Box
> And creak across my Soul
> With those same Boots of Lead, again,
> Then Space – began to toll,
>
> As all the Heavens were a Bell,
> And Being, but an Ear,
> And I, and Silence, some strange Race
> Wrecked, solitary, here –
>
> And then a Plank in Reason, broke,
> And I dropped down, and down –
> And hit a World, at every plunge,
> And Finished knowing – then –

 This subversive, oxymoronic elegy to the cruel end of knowing, told as a posthumous monologue, resonates with such terror and foreboding that only the coldest eye could have apprehended the depth of darkness and human alienation that emanate from its lines. Death functions as a muse for Dickinson in this poem. She, however, remains ambiguous about what has died. Her memory? Her soul? Her happiness? Her sanity? She feels a funeral, rather than observing it. It's palpable, internal. With Keatsian brio, she enters an interior uncertainty and never exits. The poem's structure and voice are ingeniously covert; it's a false narrative in hymnlike quatrains with an auto-elegiac speaker and cast of cerebral players/mourners as thinly disguised extras of the self. Beginning with a surreal funeral march that proceeds with moribund formality in the first three stanzas, Dickinson shifts cognitively in the last two stanzas to the speaker's metaphysical graveside, where she, or her soul, stands "wrecked" and "solitary," unfolding a proleptic vision in which she drops through worlds, until she has "Finished knowing – then." Dickinson concludes the funeral ritual at the end of the third stanza in order to concentrate on describing her existence itself as "but an Ear." She goes on then to decry the annihilation of her mind by co-opting a well-known religious image of her day, the plank of faith (from Holmes and Barber's *Religious Allegories*, published in 1848), and altering it to the "Plank of reason," only to break it over the same abyss that "the Christian" traverses successfully on the plank of faith, with Bible in hand. She shifts in mid-poem from describing an internal obsequy to chronicling her last conscious moments, turning from the funeral in her brain to a fall-by-fall, posthumous account of her actual demise.

Just as Whitman celebrates himself as a transpersonal self, down to those specific irrational atoms that "as good belong" to his reader as himself, Dickinson celebrates the courageous expedition of the lyric that goes bravely out upon circumference, beyond the last vestige of apprehension. Her dashes and blanks are no accident, creating the void that lies beyond the precipice of each of her line endings. The poem becomes brutally metaphysical at this point, in its transition from the opening symbolic funeral to the speaker's self-conscious musing on her identity as a partner only to silence; it would be easy to miss Dickinson's subtle shift away from runic narrative to lyrical fugue. All narrative scaffolding falls away into parataxis in the last two stanzas. Her last thoughts string themselves together in a series of metaphysical conceits that subvert all conventional thinking about the afterlife and faith with a searing indictment of earthly existence as no less than a hell of terrifying isolation. "As all the Heavens were a Bell, / And Being, but an Ear / And I, and Silence, some strange Race / Wrecked, solitary, here –." If Dickinson is writing about the imagined afterlife here, as some critics have suggested, the difference is moot, since, in Dickinson's thinking, death sentences reason to oblivion in *both* earthly and heavenly realms. Dickinson laments the demise of her conscious vessel, her "Brain," which is her life, aware that such lamentation in her interior uncertainty is a lyrical requirement for the life of her poetry. Oblivion inspires a dark but heroic lyricism in many of Dickinson's poems, but none concludes with a more desolate conclusion than #280.

In her descent into unknowing, Dickinson avoids conventional Protestant theology in the guise of a funeral ceremony, supplanting any notion of double predestination with her own sermon, which concludes in a chasm rather than heaven or hell. Her fall into this void curiously resembles the descent of Inanna in Sumerian mythology, where she, too, drops "down, and down," hitting worlds as she goes, removing garments along the way until she arrives naked and unknowing before her sister, Erishkegal, in the underworld. There is no direct evidence that Dickinson knew this myth, but if she didn't, she intuits its archetypal pattern with startling accuracy. She also echoes Christ's cry of utter abandonment on the cross, "My God, my God, why hast thou forsaken me?" in her assertion that the mind, even in its most visionary mode, is only capable in the end of apprehending its falling away from sense and reason, which at best either merely "seem" or "break through."

Dickinson's choice to move from one conceit to another in this poem exhibits her poetic hallmark of abandoning narrative coherence and inchoate metaphors in favor of divining multiple revelations within the same poem, rather than settling for one. She is both lyrically restless and fiercely intellectual, choosing to eulogize her last moments of ratiocination over submitting to any unthinking notion of ascendant faith. Unlike Anne Bradstreet, who adhered to religious conviction, she opts for a heretical strategy that imbues her lines with bold inversions of orthodox belief and even condescension toward stock religious images of her day. Death is indeed her impossible muse, conjuring an ultimate void while creating in the poem's interim a lyrical self-elegy that mourns the loss of knowing and the ultimate brokenness of her most vital tool for constructing poems, her "Reason," which is everything—and finally the end of knowing, which is, for all intents and purposes with regard to this speaker, nothing.

Pathos

Such intense, mortal self-consciousness as Dickinson expresses in #280 (Franklin) emanates from an ability to apprehend pathos, whether her own or another's. The lyric poet's emotional acumen for feeling *with* (compassion) or *for* (sympathy) another instills in him the mixed blessing of compound feeling. In his poem "The Poet," Hayden Carruth captures with stunning economy the unavoidable double suffering that is inherent in pathos.

The Poet

All night his window
shines in the woods
shadowed under the hills
where the gray owl

is hunting. He hears
the woodmouse scream—
so small a sound
in the great darkness

entering his pain.
For he is all and all
of pain, attracting
every new injury

to be taken and borne
as he must take
and bear it. He is
nothing: he is

his admiration. So
they seem almost
to know—the woodmouse
and the roving owl,
the woods and hills.

All night they move
around the stillness
of the poet's light.

Carruth mines stillness in this poem as a compassionate avatar of "every new injury," equating the role of the biblical "suffering servant" (Isaiah 52:13) with that of the poet. The speaker's Christlike identification with the poet as shamanistic witness to the pain of the smallest creature, a wounded wood mouse underscores the unique value of lyric poetry's redemptive labor. This poem conveys more about genuine compassion and human sensitivity to suffering than any doctrine or creed ever could, through its vivid imagery, its Zen-like awareness of the self as ultimately nothing without another, and its cognizance of the poet's vantage point as the *axis mundi*. The poem's short, mostly enjambed lines plummet down the page, leaving an indelible trail of fresh thought that ventures out to the limits of the self—to that point "Beyond the Dip of Bell" (Dickinson) where the self leaves off and the other begins. Like Habbakuk on the run, Carruth alerts the reader of "The Poet" to the spiritual necessity of hearing anew over merely reciting liturgical mantras, "admiring" over ignoring. The speaker's selfless identification with the injured wood mouse leads him to a humbling conclusion that is nonetheless revelatory: the poet is both "nothing" and "his admiration." But how can the poet be both these things at once? John Keats provided a memorable answer to this question in an 1818 letter to Richard Woodhouse:

> The poet has no identity—he is certainly the most unpoetical of all God's Creatures. When I am my own brain, then not myself goes home to myself; but the identity of everyone in the room begins to press upon me that I am in very little time annihilated—not only among Men; it would be the same in a Nursery of children.

In the spirit of Keats's poetic selflessness and essential "disinterestedness," Carruth claims in "The Poet" that the world resides in the smallest thing. Carruth depicts his poet as a witness who listens and waits, like the six-year-old speaker in Bishop's "In the Waiting Room," until his waiting turns to writing at that point when his intense listening to the smallest cries is transformed into a lyrical expression. But it is only with the awareness of his human limits that he is paradoxically able, by listening, to erase all differences between himself and his subject. In this transpersonal act of becoming his subject, he allows it—in this case, a wood mouse, which he calls "nothing" and "his admiration" simultaneously—to emphasize his appreciation of a thing so small, which looms so precious in his enlightened "human" apprehension.

Ecstasy

In turning from pathos to ecstasy, one finds that the subject of an ecstatic poem often transforms remarkably into something entirely different from what it literally is, while remaining itself at the same time. D. H. Lawrence's "Bavarian Gentians" provides a mythic example of an ecstatic poem that combines joy and madness, obsession and transcendence, in both form and content, without ever losing sight of the flower that lights the speaker's way to hell.

Beginning with a traditional iambic pentameter line, Lawrence quickly abandons blank verse in favor of a style that is consistently irregular. The poem unravels as a rich mix of metrical variation, primarily spondees, anapests, and iambs. This mercurial meter conjures both the heavy steps of the speaker's descent into hell and the leaden darkness of the underworld, as if to say that there are no received forms in the of "hall of Dis:" only stumbling and irregular feet that spur rhapsodic speech.

Bavarian Gentians

Not every man has gentians in his house
in Soft September, at slow, Sad Michaelmas.

Bavarian gentians, big and dark, only dark
darkening the daytime, torchlike with the smoking blueness of
    Pluto's gloom,
ribbed and torchlike, with their blaze of darkness spread blue
down flattening into points, flattened under the sweep of white
    day
torch-flower of the blue-smoking darkness, Pluto's dark-blue daze
black lamps from the halls of Dis, burning dark blue,
giving off darkness, blue darkness, as Demeter's pale lamps give
    off light,
lead me then, lead me the way.

> Reach me a gentian, give me a torch
> let me guide myself with the blue, forked torch of this flower
> down the darker and darker stairs, where blue is darkened on
>   blueness.
> even where Persephone goes, just now, from the frosted
>   September
> to the sightless realm where darkness was awake upon the dark
> and Persephone herself is but a voice
> or a darkness invisible enfolded in the deeper dark
> of the arms Plutonic, and pierced with the passion of dense gloom,
> among the splendour of torches of darkness, shedding darkness
>   on the lost bride and her groom.

Lawrence begins this poem on the plangent, autumnal note of the rarity of gentians in men's houses at Michaelmas, the feast day of Saint Michael the Archangel. The poem plumbs the depths of hell from the grieving groom's perspective. Unlike Demeter, Persephone's mother, who is left bereft and helpless on earth, the uncelebrated beloved descends into hell with his "torch-like" gentians. Since Lawrence's groom plays no transformative role in his infernal descent, as Demeter does in her creation of the seasons, Lawrence's groom disappears into the lost history of heartbroken lovers. Lawrence immortalizes Persephone's beloved here as a psychopomp, an Orphic character bearing gentians instead of a lyre, though he is no less lyrical than Orpheus in his song. Unlike Demeter, he is able to divine the passage to hell on his own. Lighting his way are his Bavarian gentians, aglow with the "smoking blueness of Pluto's gloom." As the instrument of his ironic light, the gentians illuminate hell itself. Lawrence obsesses on the gentians throughout the poem as both a trope of discerning blindness in the underworld and as beautiful earthly flowers. With melodic, insistent repetition, he allows the gentians to lead him to his beloved; "Let me guide myself with the blue," he says, "forked torch of this flower / down the darker and darker stairs." The poetic mantra of the gentian's color, "a burning dark blue"—and the shape of their physical appearance, "ribbed" and "flattening into points"—pierces hell itself.

The groom's descent into the underworld becomes increasingly ecstatic with each new description of the gentians, as if Lawrence's emphatic repetition of their color were oxygen to their flames. And yet there is also a limit to the groom's descent that celebrates the profligate, demonic nature of his love. He is, after all, configuring a psychic out-of-the-body body (the literal definition of ecstasy) for the purpose of traveling in a fictional yet spiritually real tableau. His irrational, utterly romantic scenario defies convention in the guise of convention, a wedding ceremony. The damned couple end up in a sepulcher "among the splendor of torches of darkness, shedding darkness." In an inversion of Milton's famous conceit for the light of hell, "darkness visible," Lawrence describes darkness as "invisible," leaving his reader in an infernal basement at a futile wedding. Yet he has seduced his reader with a conceit that is nonetheless universal. By the end of the poem, the gentians have become palpable darkness itself, both invisible and bright with burning blue. Only in the paradoxical realm of this ecstatic state can such a contradiction work. The gentians transport the reader and lover alike into a darkness that is hardly sanguine, yet irresistible for its allure and strange familiarity, its haunting lyrical depiction of Eros's depths and terrors. The groom has retrieved his bride from Pluto, but unlike Orpheus, he is doomed to remain in the "arms Plutonic," which is his choice, the ultimate limit and unknowing of his love.

Love

Love poetry swears obedience to a passionate, irrational muse. The author of the Garden of Eden creation story, known as J or Yahwist, sounds this romantic archetype in the Bible's first love story, summing up millennia of prehistoric romance with a mantra that has resonated ever since: "Bones of my bones. Flesh of my flesh." Although each age has interpreted the love muse, Erato, differently, she has remained constant in her psychic intensity and her wild conceits. Even Plato, in his subordination of Eros in *The Symposium* to the higher love of ideas, acknowledges the inexorable power of romantic love, especially as a subtext in Socrates' not-so-subtle jockeying for a seat next to his beloved Alcibiades. The Latin poets Ovid, Catullus, and Propertius reveled in their respective infatuations, in their repeated shows of lovesickness, jealousy, and rage. The Dark Ages suffered a drought of love lyrics; what poems survive from the early, Viking era are warlike (e.g., *Beowulf*, or the *Song of Roland* in 1045) or else philosophical (*The Seafarer*, *The Wanderer*), overwhelmingly narratives of male pursuits and reckonings. In 1095 William of Aquitaine's innovative poems of courtly love emerged, and shortly joined an irrepressible torrent that, as C. S. Lewis rightly claimed in his classic *The Allegory of Love*, "effected a change which has left no corner of our ethics, our imagination, or our daily life untouched."

Blazing the way for Dante and Petrarch, the troubadours and first courtly writers of France created a new lyrical mode within Western poetry that has inspired poets, for better and worse, for the past thousand years. Who could have known that the combination of the unattached Christian knight and Arabic love poetry from the Islamic caliphate of Spain would produce such a long-lasting and profound change in Western poetry?

In the medieval model of courtly love, viewed as the *sine qua non* of spiritual love, suitors were chaste or often unrequited, and the lady of the court reigned in place of the Virgin Mary. Medieval love poetry reached an ironic religious apotheosis in Dante's Divine Comedy, proving that there is a fine line indeed between the earthly and heavenly vision of the beloved. But for all Dante's efforts to restore love to its rightful religious place by transforming Beatrice into a light-bearing agent of God, love poets have failed in the intervening eight hundred years to reach these heights, preferring to devote themselves mostly to secular inspirations of what seems divine. In contrast to Dante, they have proceeded with recrudescent verve to dismiss objectivity and reason for the sake of subjective, often irrational, sense and passion, rendering Yeats's criterion for strong poetry, the "cold eye," more of a hindrance than a catalyst. The beloved has remained largely earthbound ever since, and still celebrated mostly from the male perspective.

Since the eleventh century, love poets have found themselves concocting new conceits, lyrical themes, and metaphors in each new generation. The love lyric's salt, however, resides not in its subject matter but in a specific lover's romantic experience. How then to create yet another unique poetic expression of love? To add another worthy stanza to the already vast list of love poems? As the group The Magnetic Fields sang in 1999: "The book of love is long and boring / No one can lift the damn thing / It's full of charts and facts and figures / and instructions for dancing / but I, I love it when you read to me / and you, you can read me anything." Without risking foolishness from the start, the love poet cannot deign to begin without swimming naked in the waters of his own madness, supplanting disinterestedness with intense obsession in the belief that his beloved is both particular and universal. He therefore believes that the reader stands in willingly for the beloved, for love poetry, in all its madness, makes "the divinest sense."

"I am two fooles, I know, / For loving, and for saying so," John Donne admits in his poem "The triple Foole"; "In whining Poëtry; / But where's that wiseman, that would not be I, / If she would not deny?"

Unlike the model of the evanescent poet that T. S. Eliot depicts in his essay "Tradition and the Individual Talent," the love poet eschews new critical criteria with incurable defiance and self-assertion. His audience is not the many but the one. The last thing he wishes to do is disappear before his beloved. His poetry is all personality, all I, I, I in pursuit of you, you, you. But inherent in all enduring love poetry is a critical irony, a lack of certainty in the midst of romantic thrall. Its fragile half-life is ever vulnerable to whim and chance, creating a relativity in which a few charged erotic moments can explode into a lifelong romance, as in the cases of Dante and Petrarch. It is precisely the love poet's unknowing that infuses his lyrics with a thrilling tension that combines both longing and doubt.

The love lyric suffers, therefore, from both the curse and the blessing of its subject matter and muse: Cupid. Ovid famously captures the god of erotic love's monopoly on love poetry with feigned resentment in the first stanza of his *Amores*. "Arms, warfare, violence—I was winding up to produce a / Regular epic, with verse-form to match— / Hexameters, naturally, but Cupid (they say) with a snicker / Lopped off one foot from each alternate line. / 'Nasty young brat,' I told him, 'who made you

Inspector of / Metres? / We poets come under the Muses, we're not in your mob."[1] But of course they are. Cupid is more than generous in his visitations, but the poet resigns himself immediately to the impossibility of expressing his "meanings" in any ultimate way. "The heart has its own language," the Persian Rumi wrote eight centuries ago. "The heart knows a hundred thousand ways to speak."[2] Conceits comprise an essential aspect of love's "mystic tone," capturing what Dickinson called "the internal difference, where the meanings are." These internal differences make no literal sense and are so transcendentally figurative that only the mind that has wed the heart in an experience of intense romantic love possesses the genius for grasping the metaphysical sense of such lines and stanzas as:

When I think of the state I'm in
I feel a chill within those flames of mine

(Petrarch, from Canzone 122; translation by Mark Musa)

*

If they be two, they are two so
As stiffe twin compasses are two,
Thy soul the fixt foot, makes no show
To move, but doth, if th'other doe.
...
Thy firmnes makes my circle just,
And makes me end, where I begunne.

(John Donne, from "A Valediction: forbidding mourning")

*

Your hair is like a flock of goats,
    moving down the slopes of Gilead.
Your teeth are like a flock of shorn ewes
    that have come up from the washing,

---

1. Translated by Peter Green.
2. Translated by Fatemeh Keshavarz.

all of which bear twins
    and not one among them is bereaved.
Your lips are like a scarlet thread,
    and your mouth is lovely.
Your cheeks are like halves of a pomegranate
    behind your veil.
Your neck is like the tower of David
    built for an arsenal,
whereon hang a thousand bucklers,
    all of them shields of warriors.
Your two breasts are like two fawns,
    twins of a gazelle
    that feed among the lilies.

(Song of Songs 4: 1–4; Revised Standard Version)

*

The stars be hid that led me to this pain;
Drownèd is Reason that should me comfort,
And I remain despairing of the port.

(Thomas Wyatt, from "My Galley")   *   *   *

Martin Buber was profoundly correct about the vicissitudes of love when he observed that "the particular Thou, after the relational event has run its course, is bound to become an It."[3] Eros dictates an inherent on/off or yes/no dialectic in the heart, opposing the most basic precepts of faith and marriage. *Anima* and *animus* make for fiery bed partners but near-impossible mates. We see this bittersweet dialectic played out again and again throughout mythology, literature, and history in such ill-fated couples as Innana and Dumuzi, Isis and Osiris, Solomon and the Queen of Sheba, Manjun and Layla, Orpheus and Eurydice, Catullus and Lesbia, Sappho and her beloved, Guinevere and Lancelot, Anthony and Cleopatra, Tristan and Isolde, Romeo and Juliet, Abelard and Heloise, Dante and Beatrice, Petrarch and Laura, Emily Dickinson and Reverend Wadsworth, Dr. Zhivago and Lara, Anna Karenina and

---

3. Translated by Ronald Gregor Smith.

Count Vronsky, Gatsby and Daisy, to name some of the most infamous examples. The tension between the earthly and the divine that lies at the heart of every romance derives its charge as much from absence as from presence. If presence permits lovers' consummation, absence fuels their tireless hearts.

While every love story contains a narrative of fulfillment and loss, enduring as much within oral tradition as on the page, it is the lyric that memorializes the *frissons* of erotic love in highly charged evocative lines, even fragments. But not without a price, as Sylvia Plath reminds us in "Lady Lazarus:" "There is a charge // For eyeing of my scars, there is a charge / For a word or a touch / Or a bit of blood // Or a piece of my hair or my clothes." Eros has always had Thanatos as its antinomy. No Thanatos, no charge in the wires that stretch from heart to heart. Eros consequently lives impossibly at the edge of social and physical boundaries. Dickinson described his antisocial, even criminal affliction as "The Soul's retaken moments – / When, Felon led along, / With shackles on the plumed feet, / And staples, in the Song ..."

While unrequited and lost love will, no doubt, continue to haunt lyric poets, the intensity of romantic love has diminished significantly over the last fifty years, compromised by such "modern conveniences" and anodynes as birth control, abortion, antidepressants, and the vast, accessible supermarket of video and Internet erotica. Without the risk of death, social castigation, and disease, the love lyric loses both its acetylene and its poison. But Eros is less a misfit than a witness, less a masochist than a fool. The love lyric has always reflected Eros's raw, vulnerable nature. In a society blessed with such medical sophistication as ours, however, Eros views Thanatos from a more comfortable distance. The threat of untimely pregnancy and untreatable disease no longer charges relationships with the same degree of grave danger that preyed on couples as recently as fifty years ago. Since mortality is the love poet's salt, he goes to heroic lengths both to celebrate and opine over the beloved with ecstatic inspiration. To turn his head toward what no anodyne can ultimately cure in our very midst, albeit behind a hospital curtain. One need, for instance, only read such lines as these below by D. A. Powell from his book *Cocktails*, to appreciate the ongoing vital legacy of the love lyric's mortal witness:

> I clothe his sinew and drape from it and he loves me
> here is the garland that moves not upon our head: but gigs.
>   razor thorns
> and as that crown sits firmly so I sit firm.   and if everything
>   should perish:
> as bridegroom reckoned in his likeness I go.   rock, river,
>   permeable flesh
>
> (from "[because I were ready before destruction. bearing the sign of his affliction]")

These lines, occasioned by the AIDS epidemic, return us to our most human selves with memorable pathos. Their broken but lucid syntax updates the love lyric's diachronic connection to the radical ethic of *agape*. Suddenly, all the anodynes in the world pale in the light of this great if fatal love. Indeed, we live three times in poetry such as this: first, identifying vicariously with the speaker's selfless love for his partner; second, feeling a simultaneous love of our own that emboldens us to sit as firmly "as that crown"; and third, transcending death as "rock, river, permeable flesh." A lyric that is as life-affirming as this hides in the open as a difficult, frightening, visceral expression. Yet it testifies invaluably for those who wish to turn their heads from "the shadows" to what history has proven repeatedly as an unguaranteed human commodity: namely, the existence of a soul, or whatever one might care to call that transpersonal self within a person that "assumes what [the other, the beloved] shall assume."

2009

Suspense, Suspension, and the Sublime in the Poetry of Robert Frost

Robert Frost was a sublimely gifted poet with a prodigious capacity for what John Keats called "negative capability"—that is, the ability to exist "in uncertainty, Mystery, doubt," and, I would add, *suspense* also— "without any irritable reaching after fact and reason." Frost created characters who pondered one moral and/or metaphysical question after another, most often in pastoral and domestic settings.

As famous as he was, Frost was often misinterpreted as more of a genial folk poet than a stunning witness of the sublime. He made an indelible first impression with accessible pastoral subject matter and hypnotic verbal music—"farms and forms" as the critic Christopher Benfey has referred to his topics and style. Unlike his modernist peers T. S. Eliot, Wallace Stevens, Ezra Pound, Marianne Moore, and Hart Crane, he avoided urban settings, exotic subject matter, and free verse in favor of local landscapes, rural narratives, blank verse, and rhyming iambic pentameter. In short, he discovered his "wasteland" in his own "desert places" at least a decade before his expatriate colleagues became the rage in the early twenties. Although he won four Pulitzer Prizes, the American reading public on the whole failed to appreciate what he liked to call his "ulterior meanings."

Randall Jarrell was the first important critic and fellow poet to acknowledge the sadness and terror in Frost's poems in his essays "The Other Frost" in 1947 and then "To the Laodiceans" in 1952, where he pointed out how "diabolically good" Frost's details were in his poem

"Design—how full, he wrote, of "the stilling rigor of death that 'white piece of rigid satin cloth' is." Then five years later, in 1958, at Frost's eighty-fifth birthday party at the Waldorf Astoria Hotel in New York City, Lionel Trilling echoed Jarrell's observation in a speech he called "a cultural episode." Trilling declared:

> So radical a work, I need scarcely say, is not carried out by reassurance, nor by the affirmation of old virtues and pieties. It is carried out by the representation of the terrible actualities of life in a new way. I think of Robert Frost as a terrifying poet. Call him, if it makes things any easier, a tragic poet, but it might be useful every now and then to come out from under the shelter of that literary word. The universe that he conceives is a terrifying universe.

Trilling went on in his birthday speech to site the last stanza of Frost's poem "Desert Places" as a witty *ars poetica* that exemplified what he felt was "the energy with which emptiness is perceived":

> They cannot scare me with their empty spaces
> Between stars—on stars where no human race is.
> I have it in me so much nearer home
> To scare myself with my own desert places.

Frost replied to Trilling a few weeks later with this "thank you note" from his home in Ripton, Vermont:

> You made my birthday party a surprise party. I should like nothing better than to do a thing like that myself—to depart from the Rotarian norm in a Rotarian situation. You weren't there to sing "Happy Birthday, dear Robert," and I don't mind being made controversial. No sweeter music can come to my ears than the clash of arms over my dead body when I am down.

What's worse, one wonders: to suffer scant recognition as a great poet for nearly a hundred years and then to be bastardized to boot, like Emily Dickinson, or to achieve enormous fame while going largely misunderstood throughout one's career? Both Dickinson and Frost, the most sublime American poets, along with Walt Whitman, terrified their readers, while at the same time entertaining them. But Frost was the most canny of the three in his talent for distracting the guard dogs of his readers' houses, that is, their initial wariness about any "ulterior meanings," by throwing them "bones" of blank verse, rhyme, and accessible subject matter during the erudite epoch of high modernism, while then slipping around back and breaking in with terror. The delayed recognition of Frost's break-ins signaled a telling reaction formation in his readers, namely, their immediate inclination to appreciate his poems for their familiar pastoral quality and Yankee wit, which, for the most part and rather ironically, they found comforting despite Frost's dark subject matter and terrifying conclusions.

In fact, Frost's unprecedented initial popularity grew in direct proportion to his readers' flight from the real nature of his genius. Americans loved him in the way children love *Mother Goose* when they fall under the hypnotic spell of such lullabies as "London Bridge," "Rock-a-Bye Baby," and "Jack and Jill" without realizing they're listening to one catastrophe after another. Frost loved *Mother Goose* too, and he acknowledged its influence, which one can clearly hear in the one poem out of all his work that, he felt, approached perfection, "Stopping by Woods on a Snowy Evening"—which, indeed, is no less than a haunting adult nursery rhyme in sixteen unfaltering iambic tetrameter lines. "Poetry is a way of taking life by the throat," Frost said, and so he does with his tight musical lines that grasp his reader as well by the throat and hold on, even in their unresolved conclusions. Frost also said, "In three words I can summarize everything I've learned about life: it goes on." The "promises" Frost's speaker keeps in "Stopping by Woods on a Snowy Evening" demonstrate Frost's commitment to living over dying—especially following his near-suicidal venture in the Great Dismal Swamp as a young man, following his fiancée Elinor's initial rejection of his proposal.

Place was just as important as content for Frost in the development of what he called his "quarrels with the world." Acts of gazing out from above and swinging from side to side, both physically and cognitively, recur often in his most sublime poems, where he suspends his speakers at the top of trees and staircases. His poems "Birches," "Wild Grapes," "After Apple Picking," "Mowing," "Home Burial," and "The Witch of

Coös" come immediately to mind as examples of the suspense he found in suspension. In-betweenness was his figurative study, where he either hung or stood in voluntary discomfort as he contemplated his place and condition on Earth. In this sense, he was an utterly chthonic poet who was inclined to crucify his speakers on found "crosses," where they suffer necessary pain that transports them to some higher awareness about grief, longing, or simply their innate complexity as human beings. Longinus might indeed have been describing many of Frost's poems when he wrote, in the first century CE, that a sublime poem possessed "a greatness of soul, imitation, or imagery" in which the poet, as if "instinctually," creates a work of art that uplifts "our soul" to an exalted height where "it takes proud flight, and is filled with joy and vaunting, as though it had itself produced what it has heard."

It is in Frost's suspenseful extended metaphors especially that he encounters not only joy but terror as well, which is the risk that his "lone strikers" encounter in their respective positions of suspension. I'd like to take a look at four of Frost's poems— "Mowing," "After Apple-Picking," "Birches," and "Home Burial"—as examples of his use of suspension as a device for achieving "instinctive" expressions that lead ultimately to sublime moments, whether epiphanic in their conclusions or bittersweet in their lack of resolution.

* * *

"Birches" appeared in Frost's third book, *Mountain Interval*, in 1916. Here Frost suspends himself between heaven and earth, recalling one of his favorite boyhood pastimes, swinging on birch trees. Although he enjoyed this solitary activity as a child, he finds he can't reminisce about it now in his adult life as just a daring, exciting activity and leave it at that; he has to pick a "quarrel" with the firmament, which he turns into a metaphysical plain where he experiences sublime moments as a "swinger of birches." He describes his momentary suspension at the apex of his swings as not only physically thrilling, but paradigmatic of a mortal weariness that conjures his recurrent "dream" of escaping gravity's hold by returning to his childhood where he climbed "black branches up a snow white trunk / *Toward* heaven." The more Frost recounts these days, the more he develops his poetic train of thought into a dramatic monologue, but one in which we, as his readers, experience both his quarrel with aging and his exhilarating childhood memory. We taste his euphoric communion with the sky while also identifying with his weighty return to earth. We enter his forest willingly as companion birch-climbers, hanging suspended in the same longing of childhood nostalgia when we're "weary of considerations" and wish to "get away from earth awhile / And then come back to it and begin over."

Feeling and intellect combine in "Birches" to form a sublime whole that crosses over the transom of the poet's mere personal experience to the receptive inner eye of his listener's imagination. The poem entertains first before it lowers its philosophical boom, hinting clearly enough that the speaker's reminiscence about birch-swinging is also an extended metaphor for "the Truth" that breaks in at midlife "With all her matter-of-fact about the ice-storm," or, as Frost says more plainly several lines later, when one has grown "weary of considerations, / And life is too much like a pathless wood / Where your face burns and tickles with the cobwebs." This ground-level view, harsh as it is, provides the necessary antinomy for the transcendent affirmation that Frost makes at the end of the poem in his sudden declaration: "Earth's the right place for love: / I don't know where it's likely to go better." This is a deferential, daunting truth, one that, like all of Frost's other truths, submits to human limitations while at the same time expressing intimations of an inscrutable beyond.

There is a word in this poem that emphasizes this sublime human condition as an ultimately ironic disposition for its very limitations. Frost italicizes it in an almost heavy-handed way, at least in a way that postmodernists would call unfashionably determinate. The word is *toward*. Rather than proclaim the birch tree as an earthly catapult for reaching heaven, Frost signifies the birch tree as an earthly scaffold for approaching heaven, but not reaching it, for appealing to the innate monkey in us as well as our human wonder.

We see Frost at his antinomian best in this poem, eschewing familiar religious language for his own firsthand expression that embodies, at least on the page, what Ralph Waldo Emerson called "aboriginal strength" and what Longinus defined as "great soul."

* * *

The second poem I'd like to discuss is a bit of an anomaly, for its speaker, presumably Frost, partakes in a grounded activity. I've chosen it because Frost suspends himself cognitively in this poem in the act of swinging his scythe as he contemplates the "unsayable" in the midst of work. The poem is "Mowing," a sonnet, which Frost published in his first book, A Boy's Will, in 1913.

Mowing

There was never a sound beside the wood but one,
And that was my long scythe whispering to the ground.
What was it it whispered? I knew not well myself;
Perhaps it was something about the heat of the sun,
Something, perhaps, about the lack of sound—
And that was why it whispered and did not speak.
It was no dream of the gift of idle hours,
Or easy gold at the hand of fay or elf:
Anything more than the truth would have seemed too weak
To the earnest love that laid the swale in rows,
Not without feeble-pointed spikes of flowers
(Pale orchises), and scared a bright green snake.
The fact is the sweetest dream that labor knows.
My long scythe whispered and left the hay to make.

Frost praises the unique sound his scythe makes in the field beside the woods as his first order of business. This sound is organic and mysterious—a whisper rather than just steel on grass. The scythe speaks to the farmer in the breathy voice one uses to tell secrets. Frost, the farmer, wonders just what runic sense his scythe imparts to "the ground." He confesses that he himself is ignorant of this secret, proceeding with supposition and speculation: "Perhaps it was something about the heat of the sun. / Something perhaps about the lack of sound— / And that was why it whispered and did not speak." In his metaphysical investigation into the scythe's whisper "to the ground,"

Frost observes that the scythe's voice is as full of silence as it is with sound, which is why it whispers. Frost builds poetic suspense as he continues to think about this sound as the source of a pastoral secret that only the receptive mower is privileged to hear and understand.

Turning next to ruling out possibilities for the scythe's sound, Frost eliminates a few facile options for the whisper: it is neither "the dream of the gift of idle hours," as any farmer might tell the city dweller, nor "anything more than the truth," since that would seem "too weak to the earnest love" of the laborer in the field. How fascinating that Frost writes "anything more" instead of "anything less" here, as if to say that embellishing the truth, especially with regard to labor, degrades the truth more than it enhances it.

Within the intense space of fourteen lines, Frost arrives at the answer to the mystery of the scythe's whisper in the poem's penultimate line. By combining two opposites, dream and fact, just as he had earlier with sound and silence, Frost delivers the earthly news: "The fact is the sweetest dream that labor knows." While contradictory on the surface, this line captures the ecstatic yet empirical nature of work, exemplifying what F. Scott Fitzgerald called "the test of a first-rate intelligence ... the ability to hold two opposing ideas in mind at the same time and still retain the ability to function."

Fact is dream to the laborer in the uncut field, the scythe whispers as the farmer swings it, just as Frost "swings" his lines so memorably on the page—his "ground"—back and forth between literal and figurative sense in a kind of cognitive suspension where he's thinking and working at the same time above the grass, lifting himself into revelation. His embrace of realism at the end of this poem embraces the hard truth he would follow the rest of his life, namely, the pursuit of his own poetic harvest through his hard labor as a poet—the facts that would come to him in the course of writing, wielding his pen; human facts "so much nearer home" than "the empty spaces between the stars," as he would later declare in his poem "Desert Places," interior mortal facts that would terrify him in his inner gazing.

* * *

In "After Apple-Picking," Frost writes with postlapsarian self-consciousness at the top of a ladder. The apple tree from which his speaker looks out is a metaphor as ancient as Eden itself for what J, the author of the Bible's second creation story, linked to the "awareness of death" in Eve's consciousness-raising conversation with the serpent. Suspended between Earth and "heaven still" at the top of an apple tree, Frost conveys the physical pain that accompanies the pain of his mortal awareness. It's a compounded pain in his feet—an "ache" and "pressure" that his instep keeps of "a ladder-round." As he pauses from apple-picking for just a moment, he begins musing about the inexorable force of nature that has hurtled him beyond "the great harvest [he himself] once desired." Frost expresses his festering chagrin over "the form [his] dreaming [is] about to take." Resisting mirror-gazing, he forces himself instead to gaze at the ice's mirror itself, which he then breaks—in five lines that could serve as a profound *ars poetica* for all of his poetry:

> I cannot rub the strangeness from my sight
> I got from looking through a pane of glass
> I skimmed this morning from the drinking trough
> And held against the world of hoary grass.
> It melted, and I let it fall and break.

With this description of breaking the ice in the water trough, the poet breaks the poem's form of blank verse with occasional rhyme, alternating single-stressed lines with dimeter, trimeter, and pentameter throughout the rest of the poem.

Perched at the top of his mythical lookout tree, Frost turns the "forbidden fruit" into a symbol of time and experience. Gazing down on the windfalls below, he reminisces about missed opportunities—"a barrel that I didn't fill"—and recalls a startling early-morning scene that transforms his orchard work into a personal commentary on what Robert Penn Warren called "the turpitude of time." The speaker's act of "looking through a pane" of trough ice at the "world of hoary grass" strikes him with an indelible "strangeness." Rather than gaze at his reflection, he regards the world through the glass of ice, seeing beyond himself to the white manifestation of death. The ice is a simple chilling fact, and Frost stares at it with his own "cold eye," as Yeats would say, in an anti-mimetic act of confronting nature's blank face straight on. Frost speaks here as a seer-poet who boldly forsakes any religious belief or notion of faith in favor of seeing for himself. His foreknowledge of "the form" that his dreaming is about to take casts him deeper into a brown study in which he begins to recall his myriad experiences—both good and bad—that have settled in the same "heap" in his memory. In place of any thought, speculation, or consideration about his soul's fate, he conducts a symbolic inventory of his earthly acts, which he compares to apples, all of which "struck the earth, / No matter if not bruised or spiked with stubble," ending up in "the cider-apple heap / As of no worth." Great rhyme: "earth" and "worth." Frost speaks like a modern-day Qoheleth from Ecclesiastes in "After Apple-Picking," essentially repeating that Old Testament sage's refrain, "Vanity of vanities, all is vanity," in his own New England vernacular, then adding his own deeply sardonic endnote about any prospect of afterlife or heaven:

> One can see what will trouble
> This sleep of mine, whatever sleep it is.
> Were he not gone,
> The woodchuck could say whether it's like his
> Long sleep, as I describe its coming on,
> Or just some human sleep.

A lowly woodchuck, of all creatures, as opposed to a saint or theologian or fellow "believer," serves as his authority on the afterlife. Like Emily Dickinson in her poem "I felt a Funeral, in my Brain," Frost clings stubbornly to what he knows from his earthly experience.

"After Apple-Picking" marks Frost's first sublimely "human" poem, in which he holds a heroic gaze to the ground rather than stare heavenward where his ladder's pointing, while feeling at the same time "wrecked solitary here" (as Emily Dickinson put it). He then adds an irreverent joke about the afterlife as "just some human sleep," a mortal doze from which he will fail to wake one day. Nine years later, in 1923, in his third book of poems, *New Hampshire*, Frost clarified this "sleep" at the conclusion of his poem "To Earthward," in which he traces the arc of human life from romantic love to a mortal desire strong enough to embrace the numb existence of earthly burial:

> The hurt is not enough:
> I long for weight and strength
> To feel the earth as rough
> To all my length.

What's particularly striking about the timing of "After Apple-Picking" is that it appeared in Frost's second book, *North of Boston*, in 1914, well before the United States' entry into World War I and the advent of modernism. So, not only does it presage modernism with its atheistic renunciation of an afterlife beyond human sleep, it stands as an often-misprized lyric about the mere sorrows of autumn rather than what it actually intones. It's not that dissimilar actually from Friedrich Nietzsche's religious renunciations in *Thus Spake Zarathustra*. Frost was terrifying from the start, but hardly anyone noticed.

* * *

Frost's masterpiece, "Home Burial," was also published early on in *North of Boston*. In this dramatic dialogue, Frost suspends a grieving couple separately, first the wife and then the husband, at the top of a staircase. The poem begins with Amy, the mother, at the top of the stairs, "looking back over her shoulder at some fear," which her husband informs the reader is "the little graveyard where [his] people are"—and now their child.

Frost suspends Amy in the first line of the poem in a posture that embodies T.S. Eliot's idea of objective correlative, that is, "a set of objects, a situation, a chain of events which shall be the formula of that particular emotion"—in this case, Amy's fearful backward glance out the window at the graveyard. When her husband approaches her at the top of the stairs, where "she cowered under him" with a face that "changed from terrified to dull," they stand suspended together, but with such utterly different dispositions that they can't remain together there for long. She shrinks from beneath his arm, challenging her husband to see what she sees, thinking of him as a "blind creature." He says he sees, but she disagrees: "You don't," she tells him. "Tell me what it is." He ventures an unsatisfactory answer, "Broad-shouldered little slabs there in the sunlight / On the sidehill. We haven't to mind *those*. / But I understand: it is not the stones, / But the child's mound—" Amy responds like King Lear after Cordelia's death with a slew of renunciations: "Don't, don't, don't, don't." She withdraws at this point in the poem and slides downstairs, as if floating, still suspended on her grief. "Can't a man speak of his own child he's lost?" her husband asks desperately. To which Amy responds with this brutal indictment: "You can't because you don't know how to speak. / If you had any feelings, you that dug / With your own hand—how could you?—his little grave." Frost ties feeling to language itself here, signifying poetry as a feminine strength. Amy knows how to speak, while her husband is at a loss for the right words. He concedes to his wife, "We could have some arrangement / By which I'd bind myself to keep hands off / Anything special you're a-mind to name." Which apparently would include himself, also, since he goes nameless throughout the poem. Every attempt he makes to comfort Amy only results in exacerbating her heartbreak. "My words are nearly always an offense," he confesses. "I don't know how to speak of anything / So as to please you. But I might be taught / I should suppose." But no. He is unteachable as far as Amy is concerned, as well as blind, unfeeling, and dumb. Her resentment toward him has evolved into a disconsolate, global keening that the man despairs of ever consoling:

'I shall laugh the worst laugh I ever laughed.
I'm cursed. God, if I don't believe I'm cursed.'

'I can repeat the very words you were saying:
"Three foggy mornings and one rainy day
Will rot the best birch fence a man can build."
Think of it, talk like that at such a time!
What had how long it takes a birch to rot
To do with what was in the darkened parlor?
You couldn't care! The nearest friends can go
With anyone to death, comes so far short
They might as well not try to go at all.
No, from the time when one is sick to death,

> One is alone, and he dies more alone.
> Friends make pretense of following to the grave,
> But before one is in it, their minds are turned
> And making the best of their way back to life
> And living people, and things they understand.
> But the world's evil. I won't have grief so
> If I can change it. Oh, I won't, I won't!'

The poem ends in despair, with Amy opening the door to flee aimlessly as her husband threatens to bring her back "by force." Frost, in his remarkably accurate empathy with Amy, suspends her in no-woman's land, demonstrating "greatness of soul" in his ability to grip the high-voltage wire of a mother's grief barehanded, as well as her indictment of "the world" as "evil," that is, as a place where "friends make pretense of following to the grave."

I think of the chorus's response to Gilgamesh's grief over Enkidu in *The Epic of Gilgamesh* as the kind of adequate response Amy would have liked to hear but could not hope for from her "blind creature" of a husband who was too consumed with "everyday concerns" to grasp that the loss haunted her:

> With an inner atmosphere
> Where words are flung out in the air but stay
> Motionless without an answer,
> Hovering about one's lips
> Or arguing back to haunt
> The memory with what one failed to say.[1]

Frost portrayed several female characters in extremity with rare compassion and insight in such poems as "The Subverted Flower," "Wild Grapes," "The Witch of Coös," "The Fear," "The Hill Wife," "Paul's Wife," and "Two Witches." Women speak in these poems from suspended vantage points above their patriarchal worlds with terror, fear, loneliness, and wisdom. "Home Burial," however, represents, to this reader at least, the most exquisite example of Frost's genius for negative capability as a middle-aged male poet immersing himself in the uncertainty and mystery of a grieving young mother. The impasse

---
1. Translated by Herbert Mason.

Frost creates in this poem, at the risk of losing his reader's sympathy for his protagonist, Amy, is deeply disturbing. But it's a transcendent poem for this very reason, witnessing to the inscrutable calculus of loss for which there are not only any words or solution, but no place on earth itself, much less home, for a mourner like Amy to seek refuge or understanding. The abyss into which she is about to bolt—"somewhere out of this house"— at the end of the poem leaves her husband, herself, and the reader in a state of unnerving suspense, with a Shakespearean boldness and concomitant belief in our human capacity to stare into it—that "somewhere out of this house."

* * *

Thrilling and *chilling* are the two words that describe Frost's most sublime poems, such as the four I've discussed here. Frost, perhaps more than any other American poet, mythologized a landscape that continues to be known simply as Frost country—a landscape on which he wrote his "recurrent obsessions," to borrow a phrase from the art historian Simon Schama, or as Frost himself called them, his "quarrels." These now-classic "quarrels" have made it close to impossible for any rural New England poet to follow Frost without echoing his work, if even in the slightest reference to a tree or wall or hillside. The fact that the Vermont legislature waited twenty-six years before appointing the next and only the second poet laureate of Vermont, Galway Kinnell, in 1989, testifies to the deep respect that readers of poetry and poets alike felt for Frost as the quintessential state poet.

Despite several waves of the new that have transpired since Frost's death in 1963, from postmodernism to the recent welcome explosion of multicultural voices, readers continue "to hang" with Frost in his native trees, woods, and roads, where they still feel utterly haunted by his narratives, monologues, and dramas. Frost harrows his readers with terrors that compel even nonreaders of poetry to return to again and again for more than just the mere, odd pleasure of being frightened, but to discover vicariously that their lives, our lives, are extraordinary, fragile, difficult, painful, bittersweet, contradictory, ecstatic, and grievous. Not that we didn't know these things already. By conveying the felt presence of human experience in physical interactions with the world, Frost divines passage to his readers' psyches through their bodies first and then their minds and hearts. We feel the abstractions he quarrels with in our bones, whether it's the factual dream of labor, or the limits of human consciousness, or the affirmation of Earth as "the right place for love," or the inconsolable reality of grief. Frost's language finds us, enchants us, suspends us, then leaves us captured in our own willful restraints.

2019

That Odor, That Other: On Louise Glück's "Mock Orange" and Beyond

On the occasion of the publication of Louise Glück's career-spanning volume, *Poems 1962–2012*, I was struck by just how many of Glück's poems remain not only memorable—such poems as "Celestial Music," "The Garden," "Eros," "The Drowned Children," "Vita Nova," "Gretel in Darkness," "Nostos," "Averno," "Persephone the Wanderer," "The Wild Iris"—but essential for their mythic force that continues to resonate in her deceptively simple language. Throughout her career, which has continued with both vatic and psychological force since the publication of her collected poems, Glück has written with a bold, counterintuitive voice that has challenged masculine conceits, particularly romantic conceits, with unabashed feminist fury, chthonic authority, and a spare, incisive style that is well suited to her fictive urgency that decries sincerity as a misguided poetic criterion. "The advantage of poetry over life," she wrote in her famous essay "Against Sincerity," "is that poetry, if it is sharp enough, may last. We are unnerved, I suppose, by the thought that authenticity, in the poem, is not produced by sincerity."

Accomplishing what Emily Dickinson was forbidden to accomplish by the patriarchal and conventional editors of her day (particularly Thomas Wentworth Higginson, who also refused to publish Walt Whitman, in addition to Dickinson, in the premier literary journal of the day, the *Atlantic Monthly*), namely, a celebrated public career, Glück has reprised the fiercely independent spirit of Dickinson's unpublished voice—a feminine "response" that answers the masculine love call with the surprising announcement that "Renunciation – is a piercing Virtue" (782, Franklin).

The one poem from the trove of Glück's verse I have chosen to teach most often in my contemporary American poetry class is the bold apostrophe, "Mock Orange." Of all her poems, this short lyric continues to reverberate, in confessional as well as vatic ways, with both a mythic and contemporary import that both mystifies and engages my undergraduate students most consistently.

In this poem, Glück defines a contemporary fault line between the sexes with a conceit of rebuttal to the Western legacy of mostly male love calls that embrace the beloved as the object of both love and sex. With her blunt lyrical "response" to not only "the man" whose mouth seals her mouth, but those legions of lovesick *juglares* and suitors as well who have propositioned women throughout the ages to both "live with" and "be" their loves, Glück inverts the conceits of courtly love in "Mock Orange" with apophatic savvy. How startlingly this brief lyric resounds like a sharp note that pierces the centuries-long silence of suppressed female responses. While it doesn't perhaps speak for all women, Glück voices a feminine conceit in "Mock Orange" that corrects male presumption with cold-eyed renunciation.

Mock Orange

It is not the moon, I tell you.
It is these flowers
lighting the yard.

I hate them.
I hate them as I hate sex,
the man's mouth
sealing my mouth, the man's
paralyzing body—

and the cry that always escapes,
the low, humiliating
premise of union—
In my mind tonight

> I hear the question and pursuing answer
> fused in one sound
> that mounts and mounts and then
> is split into the old selves,
> the tired antagonisms. Do you see?
> We were made fools of.
> And the scent of mock orange
> drifts through the window.
>
> How can I rest?
> How can I be content
> when there is still
> that odor in the world?

As if with Dickinson's poem "I cannot live with You" (706, Franklin) in mind, Glück updates Dickinson's anti-antiphonal confession with an unabashed brown study of her own on postcoital tristesse. By renouncing Christopher Marlowe's idyllic invitation, "Come live with me and be my love / And we will all the pleasures prove" ("The Passionate Shepherd to His Love," 1599), Glück sounds a sea change in the tradition of the love lyric. Like Dickinson's speaker in #706 and Walter Raleigh's nymph in "The Nymph's Reply to the Shepherd," Glück takes a jaundiced view toward love's pleasures without denying engaging in lovemaking. Dickinson gives several reasons for why she cannot live with her beloved, citing emotional and theological concerns.

> It would be Life
> And Life is over there
> Behind the Shelf
>
> The sexton keeps the Key to …
> Because Your Face
> would put out Jesus' …
>
> Because You saturated Sight—
> And I had no more Eyes
> For sordid excellence
> As Paradise.

Glück, on the other hand, writes from the perspective of an angel trapped in human skin, willing to partake in sex while nonetheless cognizant of the inevitable melancholy that follows sex, or as Dickinson herself so succinctly described the same bittersweet of human experience: "For each ecstatic instant / We must an anguish pay / In keen and quivering ratio / To the Ecstasy."

On the surface, "Mock Orange" reads as a mere iteration of both the good and bad news about sex. On further reading, however, one discerns Glück's refreshingly bold rebuttal as an overdue feminine objection to the poetic legacy of the prevailing male love call. No slant telling of the truth about the double-edged reality of sex here. Rather, Glück tells the truth about sex straight out in remarkably economical, exigent language that avoids addressing her speaker's lover in favor of instructing her reader about the psychic whiplash of love-making.

Glück takes Dickinson's lovesick response to her shepherd in #760 (Franklin) a step further in "Mock Orange" by ultimately renouncing both her lover and sex. By invoking a Manichean view of lust, Glück dismisses the sexual act as an inherently flawed "material" ecstasy, "a low, humiliating premise of union" that makes "fools" of lovers. How carefully Glück has chosen the word *premise* here over *promise* as a sonically clever indictment of sex's deception. Premise rather than promise escapes as the conceit of the love cry itself. While bitter kiss-off poems are as common as ecstatic love lyrics in the Western canon, from the troubadours to Thomas Wyatt's "Whoso List to Hunt" to Bob Dylan's "Boots of Spanish Leather," there are only a very few Medusa-like poems by women that turn their readers to stone. This is one of them. (Katherine Philips's "Against Love," Emily Dickinson's "I had not minded – Walls," and Sylvia Plath's "Lady Lazarus" are three others that come immediately to mind.) No less than a calling out of lust's bluff, "Mock Orange" depicts sex as an inadequate anodyne for the "old antagonisms" that return with a vengeance when lovers "split into the old selves" following sex. Although profoundly fresh, if sobering, this poem borrows strongly from D. H. Lawrence's extended metaphor about tortoise sex, "Lui et Elle," written in 1923. By employing a crucifixion trope to highlight the "fragmentariness" that sex begets, Lawrence also indicts sex as a fool-making activity.

> Alas, the spear is through the side of his isolation.
> His adolescence saw him crucified into sex,
> Doomed, in the long crucifixion of desire, to seek his consummation
>   beyond himself.
> Divided into passionate duality,
> He, so finished and immune, now broken into desirous
>   fragmentariness,
> Doomed to make an intolerable fool of himself
> In his effort toward completion again.

By impugning the mock orange, the traditional wedding flower, as a trope for sex's trickery, Glück conjures a feminine conceit that offers a devastating response to romantic custom. She equates the mock orange metaphorically with the curse of sex, picking up where Sylvia Plath left off in her poem "Tulips," namely, with a similarly defiant feminine voice that cries out "from a country as far away as health." Glück isolates sex from love as a biological act with an odor that mocks the beauty of the very flower from which it emanates, portraying it as false as the poem's eponymous flower. Glück, like Plath, employs health as a trope for convention that is anything but salubrious in her dystopic mind frame. By also dismissing the moon in the first line of the poem as a possible cause of her lyrical reconsideration, she makes sure at the start to inoculate her radical complaint from any age-old male claim of menstrual contrariness.

At the conclusion of "Against Sincerity," Glück writes that "the true, in poetry, is felt as insight." She then adds that such insight "is very rare, but beside it other poems seem merely intelligent comment." Indeed, "Mock Orange" manifests a deeply felt insight that is instructively contrary to the male tradition of courtly love. As the Lady speaks in this poem with such exquisite lyrical velocity, as if directly from the shadows of Averno, the reader hears her "felt" truth that transcends mere "intelligent comment." In so doing, he suddenly realizes that this lyric has been in the making for centuries, culling from the long silence of women's suppressed voices the right response to the beautiful but "foolish" calls of so many troubadours. How to reinvent a credible complementary romantic tradition in this century without continuing to sound foolish or oppressive or polarized? This is the implicit question that the speaker's final rhetorical question poses, since the desire for contentment, at least for men, has historically presupposed romantic inspiration—the call for the unpublished response—as one of its primary emotional staples.

The oracular voice in "Mock Orange" calls for a new male love call that transcends the conventional invitation of Marlowe's passionate shepherd with more psychologically complex poems that address Thanatos as well as Eros (as Eliot certainly did profoundly for the first time in the twentieth century in "The Love Song of J. Alfred Prufrock" in 1915), alienation as well as union. While today's poets continue to write and publish love poems, only a relative few address Glück's challenge to write beyond the immediate longings and overtures of Eros with similar apophatic strategies and conceits.

In a zeitgeist where romantic love is losing many of its former risks, primarily pregnancy, today's sexual agora has diminished Eros into more of an archaic pastime than a romantic obsession. One wonders what new love poetry will emerge that defines Eros anew within the changing cultural context of love's mores, expressions, and practices in the twenty-first century. Or will Cupid simply continue to inspire poets with his same old private obsessions that have no regard for any zeitgeist. The legacy of love poetry has favored the latter for centuries, constantly calling for bold and highly personal originality.

Glück's candid, emotionally complex "response" to the traditional antiphonal male love poem picks up where Sylvia Plath left off in "Lady Lazarus," with more renunciation than romance. One can only imagine Christopher Marlowe's passionate shepherd's response to Glück's brutal rejoinder.

"Mock Orange" has endured as an iconoclastic response to the irrepressible male love call for over half a century since it was first published in 1968, achieving iconic stature on its own as a feminine "howl," quiet though it is in lyrical savvy. Although it echoes the most strident Dear John poems of the female troubadours in the Middle Ages, it also takes rejection one step further than the *trobairises'* mere personal fury into ontological territory where romantic love is vilified in general as a deceptive phenomenon whose odor serves only to remind the disillusioned lover of "the low, humiliating premise of union." The conceit in this poem, while evocative as a reaction to the ephemeral nature of sexual ecstasy, effuses like the mock orange itself with figurative implications for extrapolating other *frissons* of human experience as equally disappointing as the "low, humiliating premise of union" that Gluck's speaker experiences in the aftermath of sex.

William Blake wrote that "the most sublime act is to set another before you." The antinomy of Glück's "low, humiliating premise of union" in "Mock Orange" resonates in conceits that look beyond the disillusionment of sex to "the other" for transpersonal ways that mitigate against the dystopia of disillusionment.

In American poetry, Walt Whitman's "have-self-will-travel" persona comes immediately to mind, as does Elizabeth Bishop's six-year-old speaker in "In the Waiting Room." More recent examples of high "premises of union" can be found in such poems as Marie Howe's "The Gate," where the mystical presence of Howe's dead brother informs her of not only what she's been waiting for, but how to wait, which is code for how to live:

> This is what you have been waiting for, he used to say to me.
> And I'd say, What?
>
> And he'd say, This—holding up my cheese and mustard
>   sandwich.
> And I'd say, What?
>
> And he'd say, This, sort of looking around.

Or Lucille Clifton's poem "John" in which Clifton prophesies "the other" as the messiah who will come

> in blackness
> like a star
> and the world be a great bush
> on his head
> and his eyes be fire
> in the city
> and his mouth be true as time

Or James Wright's "To a Blossoming Pear Tree," in which Wright's speaker acknowledges the human draw of his "dark blood" that exceeds the beauty even of the blossoming pear tree:

> Young tree, unburdened
> By anything but your beautiful natural blossoms
> And dew, the dark
> Blood in my body drags me
> Down with my brother.

But this is a subject for another essay or even book in which sex and romance don't redound as overwhelming physical and psychic forces that inveigle the poet to associate a flower, no matter how overpowering its odor, with any human intercourse.

2016

The Nature of Voice

Poetic voice is the emanation of the poet's complex spiritual energy. The words that evolve from a particular inspiration reflect the sovereign choice-making of an inner editor. Robert Frost's comment—"I have made a life study of what I can say"—depicts the tireless challenge confronting every poet to speak meaningfully in a mutable world. The doubt arises from the poet's acknowledged inability to reveal that innermost voice intact. The nature of inspiration is invariably evanescent, fading from initial clarity to inevitable obscurity. The voice that emerges in a poem is consequently a bastard voice, bounded by the limits of language.

Shelley is the champion of this romantic notion, writing in his "A Defense of Poetry" that "when composition begins, inspiration is already on the decline, and the most glorious poetry that has ever been communicated to the word is probably a feeble shadow of the original conceptions of the poet." Yet successful voice celebrates unabashedly its mortal heritage, its predestined fate to fail. It squeezes meaning out of the stone of vanity by implicating the spirit, whose sustenance is paradox and ambiguity. This condition is as often the subject of poetry as it is its inspiration. The following excerpts demonstrate three major modern poets' attempts to reconcile their writing with the inherent vanity of their undertaking. Their conclusions evoke a common pathos:

> ... Trying to learn to use words, and every attempt
> Is a wholly new start, and a different kind of failure
> Because one has only learnt to get the better of words

For the thing one no longer has to say, or the way in which
One is no longer disposed to say it. And so each venture
Is a new beginning, a raid on the inarticulate
With shabby equipment always deteriorating
In the general mess of imprecision of feeling,
Undisciplined squads of emotion. And what there is to conquer
By strength and submission, has already been discovered
Once or twice, or several times, by men whom one cannot hope
To emulate—but there is no competition—
There is only the fight to recover what has been lost
And found and lost again and again: and now, under conditions
That seem unpropitious. But perhaps neither gain nor loss.
For us there is only the trying. The rest is not our business.

— from "East Coker" (No. 2 of *Four Quartets*), by T. S. Eliot

*

What thou lovest well remains,
                     the rest is dross
What thou lov'st shall not be reft from thee
What thou lov'st well is thy true heritage
Whose world, or mine or theirs
                or is it of none?
...
But to have done instead of not doing
     this is not vanity
To have, with decency knocked
That a Blunt should open
     To have gathered from the air a live tradition
or from a fine old eye the unconquered flame
This is not vanity.
     Here error is all in the not done,
all in the diffidence that faltered ...

— from Canto 81, *The Pisan Cantos*, by Ezra Pound

*

> Those masterful images because complete
> Grew in pure mind but out of what began?
> A mound of refuse or the sweeping of a street,
> Old kettles, old bottles, and a broken can,
> Old iron, old bones, old rags, that raving slut
> Who keeps the till. Now that my ladder's gone,
> I must lie down where all the ladders start,
> In the foul rag and bone shop of the heart.
>
> — from "The Circus Animals' Desertion," by William Butler Yeats

These heroic voices proclaim the common predicament of speaking against the odds. For Eliot, it is the question of speaking or not speaking, of trying without the expectation of succeeding; for Pound, it is the threat of vanity in our lives, overcome only by loving; and for Yeats, it is the loss of his ladder, the necessity for him as a poet to lie down continually at the nadir of his emotions, "the foul rag and bone shop of the heart." Each voice is a cipher of a defiant, even absurd spirit which dares to speak in the face of oblivion, on feeble human grounds. Although given more to utterance here, these poets infer the necessity of imagination for conjuring meaning. Certainly, "to recover what has been lost" (Eliot), or to "lie down where all ladders start" (Yeats), or "to have done instead of not doing" (Pound) requires in each case the kind of industrious imagination which sustains hope.

But therein lies the liability of poetic license. When imagination is given free rein over truth-telling, it may become grandiose or illusory. It takes on the nature of genius, striving to rival vanity with inventiveness and claiming human omnipotence. Its nature is restive, uneasy in its own apotheosis, dependent on artifice for strength. It is consequently rebutted outright by the canonical voice. An exegesis of scriptural voice, for instance, substantiates the ancient conflict between idiosyncratic imagination and God's revelation, between the voice of genius and the voice of obedience.

In biblical parlance, only God's voice is omnipotent. Genesis characterizes God's acts of creation anthropomorphically as literal utterance. His voice actually brings life and matter alike into being *ex nihilo*. It reveals the subterfuge of oblivion, what James Wright called "the secret of light," with the command, "Let there be ..." The author of John's Gospel likewise writes in his opening sentence, "In the beginning was the Word" (John 1:1), reiterating the efficacy of the divine voice for which creation itself is the vocabulary. Verses three and four of the nineteenth Psalm praise this divine vocabulary as inscrutable but material:

> There is no speech, nor are there words, their voice is
> Not heard;
> Yet their voice goes out throughout all the earth,
> And their words to the end of this world.

Concerning Himself, God is divinely curt, resisting any descriptive explanation. His answer to Moses is merely, "I am that I am" (Exodus 3:14). We are to know no more than this, as Qoheleth writes in Ecclesiastes, "God has put eternity into man's mind but so he will not find out what God has done from the beginning to end" (Ecclesiastes 3:11). And Jesus, though concrete about ethics, is parabolic about his Father's kingdom. God's voice, which distinguishes itself through actual acts of creation, is therefore the antipode to the poet's voice that expresses itself through a making that is mainly representational or illusory. The poet is sadly demoted, forced by his or her condition as an image of God (as opposed to an attribute of God) to function, as Samuel Johnson wrote, "as the interpreter of nature and legislator of mankind" (*Rasselas*, 1759). The poet's voice is consequently beguiling yet mortal, representational and interpretive rather than generative, secondary rather than primary. To compensate for this insufficiency, the poet attempts the apotheosis of his or her imagination. But since this tendency requires a permissive suspension of disbelief as well as an aggressive snubbing of divine revelation, it stems more from a pagan tradition than from a Judeo-Christian one.

Vico writes in *The New Science* that "the true God" established the Jewish religion "on the prohibition of divination on which all gentile nations arose." Unencumbered by an authoritarian monotheism for which imagination is apocryphal, the pre-Christian pagan, the ancient

Greek or Roman, felt free to personify mystery, "to make things out of himself and become them by transforming himself into them." About this permissiveness, Vico says that "ignorance, the mother of wonder, made everything wonderful to men who were ignorant of everything." From this followed a poetic naïveté "not in accord with the nature of things it dealt with ... but ... a fantastic speech making use of physical substances endowed with life and most of them imagined to be divine."[1] This same myth-making which produced the pagan nations with their pantheons of cosmic personifications endures perennially in secular poetry.

The Occidental poet is thus confronted with two oracular traditions: pagan or daemonic inspiration and Judeo-Christian revelation. The pagan voice continually attempts to redefine its own genesis, while the religious strives for obedience to a higher, Other voice. As Harold Bloom argues in his book *Poetry and Repression*, "poetic strength ensues when ... lying persuades the reader that his own origin has been reimagined by the poem"—a reinvention which may be the fruit from a hybrid of both pagan and Judeo-Christian influences.

The following poems are examples of such voices, expressing idiosyncratic imaginations which are nonetheless in dialogue with biblical pathos, the mortality of human utterance. Robert Frost draws the limits of imagination in "Directive," while Denise Levertov links original sin with the origin of art. "Writing," by William Stafford, incorporates the pagan traditions of animism, metamorphosis, and personification. Since prosody, in part, generated the sound of voice, I will discuss the form as well as the content of each poem. Let us first look at Frost's "Directive."

Directive

Back out of all this now too much for us,
Back in a time made simple by the loss
Of detail, burned, dissolved, and broken off
Like graveyard marble sculpture in the weather,
There is a house that is no more a house

---

1. Translated by Thomas Goddard Bergin and Max Harold Fisch.

Upon a farm that is no more a farm
And in a town that is no more a town.
The road there, if you'll let a guide direct you
Who only has at heart your getting lost,
May seem as if it should have been a quarry—
Great monolithic knees the former town
Long since gave up pretense of keeping covered.
And there's a story in a book about it:
Besides the wear of iron wagon wheels
The ledges show lines ruled southeast-northwest,
The chisel work of an enormous Glacier
That braced his feet against the Arctic Pole.
You must not mind a certain coolness from him
Still said to haunt this side of Panther Mountain.
Nor need you mind the serial ordeal
Of being watched from forty cellar holes
As if by eye pairs out of forty firkins.
As for the woods' excitement over you
That sends light rustle rushes to their leaves,
Charge that to upstart inexperience.
Where were they all not twenty years ago?
They think too much of having shaded out
A few old pecker-fretted apple trees.
Make yourself up a cheering song of how
Someone's road home from work this once was,
Who may be just ahead of you on foot
Or creaking with a buggy load of grain.
The height of the adventure is the height
Of country where two village cultures faded
Into each other. Both of them are lost.
And if you're lost enough to find yourself
By now, pull in your ladder road behind you
And put a sign up CLOSED to all but me.
Then make yourself at home. The only field
Now left's no bigger than a harness gall.
First there's the children's house of make-believe,
Some shattered dishes underneath a pine,
The playthings in the playhouse of the children.

Weep for what little things could make them glad.
Then for the house that is no more a house,
But only a belilaced cellar hole,
Now slowly closing like a dent in dough.
This was no playhouse but a house in earnest.
Your destination and your destiny's
A brook that was the water of the house,
Cold as a spring as yet so near its source,
Too lofty and original to rage.
(We know the valley streams that when aroused
Will leave their tatters hung on barb and thorn.)
I have kept hidden in the instep arch
Of an old cedar at the waterside
A broken drinking goblet like the Grai
Under a spell so the wrong ones can't find it,
So can't get saved, as Saint Mark says they mustn't.
(I stole the goblet from the children's playhouse.)
Here are your waters and your watering place.
Drink and be whole again beyond confusion.

The voice in this poem speaks in colloquial iambic lines which resonate with what Frost called the "sound of sense," which he defined as "a strained relation" between the "very regular pre-established accent and measure of blank verse and ... the very irregular accent and measure of speaking intonation." The "sense" he wishes to convey to seekers of the figurative meanings of his poetry lies encoded in poetic language "so the wrong ones can't find it, / So can't get saved...." Frost is nowhere more overt in any of his other poems with regard to the religious import of his poetry than he is here, equating it with scriptural efficacy itself.

Like Dante, Frost has resorted to "getting lost" in order to find a greater reality beyond his familiar farm— the "farm that is no more a farm." The irony of the title, a deliberate inversion to the literal reader who expects specific, practical directions, exhibits the immediate, confident choice of the speaker. This Virgil-like guide directs his fellow traveler into the false void of the imagination where another world suddenly materializes and mere earthly transit ceases, where the hierophant and reader descend into the democratic psyche that makes no distinctions between Christian and pagan imagery, but delivers instead such archetypes as "Some shattered dishes underneath a pine," "Playthings in the playhouse of the children," and a "belilaced cellar hole." Once lost in this other world where there is "A time made simple by the loss / of detail, burned, dissolved, and broken off," where abandonment erodes our houses to "cellar holes," self-realization occurs and you "pull in your ladder road behind you / And put a sign up CLOSED to all but me." Frost's overgrown road is, like Dante's *Inferno*, an interior landscape with real objects that resonate with a private (yet universal) mythology. The odd particulars become emblematic, the voice startling and authoritative.

Frost's tragic hindsight of a world of irreparable innocence, in which even his objective correlatives for innocence—a house, a farm, and a town—have lost their original significance, is extended into his present in the image of a broken goblet. His despairing voice demythologizes childhood while simultaneously offering the possibility of revelation, an epiphany "beyond confusion." But this epiphany is separate from salvation. The aura of the Eucharist is suddenly transformed into the child's play of make-believe, a pure world which can be imagined but never attained. The voice is double-edged with sharp despondence and dull hope. It is courageously loyal to mortal reality, telling us in the memorable speech of spoken phrases that the imagination, like Moses, can only lead to a clear view, that water, not wine, is "Too lofty and original to rage." For the speaker of this poem, one thing is clear: acknowledgement of mortality takes precedence over vainglorious speculation about salvation, and this is not sacrilege, but wholeness.

* * *

In William Stafford's poem "Writing," there is also a celebration of the imagination, but no specific demarcation of its limits:

Writing

Words written on paper laid over
a fire, and just before flame breaks through
the letters awake, and everything that they tell

makes a little vibration you shiver to see:
time is so young that it never gets past
trying quick dramas like that.

Or in a mirror you glimpse a huge anchor-hook
too strong ever to bend, wrenched
and bent. That is the image where
you see anything needed: you don't need
anything lifted, but to see that some
things cannot be. A dream,
a poem, a picture gives what you need.

Or by a hand like someone's you put your
hand: nothing felt but the truth when
they touch, and unspoken questions. Answering them,
you carry forward that version of the world
that makes up its most dangerous
time, the hours of your life.

Or there is a spry little animal
the color of ink that wiggles through
perils and comforts, but never stays,
and while you whistle it along new paths
it always makes an inspired escape
and softly dives for life like this across the page.

— from *The Answers Are Inside the Mountains: Meditations on the Writing Life*

Stafford depicts the mercurial pagan voice here. Beginning by personifying words, as awakened "over a fire," he describes their telling effects as vibrating and dramatic. He asserts that writing serves a number of spiritual and emotional purposes. First, it "gives what you need" in a world where "some things cannot be." It is a "dream, a poem, a picture." Second, if the reader is in search of the kind of "unspoken questions" which only the truth can precipitate, questions whose answers create a "version of the world / that makes up its most dangerous / time, the hours of your life," then again, he or she need trust the inspired word.

And finally, writing comforts, if only briefly; it is fleeting but memorable in its escape from stasis.

The stanzas of this poem work independently as well as integrally. Each one is a complete reflection on the nature of writing. The voice is consistently generous, thinking out loud, as it were, for the sake of the reader instead of itself. It uses each stanza consummately, adding something profound to its subjects' potentially endless definition with each new "Or." And it concludes as it began, with personification. The perfect hexameter in the last line, following four stanzas of irregularly stressed lines, performs an effective metrical mimicry of the personification; the words literally do "dive for life like this across the page."

* * *

O Taste and See

The world is
not with us enough
O taste and see

the subway Bible poster said,
meaning The Lord, meaning
if anything all that lives
to the imagination's tongue,

grief, mercy, language,
tangerine, weather, to
breathe them, bite,
savor, chew, swallow, transform

into our flesh our
deaths, crossing the street, plum, quince,
living in the orchard and being

hungry, and plucking
the fruit.

— from Denise Levertov, *O Taste and See*

The voice in Levertov's poem is an admixture, too, of both pagan and biblical sensibilities, on the one hand speaking in response to scriptural dictum, while on the other championing the pagan imagination. Beginning by inverting Wordsworth's claim that "the world is too much with us," the speaker proceeds to take to heart the psalmic advice of a "subway Bible poster" as the logical next step to her opening declaration. She interprets the Lord, however, as "all that lives / to the imagination's tongue, / grief, mercy, language," etc. This exegesis marks the crucial trope in the poem, for the speaker turns away from possible devotion at this point to savor the quotidian events which compromise the rest of the poem.

The poem's free verse amplifies its dissatisfied voice with transitive enjambments and syncopated diction. Such lines as "if anything all that lives / to the imagination's tongue" and "and weather to / breathe them, bite / savor chew, swallow, transform" are strange and unidiomatic. Their uneven stresses alternate between iambs and anapests with no particular pattern. This voice is anti-Wordsworthian, building toward conclusion. Its shift from transitive verbs to participles in the last two stanzas puts an abrupt stop to the litany of preceding actions implying that human activity is ultimately fodder for entropy—which of course it is.

The voice leaves the reader back in the postlapsarian Garden of Eden, where knowledge abounds but innocence is lost. The speaker wishes for revelation but is prevented from experiencing it by her unblinking attention to the world. The imagination is the only palate for her emotional, animal, and spiritual sensation. But this palate is synonymous with original sin, since it is its consequence. Humankind is trapped, therefore, the speaker concludes, in a fallen condition—incapable of tasting or seeing the divine because of human hunger for that which satiates both the imagination and the body, which offers the pleasures of a down-to-earth communion rather than a heavenly one.

This essay has striven to identify voice without defining it. An attempt to do both would have been futile, a chimera for earnestness, as both biblical and pagan traditions reveal. Only the characteristics of voice are finally evident; that is its nature, to carry on a serious charade.

Voice is, as William Stafford says, elusive, invading the poet with unslakable demands to make new. It compels one to speak strangely about the familiar, with original honesty. It has no specific beginning or end. But it bears an implicit resemblance to light: it embraces, illuminates, warms, penetrates, weathers, and fades whatever enters its path, assuming its qualities of democracy, freedom, power, and violence. It dictates tone, diction, rhythm, and form without being those things itself. Neither extenuating circumstances nor censorship can quiet it. It seeks out the exception to the rule with brazen disrespect for pedantry. If a poet questions his or her voice, the poet is likely to suffer the immediate double loss of vision and music, becoming blind and deaf. Despite the unreadable amount of poetry already written, lasting voice remains rare, as it must, true to its spirit. In his poem "Waiting," Robert Penn Warren writes "that, at least, God / Has allowed man the grandeur of certain utterances."

1991

The Other

William Blake wrote in his book *The Marriage of Heaven and Hell* (contemporaneous with the French Revolution, in 1790–93) that "energetic creators" presided in Hell, where their proverbs ran directly counter to the "mind-forg'd manacles" of conventional morality and religion (as upheld by Dante and Milton). One of the most famous of these proverbs, which Blake claimed to have "collected" from Hell, is that "the most sublime act is to set another before you." This heavenly, or hellish, insight testifies to the transformative power of both sympathy and empathy. Yet, it also evokes terror in its challenge to encounter difference and strangeness in the other—a strangeness that incites a fear of losing one's self in someone else. This relational conceit, which lies also at the heart of democracy as a divinely imaginative idea for trusting in the collective collaboration of "the people" to determine "the common good," has obsessed poets since the time of *Gilgamesh*, if not before, and Western politicians since the time of Pericles.

Walt Whitman composed America's poetic constitution, titling it "Song of Myself." In his preface to this operatic, transpersonal poem, Whitman declares that "the genius of the United States is not best or most in its executives or legislatures, nor in its ambassadors or authors or colleges or churches or parlors, nor even in its newspapers or inventors … but always most in the common people." Whitman claimed that "Americans of all nations at any time upon the earth have probably the fullest poetical nature." For that reason alone, he felt "the United States themselves are essentially the greatest poem." Implicit in his claim for "the common people" as the country's genius lay his Blakean sensibility that apprehended the other as sublime by virtue of the other's sameness. "Every atom that belongs to me as good belongs to you," he exclaims at the outset of "Song of Myself." For Whitman, the sublime is a complex reality in which the "many are one" and difference celebrated as the paradoxical essence within commonality—an idea Whitman divined in both his poetry and his muse, the country itself as an idea and a people. So, as Whitman perceived it, irony lay at the heart of American democracy's central poetic concept—a concept that requires imagination, as well a human acumen for grasping love as "the kelson of creation." When the citizenry and government fail to appreciate this irony, as Whitman felt they did following Lincoln's assassination, the country loses its democratic magic and falls victim to wooden patriotism.

Whitman's embodiment of the other, in his transpersonal first-person speaker, not only filled him with what he called "multitudes" but established an enduring sublime charge to future generations of American poets that atomized both traditional forms and conventional subject matter. The subject of others would also become what Whitman called the "the main things" in his poem "Poets to Come" for subsequent generations of American poets, from the modernists to present-day poets, many of whose ancestors suffered alienation, ignominy, and censorship during Whitman's day—"black folks ... Kanuck, Tuckahoe ... Cuff" (from Canto 6 of "Song of Myself")—but are receiving overdue recognition today in the poetry of such poets as Terrance Hayes, Natasha Trethewey, Ray Young Bear, Yusef Komunyakaa, Tracy Smith, Patricia Smith, Kevin Young, Lucille Clifton, Ross Gay, Garrett Hongo, Li-Young Lee, Major Jackson, and Ada Limón, to mention only a few. (Clearly, if a significantly larger number than the NEA's calculation of American readers of literary fiction and poetry were to read the above poets, a less gaping cultural divide might exist between Black and White Americans.)

While there are hundreds of contemporary poems standing out as icons of alterity that I'd like to discuss, I'll begin first with an email exchange I had with friend and fellow poet Bill Tremblay on the topic of Blake's sublime influence. I quoted to him the same "Proverb of Hell" from Blake as the one I quote above, in a complaint I was making about the egregious dearth of compassion emanating from the former president (and, as this book goes to print, president-elect), Donald Trump. Bill responded with the following reflection, reminding me of how important the other is also as a correspondent who complements the writer's ideas with further thought:

> I think what poetry "conserves" is the process of reflection through representation. When we talked on the phone I mentioned that I'm a Blakean. It's in Milton that Blake lays out his version of Adam and Eve. He asks the question of what the "original sin" was; he disagrees with Milton—it was not sex, it was not that they were ashamed of their nakedness. It was instead the invention of "self and other," the split inherent in positing a subjective self which views everyone and everything as a [mere] object.
>
> Blake's project is to re-subjectify what has formerly been objectified by use of the imagination in such a way as to create compassion.
>
> Most of the "bad" things we see around us happen because the actors or agents are people who have never imagined that there are internal dimensions to objects, and that from their point of view objects are subjects; therefore, as Rilke wrote in his "Archaic Torso of Apollo," "there is no place / that does not see you." Therefore—as that poem finishes—"You must change your life."[1]

* * *

There are myriad other contemporary American poems that focus on the electric other for their sublime subject matter. Here is a very partial list of poets whose poems contain transpersonal speakers who take the risk of encountering strange others in the paradoxical, sublime, Whitmanesque practice of discovering sameness behind difference: Robin Behn ("In That Year"), Frank Bidart ("Ellen West"), Jericho Brown ("Romans 12:1"), Lucille Clifton ("john"), Carl Dennis ("The God Who Loves You"), Deborah Digges ("Tombs of the Muses"), Denise Duhamel ("Ego," "How Deep It Goes"), Bob Dylan ("The

---
1. Translated by Stephen Mitchell.

Lonesome Death of Hattie Carroll"), Martín Espada ("Alabanza," "In Praise of Local 100"), Peter Everwine ("Elegiac Fragments"), Carolyn Forché ("The Boatman"), Jeff Friedman ("Other"), Ross Gay ("Ending the Estrangement"), Allen Ginsburg ("Kaddish"), Joy Harjo ("Conflict Resolution for Holy Beings"), Robert Hayden ("Those Winter Sundays"), Terrance Hayes ("American Sonnet for Wanda C."), Jane Hirshfield ("For What Binds Us"), Ilya Kaminsky ("Deaf Republic"), Brigit Pegeen Kelly ("Song"), Galway Kinnell ("The Avenue Bearing the Initial of Christ into the New World"), Sydney Lea ("My Wife's Back"), Li-Young Lee ("The Undressing"), Philip Levine ("The Mercy"), Larry Levis ("The Oldest Living Thing in L.A.,""Elegy with a Chimney Sweep Falling Inside It"), Thomas Lux ("Pedestrian"), David Tomas Martinez ("The Only Mexican"), Marilyn Nelson ("A Wreath for Emmett Till"), Dennis Nurkse ("Introit and Fugue"), D. A. Powell ("[because I were ready before destruction. bearing the sign of his affliction]"), Adrienne Rich (*An Atlas of the Difficult World*), Jill Allyn Rosser ("As If"), Bruce Smith ("Lewisburg"), Patricia Smith ("Skinhead"), Bianca Stone ("Möbius Strip Club of Grief"), Ruth Stone ("1941"), Bill Tremblay (*Walks Along the Ditch*), and Natasha Trethewey ("Enlightenment," "The Age of Reason").

I leave it to others to add to this incomplete list. Our democracy cries out for the "good medicine" of a national readership of both eclectic and electric poems—for the interpersonal charge that transpersonal poems provide in waking citizens to others as themselves.

2019

A Tribute to the Current

Memorable language is electric by nature, conducting charged meaning from one person to another by virtue of a verbal current that alternates between the individual and the universal. If poetry as memorable language is to endure, then it must continue to carry its verbal charge to each new generation of readers, thereby transcending its provenance as timeless expression. No charge, no poetry.

Whitman captures this electric poetic principle most succinctly in his paradoxical opening to "Song of Myself": "For every atom belonging to me as good belongs to you." How the poet conveys this "transpersonal self" (Malcolm Cowley's term) is a mystery, but one that clearly involves energized language that contains a counterforce, or as Frost described it in "West-Running Brook": "… this backward motion toward the source, / Against the stream, that most we see ourselves in, / The tribute of the current to the source."

This alternating current, the verse that reverses, the language that arcs between the individual and the universal, is primary for the poet, whether she is writing about bees during the Civil War, the Vistula in communist Poland, or just the minutiae of daily life, in original language that transforms personal inspiration beyond its merely private significance into what Ezra Pound called "the news that stays news." Boris Pasternak's poem "It Is Not Seemly to be Famous…" sounds an essential caveat against the uncharged, self-reflexive narrative of fame and narcissism. "It is not seemly to be famous: / Celebrity does not exalt; / There is no need to hoard your writings / And to preserve them in a vault," he starts the poem, and concludes with this high-voltage of calling: "And never for a single moment / Betray your credo or pretend, / But be alive — this only matters — / Alive and burning to the end."[1]

The arc that connects the individual to the universal is perhaps most evident against the backdrop of a dire setting. A reader can discern the poet's distinct witnessing within her specific epoch, as well as her connection to the legacy of "memorable speech." The Turkish poet and dissident Nazim Hikmet defined and transcended his era by connecting individual sensibility to universal truths. As he wrote from prison in 1948, "Living is no laughing matter: / you must live with great seriousness / like a squirrel, for example— / I mean without looking for something beyond and above living."[2]

The poet shapes cultural memory through his unique expression, providing extraordinary sense out of transitory events. He is thus both local and catholic. Not only are our cultural memories dependent on the "sense" that poets make of their time and lives, but on our imaginations as well, for without the legacy of mythical history, which is precisely what poetry provides, we lose our vision and identity of ourselves as a people. Our moral order devolves into solipsistic relativism. Our best poetry reminds us of who we really are: Emerson's genius, Whitman's transpersonal self, Dickinson's mysticism. As Adrienne Rich conveyed so poignantly in her poem "Diving into the Wreck," if "we are the half-destroyed instruments" and "the water-eaten log," and these are the primary remnants of our national legacy, then "our names do not appear in the book of myths."

Strong poets have always eschewed "critical" help. As the poet Imlac recounts in his "Dissertation upon Poetry," in Samuel Johnson's novel *Rasselas*: "[the poet] must consider right and wrong in their abstracted and invariable state; he must disregard present laws and opinions, and rise to general and transcendent truths, which will always be the same: he must ... contemn the applause of his own time, and commit his claims to the justice of posterity." This caveat resonates with prophetic force in our present fame-mongering culture. The poet in his "abstracted

---

1. Translated by Lydia Pasternak Slater.
2. Translated by Randy Blasing and Mutlu Konuk.

and invariable state" is always solitary and ignorant of the future course of her legacy. In a poem simply called "Berryman," W. S. Merwin relates this poignant anecdote about his wise teacher:

> I asked how can you ever be sure
> That what you write is really
> any good at all and he said you can't
>
> you can't you can never be sure
> you die without knowing
> whether anything you wrote was any good
> if you have to be sure don't write

A poet writes, then, with a faith that obviates "present laws and opinions" for the sake of discovering what Emerson called her own "genius." Such faith is heroically exemplified by the Hungarian poet Miklós Radnóti, whose widow exhumed his body after World War II for the sake of salvaging his last poems, still in his back pocket, saturated with "bodily fluids." Radnóti's rescued poems, like Dickinson's and Catullus's, stand as reminders of the great poetry that must still be buried. The poetry that survives from each epoch endures not only as memorable language but as a memorial as well—a literary cenotaph—to the great poetry that remains lost. As the legacy of poetry has already proven, poetry survives as the result of a collective cultural editorship whose patience endows its wisdom with classical taste. Zeitgeists and epochs are acknowledged in this legacy for their immense particulars but are ultimately transcended by a "memorable speech" that endures for what Theodor Adorno called its "inescapable relationship to the universal and to society." It breaks what the poet and Nobel laureate Czeslaw Miłosz called "the earthly law that sentences memory to extinction." The best poems transcend the facts of their authors' biographies, achieving the status of cultural property.

Contemporary American culture's passion for reality-based entertainment poses a direct challenge to this; the public is hungry for the colorful, often bizarre facts of poets' lives, which remain perennially fascinating to the general reader, as evidenced by the commercial success of such memoirs as Deborah Digges's *Fugitive Spring* and

Stardust Lounge, Mary Karr's *The Liar's Club* and *Cherry*, Mark Doty's *Heaven's Coast*, Michael Ryan's *A Secret Life*, Molly Peacock's *Paradise, Piece by Piece*, and Nick Flynn's *Another Bullshit Night in Suck City*, to mention only a few. While most of these memoirs are lyrical and engaging, chronicling formative stages of their authors' early careers, they rarely substitute for the greater imaginative moments of poetic self-realization that transcend mere autobiography. Looking back to a previous generation for the sake of objective distance, if one were to read only Sylvia Plath's autobiographical novel *The Bell Jar* without also reading *Ariel*—or *One Art*, the letters of Elizabeth Bishop without also reading *Geography III*—they would come away from these books with only a lively, prosaic view of the poets' lives compared to the richer, disinterested revelations of their poetry, which transcend boundaries of the their literal lives into universal realms of human experience.

"'Tis pity," Frost wrote in "Revelation,""if the case require / (Or so we say) that in the end / We speak the literal to inspire / The understanding of a friend." How much more enduringly essential than mere lyricized personal experience is Elizabeth Bishop's discovery through Robinson Crusoe (a fiction himself) that Friday is a rejuvenating presence to the homesick exile simply by virtue of his tenderness toward animals: "Just when I thought I couldn't stand it / another minute longer, Friday came.... / He'd pet the baby goats sometimes, / and race with them, or carry one around." How much more profound, musical, and terrifying are these confessional but transcendent lines of Robert Lowell's from "Waking in the Blue"—

> ... Cock of the walk
> I strut in my turtle-necked French sailor's jersey
> before the metal shaving mirrors,
> and see the shaky future grow familiar
> in the pinched, indigenous faces
> of these thoroughbred mental cases,
> twice my age and half my weight.
> We are all old-timers,
> each of us holds a locked razor.

—than the lifted lines of Elizabeth Hardwick's letters in *Lizzie and Harriet*, or nonfictional accounts of Lowell's various stays in mental institutions.

Without changing his life, as Rilke so abruptly insists in the conclusion of his famous poem "Archaic Torso of Apollo," the poet is prone to forming a conventional identity. Keats was particularly aware of the unconventional nature of the poet's sympathetic personality. In an 1818 letter to Richard Woodhouse, he wrote: "...the poet has none." In place of a clear identity, the poet possesses an interior life that continually discovers its complex self in unlikely others, whether animate or inanimate, thus providing a paradoxical common ground among all things, no matter how disparate. The poet must, therefore, write about not only what he knows, but more essentially about what he *doesn't* know he knows, like Coleridge discovering "unawares," through his despondent Ancient Mariner, "the happy living things" in the disguise of hideous sea monsters. Such serendipities are the fruit of what Keats called negative capability: "being in uncertainties, Mystery, doubts, without any irritable reaching after fact and reason." How can a poet not feel that he is "irritably reaching after fact and reason" while writing his memoir? And yet it is just this nonfictional "irritable reaching" that often tempts American poets away from the more enduring "true" stories of their poetry to write commercially about their lives. The story and not the poetry, but instead the claim of poetry behind the story. This is often the ephemeral literary obsession of the American reader.

While I would not want to argue in any absolute way about the wrong-headedness of poets' memoirs—the lasting example of Whitman's transcendent *Specimen Days* comes to mind—I think it is necessary to understand in our fame-mongering culture what Whitman meant when he wrote in "Song of Myself" that his cantos were "unromantic," that is, both real and true to his ecstatic, inclusive perception of the world. How dangerously easy now for a young poet to think in a careerist way that his or her second or third book should be a memoir. It's not that the facts of a poet's life aren't important or interesting, and therefore worthy of a memoir—they of course often shed invaluable light on the poetry—but by conceding to the commercial demands of contemporary publishing, the poet limits herself. Successful memoirists, such as Whitman, escape the self-reflexive trap of literal reportage by viewing the self as a nonromantic vehicle for transpersonal awareness. By writing about the horrors of the Civil War, Whitman finds a subject outside himself that enlarges him. In *Specimen Days*, he writes with an effective disinterestedness about his role as a nurse and letter writer for the wounded, finding a context of essential connection between himself and the other:

> In one of the hospitals I find Thomas Haley, company M, 4th New York cavalry—a regular Irish boy, a fine specimen of youthful physical manliness—shot through the lungs—inevitably dying—came over to this country from Ireland to enlist—has not a single friend or acquaintance here—is sleeping soundly at this moment.... Poor youth, so handsome, athletic, with profuse beautiful shining hair. One time as I sat looking at him while he lay asleep, he suddenly without the least start, awaken'd, open'd his eyes, gave me a long steady look, turning his face very slightly to gaze easier—one long, clear, silent look—a slight sigh—then turn'd back and went into his doze again. Little he knew, poor death-stricken boy, the heart of the stranger that hover'd near.

It's not that we necessarily know more about Whitman through his diary entries than a biographical sketch might convey, but that there is simply more to know about him than about someone who hasn't yet discovered the transpersonal self. By connecting himself to a suffering stranger with such empathetic strength, he discovers "the relationship to the universal and to society," and is diminished and enlarged simultaneously. He is freed up to employ the alternating current of language within the multifaceted context of himself.

Eulogizing Gatsby in the conclusion of his great novel *The Great Gatsby*, F. Scott Fitzgerald captured the chronic misreading of American idealism in the objective voice of Nick Carraway. "He had come a long way to this blue lawn, and his dream must have seemed so close that he could hardly fail to grasp it. He did not know that it was already behind him, somewhere back in that vast obscurity beyond the city, where the dark fields of the republic rolled on under the night." The American nostalgia for the impossible dream—the beloved, the house, the happiness—continues to solicit unslaked interest in the reading public. But as Nick Carraway observes, the shadow behind the dream contains the larger, more difficult truth—the "vast obscurity" that only Dr. T. J. Eckleburg's inscrutable eyes apprehend from the start, in a gigantic ad for an oculist that evolves into a symbol for heroic poetic vision. Like Dr. Eckleburg's eyes, in contrast to the real character Dr. Eckleburg, who "sank down ... into eternal blindness," American poets must keep their eyes on the dark fields. What they discern through the darkness in these fields—inescapable relations to the universal, immense particulars—the "baby goat," the "locked razor," the "poor youth," "that whiteness," as Frost called it—is the stuff of poetry, the universal language for writing most truly about the self.

2000

Sad Friend

On March 21, 1972, Elizabeth Bishop wrote one of her most anguished letters to her old friend Robert Lowell. For the first time in the course of their long friendship, Bishop felt that Lowell had committed a serious poetic transgression by blurring the lines between the private facts of his wife's letters and the fiction of his new poems in *The Dolphin*. While continuing to admire his poetry and respect him as a dear friend, she hardened with strong resolve against the license he took with Elizabeth Hardwick's letters for the use of his poetry:

> I've been trying to write you this letter for weeks.... It's hell to write this, so please first do believe I think *Dolphin* is magnificent poetry. It is also honest poetry—almost. You probably know already what my reactions are. I have one tremendous and awful BUT ... Here is a quotation from dear little Hardy that I copied out years ago—long before *Dolphin*, or even the *Notebooks*, were thought of. It's from a letter written in 1911, referring to "an abuse which was said to have occurred—that of publishing details of a lately deceased man's life under the guise of a novel, with assurances of truth scattered in the newspapers" (Not exactly the same situation as *Dolphin* but fairly close.)
>
> "What should certainly be protested against, in cases where there is no authorization, is the mixing of fact and fiction in unknown proportions. Infinite mischief would lie in that. If any statements in the dress of fiction are covertly hinted to be fact, all must be fact, and nothing else but fact, for obvious reasons. The power of getting lies believed about people through that

channel after they are dead, by stirring in a few truths, is a horror to contemplate."

> I'm sure my point is only too plain. Lizzie is not dead, etc.—but there is a "mixture of fact and fiction," and you have *changed* her letters. That is "infinite mischief," I think.

Bishop's curious employment of Hardy in her criticism of *The Dolphin* reveals a strong adherence to the pre-modern code of Old World decency. But Bishop's reaction to *The Dolphin* is significant for more than her moral objection to Lowell's indiscriminate use of Hardwick's letters. It reflects equally her commitment to a non-confessional poetic strategy. The idea of bastardizing personal letters in one's poetry was unacceptable to Bishop for reasons that informed her own aesthetic as, in the words of Helen McNeil, a "lifelong attention to the phenomenology of perception." To better understand this aesthetic and how it grew out of Bishop's moral development, it is enlightening to review her fierce correspondence with Lowell.

In reading Robert Giroux's *One Art*, which contains Bishop's selected and edited letters, one is struck repeatedly by Bishop's fierce sanity. Although she at times envies Lowell for his family's prestige, she maintains a stalwart sense of her unassuming, perspicacious self. In a letter dated December 14, 1957, fifteen years prior to her critique of *The Dolphin*, she wrote this candid admission to Lowell:

> ... I must confess (and I imagine most of our contemporaries would confess the same thing) that I am green with envy of your kind of assurance. I feel that I could write in as much detail about my uncle Artie, say—but what would be the significance? Nothing at all.... Whereas all you have to do *is* put down the names! And the fact that it seems significant, illustrative, American, etc., gives you, I think, the confidence you display about tackling any idea or theme, *seriously*, in both writing and conversation. In some ways you are the luckiest poet I know!—in some ways not so lucky, either, of course. But it is hell to realize one has wasted half one's talent through timidity that probably could have been overcome if anyone in one's family had had a few grains of sense or education. Well, maybe it's not too late!

This said, Bishop then adds a disclaimer that preserves her sense of objectivity with a note of generosity:

> I'm not really complaining and of course am not really "jealous" in any deep sense at all. I've felt almost as wonderful a sense of relief since I first saw some of these poems in Boston as if I'd written them myself, and I've thought of them at odd times and places with the greatest pleasure every single day since, I swear.

This rare confession conveys the class disparity Bishop felt throughout her friendship with Lowell between her own middle-class orphan background and Lowell's Brahmin heritage. There are numerous other references to herself scattered throughout her letters to Lowell and others, some in fact shocking for their honesty: "I'm sorry I can't seem to say all the right things I'd like to. I really should learn to be more articulate, I know." (December 14, 1957, letter quoted above); "When you write my epitaph, you must say I was the loneliest person who ever lived." (August 15, 1957, to Lowell); "I'm getting so I can't judge the poets we know so well anymore at all.... Your life sounds very nice and well-peopled. Mine has been rather lonely and bookish, but I don't really care that much." (October 3, 1958, to Lowell).

Bishop's stability and clearheaded advice were invaluable to Lowell, prompting him even to contemplate proposing to her. In a letter dated August 15, 1957, Lowell expressed unbridled gratitude to Bishop: "Your advice about [my] going to a doctor and keeping up one's patience, sobriety, toughness, and gaiety is dreadfully true, and I am sure that all is beginning to be well." In this same letter, Lowell confessed an old desire to propose to Bishop, which he had written to her in 1948:

> The possible alternatives that life allows us are very few, often there must be none. I've never thought there was any choice for me about writing poetry.... But asking you is *the* might-have-been for me, the one towering change, the other life that might have been had. It was that way for these nine years or so that intervened. It was deeply buried, and this spring and summer (really before your arrival) it boiled to the surface.

Bishop never responded to this belated news, choosing instead to preserve the intimate, Platonic nature of their friendship.

The tension between the Bishop's diminutive sense of herself and Lowell's aristocratic swagger didn't become problematic until 1972, when Lowell published *The Dolphin*. With so little ego in her poetry, Bishop relied on clear observation, accurate description, and spare original language to achieve *frissons* of self-awareness. Lowell praised her work by referring to "the bomb in it in a delicate way." However, the idea of confession as a muse was as foreign to her as the notion of assuming an aristocratic identity. She is perhaps the most Keatsian American poet of the twentieth century, and her "negative capability," while a prodigious poetic strength, was also a reflection of her proportionate ego that relied continually on the poetic strategy of discovering itself in such unlikely objects and places as those highlighted in "In the Waiting Room," namely the "awful hanging breasts" that "held us all together."

The thought of complaining or confessing ran counter to both Bishop's central ethic of survival, which was to adopt a persevering but compassionate stoicism, and her poetic strategy, which was to discover bright truths behind the subterfuges of ordinary life and suffering. In her persona poem "Crusoe In England," Bishop constructs her most incisive idea of the solitary self as an exile subsumed by the strangeness of the world. The poem is a plangent reminiscence in which Crusoe recalls the salient features of his island, finding reminders of Home in both the landscape and the creatures of his "cloud dump."

> The turtles lumbered by, high-domed,
> hissing like teakettles.
> ...
> The folds of lava, running out to sea,
> would hiss....

He harvests the red berries of the island in order to concoct a crude cocktail:

> Sub-acid, and not bad, no ill effects;
> and so I made home-brew. I'd drink

> the awful, fizzy, stinging stuff
> that went straight to my head....

But for all his ingenuity, he remains unabashedly self-pitying in the absence of his usual comforts, confessing:

> With my legs dangling down familiarly
> over a crater's edge, I told myself
> "Pity should begin at home." So the more
> pity I felt, the more I felt at home.

He is overwhelmed by the sudden terrible awareness of his smallness on an unnamed volcanic island that he dreams is like:

> ... other islands
> stretching away from mine, infinities
> of islands, islands spawning islands,
> like frogs' eggs turning into polliwogs
> of islands ...

Crusoe suffers from an ontological insecurity that isn't assuaged until he is saved from his brown studies by Friday.

> Just when I thought I couldn't stand it
> another minute longer, Friday came.
> (Accounts of that have everything all wrong.)
> Friday was nice.
> Friday was nice, and we were friends.

By repeating "nice" in lieu of such terms as *wonderful* or *dear* or *beloved*, Crusoe is in fact making an awkward attempt at professing his deep affection for Friday. (Interestingly, Bishop's repetition of "nice" echoes D. H. Lawrence's parodic use of the word in his poem "The English Are So Nice.") Without Friday, Crusoe simply remains a pathetic castaway. Although indigenous, strange and uncivilized, Friday provides an essential human point of connection for Crusoe's lost self. He laments that Friday is not a woman since he wished "to propagate his own kind" with him, as he thinks Friday also wished to do with him. The language is remarkably elementary in the stanza about Friday, as if Crusoe is at a regrettable loss to express his innermost feelings toward his new friend. Yet his diminished sense of self is saved from the vortex of the island's ironic vastness. Back in England, his other island, Crusoe languishes with a seemingly greater ennui than the one he suffered on his "cloud dump."

> I'm bored, too, drinking my real tea,
> surrounded by uninteresting lumber.
> ...
> The living soul has dribbled away.

The poem ends with the news of Friday's death from measles "seventeen years ago come March." Ironically, unlike Crusoe, who survives the elements and the germs of his former strange new world with a knife and fortitude, Friday succumbs quickly to a common occidental disease. But a memorable epiphany resounds beyond the poem's elegiac conclusion. Crusoe was at least momentarily transformed from a whining lone survivor to a joyous friend. Bishop created an apotheosis in Crusoe of the found self within the other. Unlike the speakers in Lowell's "Skunk Hour" or "Walking in Blue," where the self remains marooned, solitary, and deranged, Crusoe finds a way out of his tortured, self-pitying self through his genuine if awkward appreciation of Friday's ordinary acts:

> He'd pet the baby goats sometimes,
> and race with them, or carry one around.

Lowell's exploitation of his wife's letters for poetic purposes bothered Bishop because he "changed" the text. Since revelation for Bishop relied on the sovereign otherness of her subject matter, she divined knowledge in an inexorable world "derived from the rocky breasts / forever, flowing and drawn, and since / our knowledge is historical, flowing, and flown" ("At the Fishhouses"). Elizabeth Hardwick's letters were not dissimilar from the "rocky breasts," for they were authored by another, to be perceived and apprehended but not changed. By changing Hardwick's letters in *The Dolphin*, Lowell was, in Bishop's eyes, committing the "infinite mischief" of both plagiarizing and superimposing his will onto his subject matter rather than allowing it to speak for itself. In addition to violating his wife's privacy, Lowell was also misrepresenting himself; by interpreting the world on his own rhetorical terms, Lowell was denying himself the opportunity of arriving at a full realization of himself as a paradoxical being, both individual and universal, as the young speaker so succinctly does "In the Waiting Room" when she proclaims "you are an *I*, / you are an *Elizabeth*, / You are one of *them*. / Why should you be one, too?"

This impasse between Bishop and Lowell was never resolved, prompting her to address it directly in her 1978 memorial poem for Lowell titled "North Haven." Setting up her farewell stanza with the recent pastoral news from Lowell's Innisfree, she concludes by addressing him directly with plangent honesty:

> You left North Haven, anchored in its rock,
> afloat in mystic blue ... And now—you've left
> for good. You can't derange, or re-arrange,
> your poems again. (But the Sparrows can their song.)
> The words won't change again. Sad friend, you cannot change.

Bishop's affection for Lowell radiates from these lines with such powerful sympathy that any residual distress she may have felt is transformed into tender elegy. Her past judgment is overridden by her repetitive acknowledgement of death's final word. She suspends her moral condemnation of Lowell's indiscriminate use of sources in order to find a way to accept his poetic tricksterism. By parenthetically echoing Keats's transhistorical nightingale, with perhaps a veiled reference to herself as "the Sparrows," Bishop proclaims with prophetic wisdom the rightful order between "words" and birdsong: the former are intransigent, while the latter is timeless and free. It is precisely this wisdom that imbues her elegy with transcendent affection and truth. She converts what would have appeared as a sharp criticism in life—"You can't derange, or re-arrange, / your poems again"—into memorable pathos.

1999

The Teasing Corner of Oblivion: On the Career and Poetry of Ruth Stone

Throughout her long career, Ruth Stone has claimed that her poems have come to her from "out there," somewhere in the universe, and that unless she's prepared herself with a writing instrument and paper to get them down as soon as they arrive unannounced, they are lost forever. She also claims that 99 percent of her poems have been lost as a result of her simply being unable to transcribe them in time. While the majority of her "transmissions" emanate with stunning verbal clarity and a tragicomic acumen, they also present a runic language that contrasts sharply with her lyrical coherence. Stone's "reflections," as she likes to call her poems, reveal the inherent paradox of her verse, as she confesses in one of her more recent poems, "All in Time":

> I sort my reflections by their titillations,
> a little pain, a little physical duress,
> a teasing corner of oblivion.
> ...
>
> What is this universe that occupies my face?
> I travel in an orderly erratic place.
> I am a particle.
> I am going toward something. I am complicated,
> and yet, how simple is my verse.

These "titillations" are indeed as "simple" as the "orderly erratic place" of the universe. But Stone also knows that the answers to her greatest mysteries, from her husband Walter's suicide in 1959 to the nature of the universe, are unattainable. Her inclination to transcribe her obscure first thoughts, as testimony to her unknowing, complements her indelibly lucid grief in both her narratives and lyrics. Stone is a very human receiver of her cosmic inspirations.

With an eye that roams both the universe and Earth, Stone melds physics and poetry in a way that weds scientific knowledge with the "still unexplained" mysteries of the cosmos. Here are a few examples of her not-so-simple verses that display her receptivity to oblivion's "teasing corner."

As Now

In times of the most extreme symbols
The walls are very thin,
Almost transparent.
Space is accordion pleated;
Distance changes.
But also, the gut becomes one dimensional
And we starve.

*

Sometimes I lift a green lacewing
Out of a trough of water
And it stretches up like a cloud
Filling the universe with a gauze torque.
I want to tell you something with my fingers.
The space between us is a crack in the ice
Where light filters green and blue
Deeper than the fissures of continents.
All of time stretched like a web between
Was sucked into that space.
I want to tell you something with my hands,
My enormous hands which lie across a broken mirror
Reflected in broken pieces of themselves.

(from "Separate")

*

Riding the Bubble

Poetry that uses non sequiturs
which are transformations
in the direction of Zen,
as the hyper-angle in Vasko
Popa's "Prudent Triangle"—
a linguistic arrangement
of infinity—
is intriguing to us

with our near sighted vision
frozen along the contiguous;
our popular choice,
a self-inflating universe.

And so far, at the farthest
visible edge, the bubble appears
to bend; light appears to speed up
because it curves away from
where it was.

The still somewhat
unexplained weak force
possibly becoming aggregate;
separating masses,
galaxies slipping
out of sight in opposite directions.

*

Then why this happiness in muted things?
Some equation of time and space,
a slowed perception of the battered brain
strips back like leaves to unexpected glittering.

   (from "Today")

Stone's metaphysical lyrics are often overlooked by her readers in favor of her accessible lyrics and narratives that chronicle the agon of her widowhood, including such poems as "The Wound," "Loss," and "Curtains." But any serious reader of Stone's poetry cannot ignore the mystical lyrics that come to her as readily as her elegies; indeed, her abstract, sometimes surreal, cryptic riddles can't be separated from her elegies and narratives any more than Dickinson's obscure lyrics can be separated from her more accessible poems.

Stone has written throughout her career in the privacy of "her own room," far from Dylan Thomas's "... strut and trade of charms / On the ivory stages." As an outlier and autodidact (she never attended college) who chose to read novels and astronomy texts instead of poetry lest she fall too heavily under the influence of either classical or contemporary poets, Stone has lived and written—when she wasn't teaching to support her family—at her home in Goshen, Vermont, a rambling early-nineteenth-century house that she bought with her Bess Hokin Prize money from *Poetry Magazine* in 1958. There she thrived as a poet while struggling to make ends meet until only a few years ago, when her deteriorating eyesight forced her to move to an apartment in Middlebury, and then to her daughter Marcia's house in Ripton, Vermont.

After sixty years of maintaining both her persistent ethic and her aesthetic in her own chosen wilderness, she has, almost while no one was looking, amassed a body of work that now manifests as a unique legacy of poetic genius in the feminine American grain—a legacy that stands in bold contradistinction to the fame-seeking business of poetry. This legacy has not gone unnoticed to Stone's readers and loyal students. Sharon Olds, speaking for many of Stone's former students, praised her teacher at Ruth's ninety-fifth birthday tribute this past June at Poets House as "the mother of mourning and the mother of humor," confessing, "I wouldn't be where I am today without Ruth Stone." After fifty years of hiding in the open amidst the burgeoning proliferation of American poetry, Stone's poetry has finally reached the national audience it has long deserved, winning such recognition as the National Book Award and the Wallace Stevens Prize. While

Stone has been blessed with longevity, living long enough to witness her overdue recognition, she nonetheless continued to feel, as she told me in my interview with her, that "men rule the world." But without the freedom and benefit of her very separate "road less traveled," Stone would not have had the advantage of the isolation and privacy in which she wrote with her cosmic muse's voice in her ear, along with the voices of her mother, grandmother, and aunt. She testifies to this matrilineal inheritance most strongly in her poem "Pokeberries": "No amount of knowledge can shake my grandma out of me; / or my Aunt Maud; or my mama, who didn't just bite an apple / with her big white teeth. She split it in two."

But Stone has complemented her mother's, grandmother's, and aunt's knowledge with her own truth-seeking amid the mysteries of the universe, while seeking to understand her husband's suicide. In the privacy of her Goshen study, far from the rages and schools of her day, she wrote, in the words of Herbert Mason's translation of *Gilgamesh*, within that "inner atmosphere ... Where words are flung out in the air but stay / Motionless without an answer, / Hovering about one's lips / Or arguing back to haunt / The memory with what one failed to say." The more inscrutable her grief grew, the more mysterious her enduring preoccupation also grew, what she specifically calls "the wild sweep of the sun, / that mysterious molecule; / this clutter of rocks, dust, / and lighter elements, like your fingernails; / like the configurations of spiral lines / on the soles of your feet, / undeciphered" (from "The Self and the Universe"). It is precisely these undeciphered spiral lines, the universe's uncracked language, that Stone pays homage to with her cold, deferential eye.

Writing in the same manner she taught her students, with a passion for divining her own language outside the influence of other poets, Stone has exercised her fierce freedom to "yip" inside what she calls her "schizophrenic night," following unwittingly in the tradition of another autodidact, Walt Whitman's, "yawping from the rooftops." Although her metaphysical "yipping" is often difficult to comprehend, it nonetheless reveals an essential aspect of her inspiration. Just as her elegies exemplify Lorca's definition of *duende* as that "despair that stems from the knowledge of death ... and colors the artist's work with gut-wrenching authenticity," her more mystical lyrics, although sometimes obscure and abstract, reflect her willingness to include such poems as "All in Time," "Riding the Bubble," and "Separate," to mention only a few, as integral counterparts to her more decipherable "yipping." Despite their occasional obscurity, Stone's homages to the universe and its mysteries, particularly the smallest things—"the infinitely small / leaping quanta"—testify to her intense wonder as an essential complement to her stunning elegiac clarity. Stone's metaphysical voice has become increasingly salient in her latter poems, where her speakers often seem only a hair's breadth away from oblivion.

Just as soon as Stone takes her reader out of the world, she brings her right back, staring chaos down, keeping the memory of Walter alive, mining the familiar as poetic gold.

2010

Swimming in the Drowned River of Contemporary American Poetry

As a poet, essayist, and interviewer for the past twenty-five years, I have struggled with a compound question that too few of my colleagues have felt emboldened, for understandable reasons, to address: namely, what is the state of poetry in America today, and what is the best way to talk about it with potential readers who feel both lost and intimidated?

Yes, poets enjoy writing for other poets who understand the inherent difficulty of their art, but what of the non-poet who is hard-pressed to hear "a voice among the crowd," as Walt Whitman wrote, for the myriad other voices shouting over each other? I understand my fellow poets' reluctance to talk about poetry's status in the marketplace. I, too, am befuddled and discouraged by the imbalance between poetry's runaway production and its actual readership. If poetry were a river in America, it would be a drowned river—that is, a river that has overflowed its banks.

So how to approach this conundrum as both a poet and a reader of poetry? How to preserve poetry as ongoing essential language? I'd like first to address the unmanageable surfeit of poetry in the marketplace today, then proceed to a suggestion for pursuing a readership strategy that is both practicable and rewarding.

Over the past thirty years, the industry of American poetry has burgeoned to an unprecedented level of trade and online publications. It is impossible to know exactly how many books of poetry are published annually in this country, especially since most poetry books and journals sell outside regular distribution and bookselling channels. Lee Ballentine, a writer for *Quora* and former publishing CEO, has observed that "most entities that publish [poetry] do not report their print quantities or sales totals anywhere. Even quantifying the number of titles published in a year would be nearly impossible, as many, perhaps most publishers are individuals, small groups, poetry clubs, etc., who often do not participate in the ISBN program." As for those publishers who *do* report their sales and are registered with an ISBN number, the numbers are still staggering. According to an article by David Alpaugh that appeared in the February 10, 2010, issue of the *Journal of Higher Education*, entitled "The New Math of Poetry": "the online writer's resource, *Duotrope*, lists more than 2,000 current markets that accept poetry, with the number growing at a rate of more than one new journal per day in the past six months. Some of these journals publish 100 poems per issue, others just a dozen. If we assume an average of 50 poems per publication per year, how many more thousands of poems have been published since *Duotrope*'s last tally in 2010?"

Desktop publishing and the internet have now made it possible for anyone who wishes to publish their poems to do just that. The publishing floodgates have opened. Ezra Pound's caveat—"the weeder is supremely needed if the Garden of the Muses is to persist as a garden"—has itself been mistaken by amateur editors for a weed itself, and summarily removed.

Conversely, one might initially sympathize with Alpaugh's opinion that "perhaps the most sinister fact about the new math of poetry is that it allows the academic oligarchy that controls poetry to impose a non-aesthetic, self-serving scoring system without attracting notice or raising indignation. Since no one can possibly read the vast number of poems being published, professionals can ignore independent poets and reserve the goodies—premiere readings, publications, honors, financial support—for those fortunate enough to be housed inside the professional poetry bubble."

While this may be somewhat true, I would add that most "academic" readers and editors (many of whom are also established poets) have spent their careers developing brilliant, open-minded aesthetics for strong poetry and should not be dismissed so easily as effete arbiters of a "self-serving scoring system." The so-called professional poetry bubble resonates more as a shibboleth than an accurate term for the diverse range of superb literary journals in that corner of the poetry market where both editorial expertise and poetic talent meet. I'm thinking of such journals as *Blackbird, Kenyon Review, New Ohio Review, Green Mountains Review, AGNI, Ploughshares, Bomb, Five Points, Antioch Review, Poetry, Southern Review, Gulf Coast, Prairie Schooner, Georgia Review, Tin House, Yale Review, Harvard Review, New England Review,* and *Iowa Review,* to mention only a relative few.

The problem for readers unfamiliar with the contemporary poetry world is that unless one attends one of the 212 MFA programs in this country, or majors in creative writing, it's difficult to know just where to turn for strong contemporary poetry. But it is there in greater numbers than ever before, primarily because more people are writing than ever before, many with the intent of publishing their work. As for those geniuses who are writing beautifully but secretly, like Emily Dickinson, one can only hope that their work comes to light in time, for these essential outliers often prove to be the very best poets.

Unlike other genres of literature, poetry indulges in riddles and for this reason is often viewed as a difficult, even hostile art form. Robert Frost acknowledges this in the conclusion of his poem "Directive": "I have kept hidden in the instep arch / Of an old cedar at the waterside / A broken drinking goblet like the Grail / Under a spell so the wrong ones can't find it, / So can't get saved, as Saint Mark says they mustn't." Such lines corroborate William Carlos Williams's claim that "it is difficult to get the news from poems." As often as not, poetry is difficult by design.

Is it any surprise, then, that despite the abundance of poetry being published today, its readership, according to the most recent National Endowment for the Arts poll, has plummeted to 9.2 percent of the reading public? Not at all, I would answer, especially in this cyber age of text messaging and social media when most people view "news" as an immediate, accessible commodity.

But does this mean that poetry has arrived at its own swan song? In responding to an article by Christopher Ingraham titled "Poetry Is Going Extinct, Government Data Show" that appeared in the *Washington Post* on April 24, 2015, I wrote an essay for *The Cortland Review* that begins:

> Nothing has changed about the character or necessity of poetry as "the news that stays news" (Ezra Pound), as "the best words in the best order" (Samuel Taylor Coleridge), as "memorable speech" (W. H. Auden), as "prayers to the unsayable" (unknown), as "the maximum efficiency of language" (William Corbett). Poetry is like a jealous lover; it demands full and uninterrupted attention. It insists on being memorized and studied over and over. Like Eros, it was born poor and has remained so to keep its blessing. It is archetypal at its core, dismissing mere information as a potentially fatal distraction when viewed as more than subject matter.... I hear poetry kicking and screaming as our high-tech culture lowers it slowly into the acid vat of synchronicity, where no news remains memorable for long as mere information. Strong poetry is still being written, but how to preserve it in the blue light? How to keep up with our wizardry without sleeping with it? How to remember that just a few good lines are worth more than a million bytes?

With regard to a strategy for reading poetry today, I would simply suggest slowing down instead of speeding up, finding one poet who suggests another, then reading him or her closely. Here is a very partial list of Vermont poets with whom one who feels alienated from contemporary poetry might begin: Robert Frost, Galway Kinnell, Ruth Stone, Mary Ruefle, Stephen Sandy, Major Jackson, Martha Zweig, Jay Wright, Jay Parini, Sydney Lea, Ellen Bryant Voigt, Hayden Carruth, David Budbill, Paige Ackerson-Kiely, Karin Gottschall, Dennis Nurkse, Cleopatra Mathis, Verandah Porche, Cynthia Huntington, Kerrin McCadden, Elizabeth Powell, Grace Paley, Louise Glück, and Bianca Stone.

A small culture of poetry exists inside the cacophonous culture of "po biz," a deeply personal culture that every reader of poetry must create in the privacy of his or her own reading chair—in what Ralph Waldo Emerson would call the realm of "one's own genius." The great paradox of this culture lies within its power of one, which transcends the dire statistics of government data.

2016, 2018

Like a Book at Evening Beautiful but Untrue, Like a Book on Rising Beautiful and True

In the eighth section of Wallace Stevens's magnificent poem "The Auroras of Autumn," Stevens arrives at a beguiling complementary simile in the style of Hebrew parallelism about the nature of truth: "Like a book at evening beautiful but untrue, / Like a book on rising beautiful and true." So how can something be both untrue and true at the same time? Truth is as mercurial as human emotions and hardly dependent on fact, as Mark Strand points out so evocatively in his poem "Elegy for My Father": "Why did you lie to me? / *I always thought I told the truth.* / Why did you lie to me? / *Because the truth lies like nothing else and I love the truth.*" So how to capture the elusive, supremely fictive, paradoxical, immortal truth in a work of art, specifically a poem? Because of its inherently manifold nature, it covers the full range of human emotions, from humor to horror. Humor invites the "witness" first with risible instruction at the highest cognitive level, often employing a strategy of *via negativa*. I think, for instance, of the joke in which a young American truth-seeker ventures halfway around the world to learn the truth from a wise man in the foothills of the Himalayas. After arriving at the man's dirt-floor hut, he humbly asks the wise man to impart the truth in a single utterance. The wise man awakens from his deep meditation and responds haltingly, "Truth ... is ... a ... deep ... well." The young American recoils in rude disappointment at this news, at which the wise man comments, "You mean it isn't?" As immediately old as this joke becomes the second it's told, it nonetheless conveys two essential truths about truth-telling that are critical to the poet's understanding: first, that truth is experiential, and second, that the wise man or woman knows implicitly that truth is too large and complex to be contained in the merely factual. Call it the Murphy's Law of Truth, that there is little the truth-teller can say to the literal-minded pilgrim about his or her inability to instill the truth in another except come back with rhetorical ripostes. "You think it's more mind-blowing than that?" "You think it's not shockingly disappointing on first hearing?" "You think I can tell you?"—questions that remind me of Yahweh's divinely wiseacre responses to Job's complaints about his mysterious sudden rash of personal tragedies and physical maladies: "Can anyone capture the Behemoth by the eyes or trap it and pierce its nose? … Can you bind the chain of the Pleiades? … Can you tilt the waterskins of the heavens?"

So, how then does one move beyond jokes and satire to the more sober undertaking of what Carolyn Forché calls "the poetry of extremity" in her game-changing anthologies of the poetry of witness? The poet Ruth Stone makes the argument that the poet must always maintain his or her sense of irony and figurative acumen, whether it's comical or not. That without humor and figurative language, the truth of horror and grief remains only half told. "See what you miss by being dead," Stone chides her deceased husband in her heroic poem "Curtains" after telling a heart-wrenching story about how difficult life is for her as a widow with a landlord who forbids pets. In that one outburst to her husband, she captures the double-edged truth of why she's chosen to go on living despite life's almost unbearable hardships, unlike her husband, Walter, whom she is still in love with, but also angry at for ending his life.

In our present age, an explosion of indeterminate, post-avant-garde, fiercely iconoclastic poetic expression has largely supplanted the language of overarching universals and sense-making. The question of truth—which Pontius Pilate put most succinctly over two thousand years ago in his response to Jesus' claim that he was a "witness to the truth": "Truth. What is truth?"—has devolved in the literary marketplace into what Stephen Colbert calls "truthiness." Although a comedian, Colbert has the instincts of a poet, trusting his audience to grasp the validity of his satire without insisting on calling it "the truth." For truth may be too large a word today to resonate universally. In the polarized zeitgeist of today's politics and social media, in which religious absolutism wages war against secular indeterminacy, truth-telling falls between the cracks of belief and fiction, doctrine and art, cynicism and fundamentalism.

As recently as fifty years ago, a number of American poets who followed the Modernists aspired to embrace fully the truth of their age and lives in "memorable speech." They embraced their "vanity of vanities" with extraordinary chutzpah and originality amid enormous political and social upheaval, while also somehow maintaining faith in divining truths that crossed over from their poetry with a Whitmanesque current and currency to both their readers' psyches and their bones.

As a poet of the generation following these poets, most of whom were born in the 1920s, I was curious to talk to several of them about their "broken" yet tensile language. So, as I sat before Galway Kinnell, Ruth Stone, Maxine Kumin, Robert Bly, Gerald Stern, Philip Levine, Jack Gilbert, Lucille Clifton, and Donald Hall on the figurative dirt floors of their respective book-filled huts during the interviews I conducted with them between 2008 and 2011, I learned like a fool that the truths they imparted were unteachable, despite their memorable "music," residing solely within them as unique, original expressions that they had forged in the darkness of their "deep wells." Their wisdom made memorable sense, but it wasn't mine, and, yes, I was often initially shocked by their answers. Kinnell's claim, for instance, that he dare not call himself a poet, for being a poet "is so wonderful an accomplishment it would be boasting to say it of oneself," and Ruth Stone's admission that "the writing is separate.... I don't write out of the memory of experiencing a memory." They had learned something crucial about truth and how to tell it—to wit, that no one possesses it absolutely, and that when one tries to tell it too self-consciously or pridefully, it disappears. Or as Jack Gilbert opined, "Real pride gives up. False pride keeps performing." I exited my subjects' studies feeling chastened, enlightened, foolish, disappointed, and challenged in unexpected ways—ways that crushed my preconceived notions about truth-telling beneath the weight of their spare, self-effacing language.

One wonders in today's synchronic zeitgeist who is prepared to hear the truth, to sustain the truth with listening. This is not just a topical question, but one that has resonated throughout human history. The despondency of Elijah on Mount Horeb or Jonah's suicidality in the desert testify to the perennial prophetic condition of the truth-teller. If the present generation of poets and readers of poetry have become deaf to Old World "singing," then the contemporary poet is left to overhearing himself as an audience of one, or at most "a diminished thing" with a more resonant voice than the "other birds," as Robert Frost declaimed in these lines from his 1920 poem "The Oven Bird" following the earth-shattering devastation of World War I:

> The bird would cease and be as other birds
> But that he knows in singing not to sing.
> The question that he frames in all but words
> Is what to make of a diminished thing.

In a new era that's nonetheless similar to the period following World War I for its lack of sense and meaning—in which one might still claim, as Yeats did around the same time Frost wrote "The Oven Bird," that "the falcon cannot hear the falconer"—one wonders also who hears the "the still quiet voice" of the "diminished thing," and just who is "singing not to sing."

* * *

I'd like to discuss three poems—two narratives and one lyric—in which the poets tell the truth in dramatically different ways that employ both fictive and literal strategies. I recall something that Jack Gilbert said in my interview with him as a starting point for thinking about all three of these examples: "The mechanics of poetry have so little to do with design. There is no pressure, it seems to me, to write poems that matter today." The poems I have chosen to write about still matter for reasons that have more to do with design than mechanics—designs that emanate mortal pressure, or what Federico García Lorca called *duende*. The first poem I'd like to take a look at is Randall Jarrell's supreme fiction, "The Woman at the Washington Zoo."

The Woman at the Washington Zoo

The saris go by me from the embassies.

Cloth from the moon. Cloth from another planet.
They look back at the leopard like the leopard.

And I....
        this print of mine, that has kept its color
Alive through so many cleanings; this dull null
Navy I wear to work, and wear from work, and so
To my bed, so to my grave, with no
Complaints, no comment: neither from my chief,
The Deputy Chief Assistant, nor his chief—
Only I complain.... this serviceable
Body that no sunlight dyes, no hand suffuses
But, dome-shadowed, withering among columns,
Wavy beneath fountains—small, far-off, shining
In the eyes of animals, these beings trapped
As I am trapped but not, themselves, the trap,
Aging, but without knowledge of their age,
Kept safe here, knowing not of death, for death—
Oh, bars of my own body, open, open!
The world goes by my cage and never sees me.
And there come not to me, as come to these,
The wild beasts, sparrows pecking the llamas' grain,
Pigeons settling on the bears' bread, buzzards
Tearing the meat the flies have clouded....
                                    Vulture,
When you come for the white rat that the foxes left,
Take off the red helmet of your head, the black
Wings that have shadowed me, and step to me as man:
The wild brother at whose feet the white wolves fawn,
To whose hand of power the great lioness

> Stalks, purring....
>   You know what I was,
> You see what I am: change me, change me!

This persona poem is remarkable for the transpersonal self that crosses over from its author to an other, a woman at the Washington Zoo. Jarrell imagines most accurately what it's like to be a person of the opposite sex trapped in her "null navy" uniform, no less a captive (and serviceable, too, with all the sexual connotations this word suggests) than the animals at the zoo. Jarrell must have known Rainer Maria Rilke's poem "The Panther," in which Rilke captures exquisitely the tragic stasis of a caged panther. He finds a truth here that he couldn't have found without assuming the identity of another, extrapolating from the boredom of the zoo animals that of the woman imprisoned in "the cage" of her job. By concocting this fiction, Jarrell has told an untrue story that nonetheless tells a memorable truth about the torture of imposed restrictions on the spirit of both animals and humans. Like Whitman, he is large, containing multitudes in a particular other who bestows a vision of an entirely different experience from his own that nonetheless becomes his own in an act of painstaking empathy, or what John Keats would call "negative capability." By wedding his imagination with his compassion in writing about someone utterly different from himself, Jarrell discovers the transformative, ironic truth of himself, and in doing so ends up experiencing a second transcendent vision of seeing through and beyond his imagined persona to the mystical nature of the caged vulture as "the wild brother" worthy of his speaker's prayer and hope for "change."

* * *

Emily Dickinson's poem #554 (Franklin) provides a trenchant example of the function of the imagination's role as a verbal catalyst for conveying emotional and psychic truth. Dickinson charges an imagined erotic encounter with such intense lyrical language that the poem ultimately turns from an archetypal call-and-response lyric into an ironic ars poetica that weds her "veiled" face to her fire-breathing muse "in the crease."

554

I had not minded – Walls –
Were Universe – one Rock –
And far I heard his silver Call
The other side the Block –

I'd tunnel – till my Groove
Pushed sudden thro' to his –
Then my face take her Recompense –
The looking in his Eyes –

But 'tis a single Hair –
A filament – a law –
A Cobweb – wove in Adamant –
A Battlement – of Straw –

A limit like the Veil
Unto the Lady's face –
But every Mesh – a Citadel –
And Dragons – in the Crease –

In the first half of this poem, Dickinson celebrates her desire to answer the mating call of a potential suitor across the street—in fact, to tunnel till her "Groove / Pushed sudden thro' to his." (Interestingly, this language is every bit as "disgraceful"—the term Dickinson used in a letter to Thomas Wentworth Higginson at the *Atlantic Monthly* to describe Walt Whitman's sexually explicit verses—as anything Whitman ever wrote.) There was no potential suitor who actually lived "the other side the Block" from Dickinson, but he lived in her head, and she heard him calling to her. So the fictive quality of this poem, mixed with its speaker's staunch reticence about actually meeting this suitor in the second half of the poem, is stunning. Only poetry this pithy and electric can convey the explosive truth of the heart's alternating current: attraction one second and flight the next. "But 'tis a single Hair – / A filament – a law – / A Cobweb wove in Adamant – / A Battlement of Straw." Modesty and apprehension trigger Dickinson's sudden faint, prompting her to recoil behind her "veil."

Indeed, Dickinson felt utterly abashed by her own visage, referring to her "external face" as "sight's ineffable disgrace." In a flash, she reverses her strategy of call-and-response to characterize the truth of her more pressing *agon*—namely, the labile phenomenon of her emotions in the clutches of romantic attraction. No constant truth here, but rather a psychic volatility capable of shifting from one extreme to the next in an instant. Dickinson conveys romantic love's complex nature in broken yet highly charged lines. With a sudden lyrical surge in the last stanza, Dickinson employs brilliant ambiguity in her description of "the lady's veil" as a veiled description also of the female genitalia, as if her sex itself were speaking as that "mesh" and "citadel"—her feminine redoubt— "with Dragons – in the Crease." She found her most multivalent, devastating voice as a woman in this poem by discovering before her and her reader's eyes something remarkably true that she didn't know she knew, that her sex and her veil are one, replete with dragons in the folds, her fire-breathing poetry.

No other art form besides poetry can tell the truth as complexly or as powerfully as this. "Tell all the truth," Dickinson wrote in another poem, "but tell it slant." Her volatility, her fictions, her tropes, her veiled revelations, and her nuclear economy comprise the poetic devices of her "slant" telling in this poem that ends up walloping us so artfully.

* * *

Lastly, I'd like to discuss the function of literal expression as a complementary means of truth-telling. This poem, a passage from *Gilgamesh* that's uttered by the chorus following the death of Enkidu, is between three and four thousand years old.

> All that is left to one who grieves
> Is convalescence. No change of heart or spiritual
> Conversion for the heart has changed
> And the soul has been converted
> To a thing that sees
> How much it costs to lose a friend it loved.

It has grown past conversion to a world
Few enter without tasting loss
In which one spends a long time waiting
For something to move one to proceed.
It is that inner atmosphere that has
An unfamiliar gravity or none at all
Where words are flung out in the air but stay
Motionless without an answer,
Hovering about one's lips
Or arguing back to haunt
The memory with what one failed to say,
Until one learns acceptance of the silence
Amidst the new debris
Or turns again to grief
As the only source of privacy,
Alone with someone loved.
It could go on for years and years,
And has for centuries,
For being human holds the special grief
Of privacy within the universe
That yearns and waits to be retouched
By someone who can take away
The memory of death.[1]

Nothing is made up in this poem—just plainspoken advice and commentary on the nature of grief, and yet it is undeniably a poem by virtue of its "memorable speech," its "maximum efficiency of language," and its "best words in the best order." When reading this ancient poem I'm reminded of a few lines from Philip Levine's poem "The Simple Truth":

> Some things
> you know all your life. They are so simple and true
> they must be said without elegance, meter and rhyme,
> they must be laid on the table beside the salt shaker,
> the glass of water, the absence of light gathering
> in the shadows of picture frames, they must be
> naked and alone, they must stand for themselves.

---

1. Translated by Herbert Mason.

Levine captures beautifully the poetry of *Gilgamesh's* anonymous author. Spoken as one voice in a choral setting, the above lines emanate a deep knowledge of grief that seems eternal in the simplicity and truth they express. This pericope from the oldest extant text of Sumerian literature captures the literal truth about the very abstract feelings of grief, as well as the indeterminate span of its affliction. There is truth here that resonates with a human freshness that transcends time and place. It is lyrical as well as factual in its description of emotional inertia, capturing in precise words the otherwise nebulous phenomenon of grief. It serves as a vital, defining witness to one of the most profound features of our human nature. As Harold Bloom has written about Shakespeare's language, it reads us—as if some collective of human authors gathered as a harmonious, inspired collective to depict our deepest and most complex emotions.

So how to conclude about truth? Certainly, there's no feasible way without a context or admission that as a human being one can only approximate it. That Pilate was right in his jest. But perhaps it's safe to attest that truth is both constant and fluid, both concrete and abstract, moving like mercury, disappearing like smoke, singing most beautifully and harshly, defying craft for craft's sake while sleeping comfortably at the same time in its double bed. It is a creature for all intents and purposes—both human and animal—in whose pocket sits an ancient, double-sided coin with a fictional image on one side and a factual relief on the other: Orpheus and Catullus, Eve and Joan of Arc, Hamlet and Caesar. This creature who borrows our names if we speak the truth appears disguised in our dreams, disappears in the klieg lights, and lives in the rich poverty of knowing that her coin is rarely recognized at first for its actual value. Witness the literal debt that poets and prophets have incurred before their coins have rolled back to them with infinite worth. Witness the contumely and neglect they have suffered for their timeless verses before they turned to gold.

2015

The Tradition of Resistance and Independence in American Poetry

The legacy of resistance inherent in American poetry that began with Walt Whitman and Emily Dickinson reemerged with new force in the second half of the twentieth century. Those poets born primarily in the twenties and thirties maintained and renewed a rebellious eloquence that was as subversive in its form as it was in its content. Like Whitman and Dickinson, many of the major American poets born in the decades between 1915 and 1935 employ a "transpersonal self" that yawps "barbaric" but thrilling renunciations, paeans, confessions, pastorals, and jeremiads.

In their unorthodox conceits, Whitman and Dickinson effected a quality of terror Longinus claimed was beauty's essential alloy. Their new forms, though vastly different from each other—Whitman's prosaic "meter-making arguments" in contrast to Dickinson's essential epigrammatic lyrics—nonetheless emanated a common *duende*, that modernist yet also ancient concept that the Spanish poet Federico García Lorca would define in the early twentieth century as "dark sounds [that are] the mystery ... from which we get what is real in art ... not a matter of ability, but of real live form; of blood; of ancient culture; of creative action."[1] These "dark sounds" have inspired at least five generations of American poets since Whitman and Dickinson to undertake wild explorations of unconventional subject matter. Coleridge called these raw inspirations a century and a half prior to Lorca "fugitive causes," a

---
1. Translated by A. S. Kline.

phrase inspired by his upper school teacher, James Boyer, who instilled in the young poet the muse's mercurial nature. Coleridge learned from Boyer "that poetry, even that of the loftiest and seemingly that of the wildest odes, had a logic of its own, as severe as that of science; and more difficult because more subtle, more complex and dependent on more, and more fugitive causes."

During an interview with Galway Kinnell in 2009, I observed: "A consistently raw quality runs throughout your work, resounding with primordial energy. It's almost as if you write with dirt in your mouth, figuratively speaking of course." His response confirmed my appreciation for the grounded energy in his work. Laughing, he replied, "That's pretty good." This figurative dirt is not only reminiscent of what John Keats called "the poetry of the Earth" in his poem "The Cricket and the Grasshopper," but also the earthy language of those Whitman identified as the "powerful uneducated persons" one should "go freely with." It was precisely this earthy vernacular that Whitman believed renewed language with his definition of "wit": "the rich flashes of humor and genius and poetry—darting out often from a gang of laborers, railroad-men, miners drivers or boatmen!" In short, the "slang" or "earthy chants" that Whitman celebrated so acquisitively—like no other American poet before or since—enriched his new expansive idiom with what he called "the lawless germinal element, below all words and sentences, and behind all poetry." I think this is precisely the connotative meaning of dirt that Kinnell responded to with such immediate affirmation in his interview, a meaning that harkens still so immediately to Whitman in the arc of dark chthonic sounds in American poetry.

In 1955, exactly a century after the first publication of *Leaves of Grass*, Allen Ginsberg refreshed "the wholesome fermentation" of Whitman's expansive language in his groundbreaking poem, "Howl," a poem that led to the landmark Supreme Court decision *The People [of the State of California] v. Lawrence Ferlinghetti* (the publisher of "Howl") and, eventually, Ferlinghetti's exoneration from obscenity charges. Ginsberg had upped Whitman's ante from slang to perceived "obscenity" in his attempt to reprise "the wholesome fermentation or eructation of those processes eternally active in language" (Whitman). Several bold, innovative books of free-verse poetry followed "Howl" in the early sixties: James Wright's *The Branch Will Not Break* (1961), Galway Kinnell's *What a Kingdom It Was* (1960), W. S. Merwin's *The Drunk In the Furnace* (1960), Adrienne Rich's *Snapshots of a Daughter-in-Law* (1962), Ruth Stone's *In an Iridescent Time* (1960), and Sylvia Plath's *Ariel* (1961). Turning away from the academic poetry of the fifties, this generation of contemporary poets following on the heels of the first generation of postmodernist poets—Robert Lowell, Elizabeth Bishop, Randall Jarrell, and John Berryman—reconceived the mystical conceits of Whitman's and Dickinson's respective manifestations of *duende* with their own iconic tropes: "that sticky infusion, that blood by which I live" (Galway Kinnell, "The Bear"), the "gross, hysterical, nude" disposition of the beat outlier (Allen Ginsberg, "Howl"), "the wreck" (Adrienne Rich, "Diving into the Wreck"), "the afrikan in me / still trying to get home" (Lucille Clifton, "hag riding"), and "the oil-stained earth" (Philip Levine, "They Feed They Lion"). Although these poets crafted their own particular styles, they each shared a common spiritual aesthetic in which the unconscious communes with nature, the commonplace turns strange, the unsayable echoes in silence, and truth lives in doubleness.

While there exist many contemporary poets whose work I enjoy and admire, I suffer from the impression, however valid, that today there are more poets than readers of poetry. Perhaps American poets have always suffered from this illusion, since the most passionate readers of poetry in this country are often secret readers. At least five thousand new titles of poetry are published every year in the United States. How to hear the soul-waking "howl" anymore "in the midst of the crowd"? Maxine Kumin commented to me during my interview with her in 2010 that "it will all get sorted out in time." While I took solace in her prediction, I'm still not so sure that it will. If today's poets are to understand the paradoxical nature of their particular marginalization, it is important to trace the arc of renunciation in American poetry from its provenance in 1855 with the first publication of *Leaves of Grass* to the present plethora of so much eclectic poetry. Whitman and Dickinson wrote against the conventions of both Puritanism and prosody, the modernists against the annihilation and nihilism of the First and Second World Wars, the contemporary poets against patriarchy, the influence of the modernists, the military–industrial complex, racism, and the academic poetry of the fifties.

The particular *agon* of today's poets is overwhelming: a seemingly impossible struggle against the forces of commercialism that have infected the counter-tradition of American poetry with corporate takeover and exploitation. The MFA and the writing industry in general, while providing valuable apprenticeships for beginning writers, has also created a theory-driven climate that undervalues what Emerson, in his essay "Self-Reliance," called the innate "genius" of every person. Most of the senior poets I cite above never attended MFA programs. So how should today's poets resist the corporate leviathan they've helped create? How "to have the wilderness pure" again (Robert Frost) in which resistance, independence, and difficulty run like "the west-running brook"?

Each new generation of groundbreaking poets since Whitman and Dickinson has consisted mostly of outliers. The same is true of the fathers and mothers of jazz, and rock and roll. A culture existed between 1855 and 1980 that allowed poets to flourish in their resistance to the dehumanizing and artistically desiccating forces of their day. James Wright's philippic "Ars Poetica, Some Recent Criticism," echoes today with the same elegiac resonance that it did in 1973, "Reader, we had a lovely language. / We would not listen." The "lovely language" of the past can't be repeated, nor should it be, but today's poets "repel the past" (Whitman) at their own expense. By cynically dismissing their forebears' ageless and subversive music, they run the risk that future generations of poets will dismiss *them* as well. Recognition of the past is essential for preserving the vital tradition of difficulty and resistance in American poetry.

Allen Ginsberg wrote these lines in 1958:

> And all these streets leading
>   so crosswise, honking, lengthily,
>   by avenues

>   stalked by high buildings or crusted into slums
>   thru such halting traffic
>   screaming cars and engines
>   so painfully to this
>   countryside, this graveyard
>   this stillness
>   on deathbed or mountain
>   once seen
>   never regained or desired
>   in the mind to come
>   where all Manhattan that I've seen must disappear.

    (from "My Sad Self")

    Is this the last time a poet called so stridently for the disappearance of the mecca of finance? Ginsberg defined his great ambition as a poet "to pierce the world." Is this still possible? Does contemporary American poetry suffer from too much good writing that's often lost or obscured among the glut of weak writing? Are we drowning in it? No one gets censored for obscenity anymore. But what now? Without national denial in the guise of American innocence and naïveté—a three-hundred-year-old soufflé that fell in the 1950s—is there little or no opportunity for a new poet/prophet to compose a redeeming jeremiad or vision that serves as a foil to the real obscenity of national prevarication and lethal domestic and foreign policy? To conjure the new "main things" with a "fresh meter-making argument"?

    These are obvious but wrong questions. The new soulless obstacle for American poets to write against appears to be their own Trojan horse: "po biz" itself with all its competitions, fiefdoms, and programs. How ironic in light of America's rebellious poetic tradition that today's captains of po biz and business would end up in the same procrustean bed. But perhaps this was inevitable after Paul Engle and Wilbur Schramm laid the groundwork for the lucrative future of MFA programs in 1935 by founding the Iowa Writers Workshop. As early as 1934, the critic Edmund Wilson claimed in his essay "Is Verse a Dying Technique?" that Romanticism's emphasis on intensity had made poetry seem too "fleeting and quintessential." These criticisms have only intensified in the ensuing decades, culminating most famously in Dana Gioia's 1991 essay "Can Poetry Matter?," in which he observes "that the voluntary audience of serious contemporary poetry consists mainly of poets, would-be poets, and a few critics. Additionally, there is a slightly larger involuntary and ephemeral audience consisting of students who read contemporary poetry as assigned coursework. In sociological terms, it is surely significant that most members of the poetry subculture are literally paid to read poetry: most established poets and critics now work for large educational institutions. Over the last half century, literary bohemia had been replaced by an academic bureaucracy."

What then specifically steers many American poets today away from writing more boldly about those "fugitive causes" that precipitate visions with a memorable "logic" of their own? What tendentious weaknesses specifically continue to incite conservative critics to sound the death knell of poetry in America? And where are the raw, erudite, rejoinders to these critics from today's poets that resonate with both the learning and innovation that James Wright's poem "Ars Poetica, Some Recent Criticism" did in 1973? It's easy to accuse conservative critics of indulging in a treacherous nostalgia for the golden period of modernism. But despite the strong poetry emerging today throughout the country, the forces of po biz continue to homogenize, commodify, institutionalize, professionalize, dehistoricize, ghettoize, and theorize poetry into a literary industry of low expectations in which fewer and fewer poets entertain "high ambition," an observation Donald Hall made as far back as 1988 in his famous essay "Poetry and Ambition," which he concludes with this observation: "Ambition is appropriately unattainable when we acknowledge: No poem is so great as we demand that poetry be."

How many poet/teachers today are emphasizing the redemptive efficacy of the poet's paradoxical task of stripping herself of knowing, while simultaneously resisting the supposed imperative to repel the past? How many MFA "mentors" are encouraging their apprentices to attain the shamanistic wisdom of the "gross, mystical," and "nude" seer, or to risk placing their full intellectual weight on the "plank of reason" to break it purposefully, then fall through "worlds" until they have "Finished knowing—then"? Ginsberg refers to Whitman as his "courage teacher" in his poem "A Supermarket in California." For poets to escape po biz's "perfumed rooms," they must trust in Ginsberg's same courage teacher enough to suffer anonymity and even ignominy for their daring, just as Whitman and Dickinson did, just as Allen Ginsberg and Robert Bly did, just as James Wright and Sylvia Plath did, just as Lucille Clifton and Etheridge Knight did, just as Adrienne Rich and Ruth Stone did. In this regard, they must become prophets as well as poets in identifying the illusory "gift" in their midst as a wooden subterfuge, and then write against it in a strange, new way that is also immediately familiar, contemporary, and transformative.

2014

Getting It Right

Poetry, at least good poetry, is hard, if not impossible to write, which is why poets feel so compelled to write the next poem—"to get it right," as Jack Benny remarked about his joke-telling. You hear or read a good poem and think, *I could have written that*, and then you try, only to find out just how squirrely inspiration really is. "That is not what I meant at all," T. S. Eliot laments in the thin disguise of J. Alfred Prufrock. How true. You might ask, *What happened to all the sense and music I was going to make?* Yes, occasionally a good poem arrives on your psychic doorstep as a gift and you think, *Now that was easy. Too easy.* I recall such a visitation occurring to me when I was at divinity school several decades ago. I had just attended a lecture on the Genesis creation stories and was exiting the lecture hall when these words suddenly echoed in my head: "And Adam fell to his knees / and prayed, Lord, Lord please, / please forgive me, / while Eve lit a cigarette looking on / waiting for him to finish so they could move along." Just a ditty, but I think these jaundiced lines played a big part in helping me decide to become a poet instead of a priest—just this poetic charge of a short four-line poem, but enough to encourage me to try again, and then again, until I was hooked like an addict on the opiate of poetry.

    The muse is just this generous and cruel, enticing her scribes with a few memorable lines, then casting them into what an anonymous mystic in the late fourteenth century called "the cloud of unknowing." And doubt, too, I would add. Every poet who has emerged from his or her adolescence with a need to continue writing has experienced this initiation. She works at her desk in a well-lighted study but writes in the dark of witnessing her inspiration turn from what she thinks might be immortal poetry to a jumble of words on the page. Perhaps Percy Bysshe Shelley described the trouble with writing best in his essay "The Defence of Poetry": "It didn't take much for poetic inspiration to come, just like a blow of a wind … as soon as you start composing a poem, the inspiration is gone."

Writing poetry is a Sisyphean task. No poet ever writes the poem to end all poems. The poet, therefore, must love pushing her boulder up the proverbial hill. It's about the pushing, and then listening as the boulder descends back down the hill. If the poet ever comes to think there is an opposite side of the hill, then she writes under the delusion that she can say the unsayable, or that the truth is ultimately sayable, or that it is possible to escape the human condition and still write about it. The memorable poem is as mortal as the poet, as multifaceted as the truth, and as surprisingly beautiful. It all but touches the divine.

Ruth Stone, in her interview with me, went so far as to say, "Even as a child, I would hear a poem coming toward me from across the universe. I wouldn't hear it, I would feel it, and it would come right toward me. If I didn't catch it, if I didn't run in the house and write it down, it would go right through me and back into the universe. So I'd never see it again. I'd never hear it again. I've lost about 99 percent of my poems this way." The inherent "trouble" with poetry for both the poet and her reader, as Stone's comment testifies to has a lot to do with its inscrutable mystery. But this mysterious trouble is also poetry's mystical strength. Yes, the strong poet's boulder resounds with brilliant new poetry as it rolls back down the hill, but any widespread confirmation of its music by critics and readers alike often takes a while, in some cases a long while, as evidenced by American readers' remarkably slow embrace of the genius of Emily Dickinson and Walt Whitman.

The poet writes in the dark, then, with an incurable obsession. Rilke famously dramatizes his obsession in a letter to the young Mr. Kappus in this way: "This most of all: ask yourself in the most silent hour of your night: *must* I write? Dig into yourself for a deep answer. And if this answer rings out in assent, if you meet this solemn question with a strong, simple '*I must*,' then build your life in accordance with this necessity...."[1] Needless to say, if the answer doesn't "ring out in assent," then one doesn't possess the blind faith necessary to keep rolling his boulder up the hill, which is more than understandable and forgivable. Poetry's not for the meek—maybe it's for the foolish by all worldly standards, but not the meek.

So far, I've made the task of writing poetry sound counterintuitive and masochistic, stressing a few of its most difficult realities, namely its dearth of both monetary and literary rewards and its lamentably scant readership. So, what exactly is in it—the act of writing—for the poet? "I'm Nobody! Who are you?" wrote Emily Dickinson. But Miss Nobody wrote nearly two thousand poems. Reading Dickinson's letters to the editor of the *Atlantic Monthly*, Thomas Wentworth Higginson, about publishing reminds me of this succinct joke. "Hit me," said the masochist to the sadist. "No," responded the sadist. Little did Higginson know that Dickinson already knew the joke. Publishing was as far from her mind as "firmament to fin." Her submissions were ruses. But for most poets, especially today, publishing is their obsession and all too often a premature goal, while editors' acceptances of nascent work are too often unwitting refutations for those poets who seek notoriety over quality. Better an immediate no, like the sadist's response to the masochist, than an undiscerning yes.

But back to the struggle poets put themselves through to get it right. This *agon* is a double-sided currency with the *agon* of configuring the best words in the best order on one side and the ecstasy of approaching this impossibility on the other. Or as Dickinson wrote: "For each ecstatic instant / We must an anguish pay / In keen and quivering ratio / to the Ecstasy." It is a selfless, solitary ecstasy at first, the sense that you've got something down in any form—formal or free, verse or prose—that's memorable, definitive, beautiful, musical, and resonant with what the great prose poet Russell Edson called "poetry mind." Enough to keep you going. A big secret you've told yourself simply because you've found the words for "it." So, you're perennially on a spiritual diet as a poet—your spiritual body innately thin. "Who will have me?" asks Ruth Stone

---

1. Translated by Stephen Mitchell.

in her poem "Bargain"; "'I will,' said Poverty." The poet doesn't have a choice, as Rilke informed the young Mr. Kappus. She's like Jonah, on a mission in which she can't avoid trying to define what's most human and verbally beautiful in essential language, even if she doesn't want to. Even if she finds herself in the desert with no relief except for an occasional shade tree that also shrivels in the heat. So she's prophetic by default, in addition to being artistic.

These facts about the nature of poetry were confirmed for me in a series of interviews I conducted with seven eminent senior poets (Jack Gilbert, Maxine Kumin, Robert Bly, Galway Kinnell, Ruth Stone, Lucille Clifton, and Donald Hall) between 2004 and 2011 and then published in 2012 in a book titled *Sad Friends, Drowned Lovers, Stapled Songs*. I'd like to cite a few of the comments from these poets on the surprising, ironic, humbling, ecstatic, and grievous experience of writing, beginning with Jack Gilbert:

CD: Why do feel your pride and strength were also your weaknesses?

JG: I came to see what performance does to someone. It rots you. You become so vain. This is why I refuse to give readings. Because I am weak, it's hard to resist the power. You're like an actor who can capture the audience with your words, your style, your appearance.

CD: Then where does your real power come from?

JG: I don't trust myself. I love the effect so much. It's like if you have the power to make women fall in love with you. I don't want to become that person, that performer, that figure who can intoxicate his audience. If I wanted to, I could make a lot of money. But then I wouldn't want to give it up.

CD: What is the power in you to resist the power?

JG: I would like to think it's the strength of real pride.

CD: How do you distinguish real pride from false pride?

JG: Real pride gives up, false pride keeps performing.

CD: How do you feel now in looking back on your life, your career?

JG: Grateful. I lived my life so richly in so many ways. By falling in love. By being poor. I lived my life in such a wide range of being me.

Maxine Kumin:

CD: Were you emboldened by Anne [Sexton] to write [such poems as] "Sperm," "The Thirties Revisited," "Heaven and Anus," "Life's Work," "The Jesus Infection," and "Song for Seven Parts of the Body," especially after her death?

MK: When Anne [Sexton] killed herself in October of 1974, I felt for a long time that the "fun" had gone out of writing poems. The fun of sharing early worksheets, the fun of reshaping, cutting, adding, the whole sport of revving up, of developing the poem. And the other loss—I am speaking of our professional relationship—was that she would not be there as we spread the poems for the next book out on the floor and tested what poems went with what others, what comprised a section, etc. The fun of format, if I may call it that, something we had always done for and with each other.

Galway Kinnell:

CD: One thing that struck me when you visited my creative writing class last year was your comment that you were reluctant to call yourself a poet.

GK: A poet should not call himself a "poet." Being a poet is so marvelous an accomplishment that it would be boasting to say it of oneself. I thought this well before I read that Robert Frost took the same view.

CD: In the last poem of *Strong Is Your Hold*, a poem titled "Why

Regret," you write, "Doesn't it outdo the pleasures of the brilliant concert / to wake in the night and find ourselves holding hands in our sleep." These are actually the last two lines of the poem. They make the valiant claim about what means most to you, not the brilliant concert, or perhaps poem also by implication, but waking in the middle of the night to find yourself holding hands with your beloved.

GK: Is it a valiant claim, or is it a wonderful, surprising realization? Isn't to find in a moment that we, who chose years ago to live as a couple, are still thrilled to be with each other, isn't that about the most blessed thing of all?

CD: Yes, and especially heartening to hear from someone who has achieved as much as you as a poet.

GK: Art is wonderful, but the moment love is smashed, darkness falls, deafness falls, nothing survives as it was.

Donald Hall:

Poetry is a device for saying something and taking it back at the same time. It's the device for double-mindedness or many-mindedness. No emotion is pure, but frequently we are aware of one and not the other. In poetry somehow you come out with both.

Ruth Stone:

When I'm writing I'm not experiencing anything. It's funny. The writing is separate. I don't write out of the memory or experiencing a memory. The writing is separate.

Robert Bly:

CD: Could you describe exactly what you meant by the "new imagination" in your 1958 essay that appeared in your journal *The Fifties*?

RB: It's an imagination that allows the unconscious to come in with its various ignorances and brilliances. And when Jim [Wright] and I grew up, the poems, as in the *Kenyon Review*, were well controlled by the rational part of the mind, which had only a little bit of playfulness. But that's a little different than letting the wolf in the house.

Lucille Clifton:

LC: Poets have to speak out of what is truth for them. Everything we say has so many meanings. I'm shy. I'm really quite shy. Nobody believes it.

CD: But you're sane ... you've been sane the whole time we've been talking.

LC: Thank you. To be sane in this world is crazy.

Now that Ruth Stone, Lucille Clifton, Jack Gilbert, and Galway Kinnell have all passed, I wonder how they would respond to an article titled "Poetry Is Going Extinct, Government Data Show," which appeared in the *Washington Post* on April 24, 2015. I would like to presume in answering for them, after listening to their answers to my questions about the state of contemporary poetry in America, that nothing has changed about the character or necessity of poetry as "the news that stays news," as "the best words in the best order," as "memorable speech," as "prayers to the unsayable," as "the maximum efficiency of language." But what has changed as the result of the internet, along with the ever-expanding proliferation of literary journals and the plethora of MFA writing programs, is its quantity—to the point that it's impossible now, as it has been for several decades, to wade through its unmanageable surfeit with any satisfactory absorption or fair critical assessment.

Poetry is like a jealous lover; it demands full and uninterrupted attention. It insists on being memorized and studied over and over. Like Eros, it was born poor and has remained so to keep its blessing. A star major-league pitcher makes more in one game than a poet does in a lifetime. It's diachronic at its core, dismissing mere information as a potentially fatal distraction when viewed as more than subject matter.

We now live in an unprecedented time of surfeit for poetry's readership: so many voices behind the microphone in a crowded room, too much to hear, read, and process in the way that poetry requires. Devoted readers of poetry feel like they have to be cyber wizards with a Luddite's mentality, and for many that seems often impossible. I hear poetry kicking and screaming as our high-tech culture lowers it slowly into the acid vat of synchronicity where no news remains memorable for long as mere information.

Like the speaker in Whitman's Canto 32 of "Song of Myself," the poet uses the stallion but a minute, then resigns the horse with a rhetorical question: "Why do I need your paces when I out-gallop them? / Even as I stand or sit passing faster than you." Of course, the flip side of this is the reality that poets rarely if ever know for sure when they're actually outpacing the stallion. How easy indeed it is to write bad poetry when you think you're writing good poetry at the speed of light! But even bad writing is often a necessary, even essential catalyst in the poet's surprising progress toward strong writing. I'm thinking of the scribbled note written in haste, or the embarrassing awkward admission that ferments into such memorable language as D. H. Lawrence's confession at the conclusion of "Snake": "And I missed my chance with one of the Lords / Of life / And I have something to expiate: /A pettiness." Or Elizabeth Bishop's early talky drafts of "One Art" that show no sign of that poem's eventual formal eloquence. Like Whitman, both Bishop and Lawrence superseded "the stallion" in their final drafts, proving the human alacrity of their verbal stallions, which transcend literal speed with memorable speech.

But what if, as Christopher Ingraham seems so eager to announce in his citation of government data concerning poetry, poetry's readership is "going extinct"? His extrapolation from poetry's readership to poetry itself betrays a telling error, a crooked focus. Is he so eager, like other doomsayers of poetry (there have been many since Dana Gioia's essay "Can Poetry Matter?" appeared in *The Atlantic* in 1991), to announce poetry's demise in this country? Anyone who loves poetry knows it's alive and well as essential language. "The proof of the poet is that his country absorbs him as affectionately as he absorbs it," Walt Whitman declaimed in his preface to *Leaves of Grass* in 1855. An unprecedented amount of new music resounds today in the descents of strong poets' boulders from the summits of their respective mountains. But America's best poets don't await the proof of their country's affectionate absorption of their work behind their boulders. They can't. It would be an enervating distraction from the poems they need to write, as well as an affront to their muse. So they must endure the contumely of the government's data as well as the mystery of their poems' destiny.

Who could blame American poets, or any poet, for whining like Elijah on Mount Horeb before he hears the "still small voice" that tells him to get off the holy mountain that there are, in fact, far more "faithful" in the land than he realizes? Such whining by poets or prophets is as off-putting as myopic government data or poets writing merely for other poets. Poetry's "holy mountain" is a figurative and sometimes literal monadnock in a landscape of hidden readers—a desolate *topos* that's also the *axis mundi* where poets experience a revelation that sanctifies their barren summits. Terrence Des Pres writes most profoundly about this ironically transcendent place in his essay on C. P. Cavafy's poem "Dareios," which appeared in his superb book *Praises and Dispraises* (1988):

> Released from his self-serving plans ... the poet can assume his true office. He can allow the poetic idea its hegemony and write the real thing, a poem alive with its time and the true concerns of its audience. Most interesting is the way "the poetic idea" persists, awaits the coming of its incarnation. When it asserts itself it lifts the poet beyond his fear, beyond his pettiness and mere ambition.

2014

Silence Amidst the Crowd: Philip Levine's "The Simple Truth" and "Call It Music"

Although they appeared ten years apart, in 1994 and 2004 respectively, Philip Levine's poems "The Simple Truth" and "Call It Music" share a quality of patience even amid the bumptious culture of America. These two lyrical narratives defer in their conclusions to the silent "voice" behind speech, moving from remorseful ars poetica in "The Simple Truth" to mystical reverie in "Call It Music." In both poems, the catalyst that inspires Levine to humble himself before silent truths lies in his placing others—a potato vender in "The Simple Truth" and Charlie Parker in "Call It Music"—before him with Whitmanesque awe and empathy. It is Levine's "negative capability" in identifying with these sacred ordinary others that spawns his awareness of the power of the unsayable.

The Simple Truth

I bought a dollar and a half's worth of small red potatoes,
took them home, boiled them in their jackets
and ate them for dinner with a little butter and salt.
Then I walked through the dried fields
on the edge of town. In the middle of June the light
hung on in the dark furrows at my feet,
and in the mountain oaks overhead the birds
were gathering for the night, the jays and mockers

squawking back and forth, the finches still darting
into the dusty light. The woman who sold me
the potatoes was from Poland; she was someone
out of my childhood in a pink spangled sweater and sunglasses
praising the perfection of all her fruits and vegetables
at the road-side stand and urging me to taste
even the pale, raw sweet corn trucked all the way,
she swore, from New Jersey. "Eat, eat," she said,
"Even if you don't I'll say you did."
                              Some things
you know all your life. They are so simple and true
they must be said without elegance, meter and rhyme,
they must be laid on the table beside the salt-shaker,
the glass of water, the absence of light gathering
in the shadows of picture frames, they must be
naked and alone, they must stand for themselves.
My friend Henri and I arrived at this together in 1965
before I went away, before he began to kill himself,
and the two of us to betray our love. Can you taste
what I'm saying? It is onions or potatoes, a pinch
of simple salt, the wealth of melting butter, it is obvious,
it stays in the back of your throat like a truth
you never uttered because the time was always wrong,
it stays there for the rest of your life, unspoken,
made of that dirt we call earth, the metal we call salt,
in a form we have no words for, and you live on it.

                              *

Call It Music

Some days I catch a rhythm, almost a song
in my own breath. I'm alone here
in Brooklyn, it's late morning, the sky
above the St. George Hotel is clear, clear
for New York, that is. The radio is playing
Bird Flight. Parker in his California
tragic voice fifty years ago, his faltering

"Lover Man" just before he crashed into chaos.
I would guess that outside the recording studio
in Burbank the sun was high above the jacarandas,
it was late March, the worst of yesterday's rain
had come and gone, the sky was washed. Bird
could have seen for miles if he'd looked, but what
he saw was so foreign he clenched his eyes,
shook his head, and barked like a dog—just once—
and then Howard McGhee took his arm and assured him
he'd be OK. I know this because Howard told me
years later, told me he thought Bird could
lie down in the hotel room they shared, sleep
for an hour or more, and waken as himself.
The perfect sunlight angles into my little room
above Willow Street. I listen to my breath
come and go and try to catch its curious taste,
part milk, part iron, part blood, as it passes
from me into the world. This is not me,
this is automatic, this entering and exiting,
my body's essential occupation without which
I am a thing. The whole process has a name,
a word I don't know, an elegant word not
in English or Yiddish or Spanish, a word
that means nothing to me. Howard truly believed
what he said that day when he steered
Parker into a cab and drove the silent miles
beside him while the bright world
unfurled around them: filling stations, stands
of fruits and vegetables, a kiosk selling trinkets
from Mexico and the Philippines. It was all
so actual and Western, it was a new creation
coming into being, like the music of Charlie Parker
someone later called "glad," though that day
I would have said silent, "the silent music
of Charlie Parker." Howard said nothing.
He paid the driver and helped Bird up two flights
to their room, got his boots off, and went out
to let him sleep as the afternoon entered

the history of darkness. I'm not judging
Howard, he did better than I could have
now or then. Then I was 19, working
on the loading docks at Railway Express,
coming day by day into the damaged body
of a man while I sang into the filthy air
the Yiddish drinking songs my Zadie taught me
before his breath failed. Now Howard is gone,
eleven years gone, the sweet voice silenced.
"The subtle bridge between Eldridge and Navarro,"
they later wrote, all that rising passion
a footnote to others, I remember in '85
walking the halls of Cass Tech, the high school
where he taught after his performing days,
when suddenly he took my left hand in his
two hands to tell me it all worked out
for the best. Maybe he'd gotten religion,
maybe he knew how little time was left,
maybe that day he was just worn down
by my questions about Parker. To him Bird
was truly Charlie Parker, a man, a silent note
going out forever on the breath of genius
which now I hear soaring above my own breath
as this bright morning fades into afternoon.
Music, I'll call it music. It's what we need
as the sun staggers behind the low gray clouds
blowing relentlessly in from that nameless ocean,
the calm and endless one I've still to cross.

These two poems develop similar paradoxical themes on the nature of Levine's inscrutable muse. While issuing a prophet-like caveat at the close of "The Simple Truth" about the impossibility of ever speaking truths he's known "all his life," despite their life-sustaining presence "in the back of your throat," in "a form we have no words for," Levine defines this unspeakable but palpable truth in "Call It Music" as "a silent note / going out forever on the breath of genius." Although generally not given to philosophical flights in his recurring lyrical narratives and jeremiads about factory work, family history, anti-Semitism, the legacy of poetry, and rites of passage, Levine conjures a metaphysical conceit for music that is similar to his conceit for truth—an abiding, mystical silence. A close reading of these poems reveals an overheard voice that engages Levine in a poetic conversation with himself about just what he can and cannot say. But his subject, which is also not a subject—namely, those truths that are inexpressible—remains the inscrutable subtext of both poems and consequently Levine's essential struggle in the making of these poems.

Levine divides "The Simple Truth" into two sections with the strategy of broaching his impossible subject by first engaging his reader with personal narrative. In the first seventeen lines of the poem, he recounts a recent purchase of "a dollar and a half's worth of small red potatoes" from a Polish woman—"someone out of [his] childhood"— and then walking through "the dried fields / on the edge of town" in June. While this vignette is rich with pastoral detail, recalling a scene out of Dos Passos's *USA* or a passage from Whitman's "Democratic Vistas," it doesn't present much more than a vivid account of Levine's encounter with a Polish vender at a roadside vegetable stand who urges him to eat her fruits and vegetables. This woman's look, accent, and playful rejoinder bring back memories of Levine's childhood, prompting him to turn his reflection into philosophizing. Moving from the Polish woman's command to "eat, eat" to the general observation that there are "some things / you know all your life," Levine unravels an *ars poetica* that redounds on the very real grounds he describes so evocatively in the first half of the poem. The literal potatoes become metaphors for the unsayable, which are those "things" one knows all his life. This *a priori* epistemology becomes the real subject of the poem, addressing the poet's primary responsibility to innate knowledge: to forgo "elegance, meter and rhyme" when speaking of those things "so simple and true." What remains mysterious, however, is why this awareness about the simple truth leads to suicide and betrayal. Levine confesses his and Henri's betrayal of their love, along with Henri's suicidal downward spiral, as a seemingly direct consequence of his awareness of the truth's need for simple, unadorned form. "My friend Henri and I arrived at this together in 1965 / before I went away, before he began to kill himself, /

and the two of us to betray our love." Levine leads his reader to assume from these tragic consequences of arriving at the simple truth, that it, whatever "it" is, is both revelatory and destructive.

Levine's shift from literal storytelling to figurative witnessing turns on his phrase "some things" in line 18. By implication, these "things" are antipodes of formal poetic expression, free of meter and elegance. Things (lines, phrases, silence) "on the table beside the salt shaker," that "must stand for themselves," "naked and alone." But Levine never says what these things are specifically, leaving his reader to surmise for herself. He does, however, provide gustatory clues that hearken back to the potatoes he bought from the Polish hierophant at the roadside vegetable stand and then cooked for dinner "with a little butter and salt." These same potatoes are now "like a truth / you never uttered because the time was always wrong." The same food that's celebrated for its sustenance at the start of the poem has now become "like a truth" "in the back of your throat." We now see what Levine was up to in the first part of the poem, setting up the physical "that" with his potato vignette in a dialectic that concludes with a metaphysical "this" that incorporates the same potato. Patience leads to prescience in this compound narrative where earth is wed to truth "in a form we have no words for" but nonetheless exists as a vital sustenance that one lives on—or not. The elusive simple truth that Levine leaves his reader with resonates more as a spiritual cognizance than any possible truthful utterance. The fact that the "time is always wrong" for uttering those things one knows all his life belies any absolute efficacy of language, leaving silence as truth's most authentic realm and poetry's inscrutable, ironic source.

A decade after writing "The Simple Truth," Levine returned to silence, in his poem "Call It Music," as a realm that evinces more than a mere absence of sound, but a mystical music as well that resonates first from random things in "the bright world," then finds its way through the receptive ear and eye of the musician to an adequate instrument: Charlie Parker's saxophone. And even though this silent music emanating from mere ordinary things pours out ultimately from Parker's sax, Levine claims that it somehow also remains "silent":

> Howard truly believed
> what he said that day when he steered
> Parker into a cab and drove the silent miles
> beside him while the bright world
> unfurled around them: filling stations, stands
> of fruits and vegetables, a kiosk selling trinkets
> from Mexico and the Philippines. It was all
> so actual and Western, it was a new creation
> coming into being, like the music of Charlie Parker
> someone later called "glad," though that day
> I would have said silent, "the silent music
> of Charlie Parker." Howard said nothing.

Whether intentional or not, Levine echoes here the same ancient conceit that King David employs in verses 2 through 4 of Psalm 19: "Day to day pours forth speech, / and night to night declares knowledge. There is no speech, nor are there words; / their voice is not heard; / yet their voice goes out through all the earth, / and their words to the end of the world." Substitute Parker's saxophone in this psalm for "day" and "night," and one becomes the other. This metaphorical synergy, which Levine's friend Larry Levis called "glad music," does indeed play out as "day's speech" and "night's knowledge" in "Call It Music," revealing his inherent awareness—not unlike David's—of the ultimate "silence" of his own words within time's cosmic sweep. But it is this particular submission and admission that imbue Levine's lines in the here and now with valiant witness to the "bright world," the glittering minutiae and "glad music" that are memorable, at least for as long as his "voice" and lines remain in the memories of his readers.

Levine repeats the same gustatory metaphor in "Call It Music" that he used in "The Simple Truth": "I listen to my breath / come and go and try to catch its curious taste, / part milk, part iron, part blood." Can one then infer syllogistically that truth is breath for Levine? Or does he merely wish to use the same metaphor to describe both truth and breath while ascribing different meanings to these two subjects? He does add milk and blood to the list, so there are a few additional flavors in his organic taste. But Levine never makes any definitive claim about truth being breath, or vice versa, choosing instead to distill his tropes in "Call It Music" (the last poem in his most recent book, *Breath*) down to four things: "automatic" breath, a "curious taste," "silent music," and the "breath of genius." Levine writes about these four endogenous and metaphysical things as if he has known them all his life, but is just now finding the right words for his mystical knowledge. He talks to himself throughout much of the poem, overhearing himself say that his breathing is not he, that Charlie Parker's music is "silent," that his late friend Howard McGhee, a jazz musician, teacher, and disciple of Charlie Parker, did the best he could in attending to Parker, despite Parker's institutionalization and early demise, and that the word for the "whole process" of breathing "means nothing" to him. In a show of exemplary deference, Levine humbles himself before Parker's music at the end of the poem, perceiving from his humility's ironic alembic just what ineffable quality Parker's music possesses that inspires him in turn to call it "silent"— which is its genius "above [his] own breath." Levine qualifies this music as necessary, not just for him, but for his reader as well. "It's what we need / as the sun staggers behind the low gray clouds / blowing relentlessly in from that nameless ocean."

The poem has been personal up to this point, elegizing the lives and music of Howard McGhee and Charlie Parker. Levine's leap from I to we at the end exhibits his subtle but effective shift away from the personal to the universal, saving the poem from mere private reminiscence about his two late friends and his own imminent demise. Unlike his speaker in "The Simple Truth," who leaves his reader with a palpable metaphor for the "unsayable," in the conclusion of "Call It Music" Levine avoids the topic of telling "the simple truth" altogether in favor of evincing the power of breath alone as that transcendent ether that both vivifies the body and sounds "the silent notes" of genius.

The metaphor in the poem's diminuendo is revelatory for Levine. Charlie Parker the man, who is also "a silent note going out forever on the breath of genius," leads Levine like an angel to the inner sanctum of silent music where he hears Parker's breath "soaring above [his] own" at day's end. This music's inherent grace, in turn, bestows a mortal vision to Levine of an empyreal ocean, "the calm and endless one [he has] still to cross." Like Dickinson's psychopomp, a fly "with blue uncertain stumbling buzz" in her poem "I heard a fly buzz," Parker's music leads Levine to that point where he "cannot see to see." And yet he does see a final time and place, at least in his mind; it is a cloudy afternoon at the beach, but like the truth he cannot utter in "The Simple Truth," the ocean over which the clouds blow in concealing the sun remains nameless.

Levine's patience lies in his wisdom to submit to truths he knows but cannot express, "without any irritable reaching after fact or reason," and his willing surrender to "the silent note." In a letter Levine wrote to me about this poem in response to a first draft of this essay, he provided this note on the inspiration of Parker's music within the tragic context of his abbreviated life:

> The silent music of Charlie Parker. Have you ever heard the recording—that famous infamous one—of "Lover Man"? It's one Bird wished was never released. It was Larry Levis who used the term "the glad music" of Bird. I say silent because that solo says so much about silence, and then it was followed by months of literal silence because Parker was confined to a mental institution in Camarillo, California, for close to six months. When near the end of the poem I hear Bird's voice soaring above my own, I'm hearing his music; in the beginning of the poem I refer to "Bird Flight"—that's a weekday radio broadcast hosted by Phil Schaap on WKCR; it lasts over an hour and is dedicated to the music of Charlie Parker.... The poem is about what cannot be said. I have for some years been writing about just this theme.

Levine is not alone among poets of his generation in his homage to the unsayable. Adrienne Rich and W. S. Merwin corroborate his paradoxical embrace of the unsayable in recent testimonies of their own. Adrienne Rich concludes her 2006 essay "Poetry and Commitment": "Finally: there is always that in poetry which will not be grasped, which cannot be described, which survives our ardent attention, our critical theories, our classrooms, our late-night arguments. There is always (I am quoting the poet/translator Americo Ferrari) 'an unspeakable where, perhaps, the nucleus of the living relation between the poem and the world resides."' Merwin echoes Rich's sentiments in a prepared statement on this subject that appeared in the *American Poetry Review*'s twenty-fifth anniversary issue (June/July 2008). Responding to the question, *How does poetry help people to live their lives?*, Merwin answered, "The source that rises unbroken from the unsayable speaks to us of the impulse and mystery that we share with every living creature. The urge is meaningless, like the unknown itself, and in the end remains, by nature, unsayable."

While these statements reaffirm in eloquent prose what is most sacred about the wellspring of poetry, Levine's testimonies to what Qoheleth described in Ecclesiastes as the "eternity that God has put into the minds of men, but so he cannot figure out what has happened from beginning to end," provides a timely poetic update on the inviolate silence that resounds between the lines of memorable poetry.

2009

The Poetic "Engine" in Flannery O'Connor's Fiction

Flannery O'Connor charged her prose with poetry that electrified her fiction. Both her narratives and her characters' speech underscores the kind of verbal quality that, as W. H. Auden claimed, defined poetry itself: language that achieves "memorable speech." In a short essay titled "A Reasonable Use of the Unreasonable" that O'Connor wrote to help her students understand her work, she defined the vatic force in her stories as "belief," describing it metaphorically as "the engine that makes perception operate." By infusing her fiction with poetic phrases and passages at strategic moments, O'Connor charged her fiction with "memorable" invectives, startling revelations, mystical visions, and oracular conclusions that shock her readers with stunning truths. Dynamic poetic one-liners typify the dialectical exchange of O'Connor's muse, who moves boldly between belief and unbelief: "Go back to hell, you old wart hog" (from "Revelation"); "'Oh Lord!' he prayed. 'Break forth and wipe the slime from this earth!'" (from "The Life You Save May Be Your Own"); "No pleasure but meanness" (from "A Good Man Is Hard to Find")"; "I been believing in nothing every since I was born!" (from "Good Country People"); and "Christ will come like that!" (from "The Displaced Person"). The "memorable speech"—the poetry—in these lines provides an extra cylinder to O'Connor's fictive "engine," giving it a power that "makes perception operate" at a highly moral and spiritual level. She also referred to the salvific paradox that underlies the mystical praxis of many of her stories as "a reasonable use of the unreasonable."

In what is perhaps her most famous story, "A Good Man Is Hard to Find," O'Connor creates a character, the Grandmother, who O'Connor explains, in her essay "On Her Own Work," "experiences that special kind of triumph which instinctively we do not allow to someone altogether bad." She goes on to comment on the startling transformation of the Grandmother's character: "I often ask myself what makes a story work and what makes it hold up as a story." She answers her own question by concluding

> ... that it is probably some action, some gesture of a character that is unlike any other in the story, one which indicates where the real heart of the story lies. This would be an action or gesture which was both totally right and totally unexpected; it would have to be one that was both in character and beyond character; it would have to suggest both the world and eternity. The action or gesture I'm talking about would have to be on the anagogical level, that is, the level which has to do with the Divine life and our participation in it.

The Grandmother's "gesture" of touching "The Misfit" on the shoulder, in conjunction with her sudden recognition of him as "one of [her] babies" just before he shoots her three times in the chest, resonates with absurd affection and converts her from a two-dimensional termagant into a three-dimensional agnostic who doubts God's miraculous powers. "Maybe God didn't raise the dead," she concedes to The Misfit, as if to say that doubt—that "engine" that drives her fiction—compromises belief. In just one electric, poetic line, accompanied by a compassionate gesture, O'Connor both reverses the odious, shallow character of the grandmother to a shockingly saintly figure, and counters The Misfit's nihilism with her own profoundly truthful doubt. O'Connor wrote about the Grandmother's abrupt sense of "kinship" with The Misfit in "On Her Own Work":

> Her head clears for an instant and she realizes, even in her limited way, that she is responsible for the man before her and joined to him by ties of kinship, which have their roots deep in the mystery she has been merely prattling about so far. At this point she does the right thing, she makes the right gesture.

In one of her letters, quoted by Ralph Wood in his book, *Flannery O'Connor and the Christ Haunted South*, she comments, "Grace is never received warmly. Always a recoil...." O'Connor never wrote a more Catholic story, in which the transactional concept of absolution played more of a dramatic role as the result of her anagogic gesture.

O'Connor's observation near the end of "On Her Own Work" disturbs and enlightens simultaneously in its claim that violence is "strangely capable of returning [her] characters to reality and preparing them to accept their moment of grace." Her poetic wit spices The Misfit's speech with zingers that continue to echo long after the Grandmother has died: "There never was a body that give the undertaker a tip." "It's no real pleasure in life." "They never shown me my papers." "She would of been a good woman if it had been somebody there to shoot her every minute of her life." These retorts shift O'Connor's fictive transmission into its highest poetic gear. The paradoxical manner in which she does this, however, confounds many of her readers at first, in the same way that poetry often confounds and repels readers with irony, abstraction, and figurative language.

This is why it's easy to speculate that O'Connor felt compelled to write "On Her Own Work" in an attempt to explain the mechanics of her operative "engine." Her explanation of the philosophy behind The Misfit's nihilism and turpitude, along with her tacit approbation of the grandmother's final Christian "gesture," creates a theology that translates terror into epiphany. Both the grandmother and The Misfit are antiheroes, inspiring little if any sympathy throughout most of the story, although The Misfit's nihilistic philosophizing mesmerizes with disturbingly alluring logic. O'Connor dares to walk a high tightrope throughout "A Good Man Is Hard to Find," aware that at some point she has to turn either the Grandmother or The Misfit into a credible three-dimensional character in order to make her point about "belief." The suddenly weird, out-of-character epiphany the Grandmother experiences when "her head clears" in her outlandish identification with The Misfit as "one of [her] babies," along with her attempted "gesture" "to touch" him, releases the operative power of her fictive "engine."

O'Connor keeps both her religious and poetic balance on the high wire of her belief in the Grandmother's "gesture" that serves as the mystical climax of the story. The manner in which the Grandmother dies, collapsing into a "cross-like" position with her knees folded beneath her, serves as a capstone image of her final Christlike gesture to the atheistic Misfit.

Although a devout Catholic in practice, O'Connor's religious sensibility resonates in her poetic epiphanies in more of a philosophical than conventionally religious way. Several of her other characters, such as Hazel and Tarwater in *Wise Blood*, Hulga and the Bible salesman in "Good Country People," and Parker in "Parker's Back," also exemplify a postlapsarian zeitgeist. O'Connor relied on lurid realism in developing her philosophically complex characters in the mid-twentieth-century agrarian South. As Ralph Wood points out, she was enamored with the godless views of both Nietzsche and Heidegger, "who were not involved in a shouting match with the Almighty," but more intent on "protesting the massive vacancy of the soul that, largely unrecognized, characterizes modern religious life in the West." O'Connor was also fascinated by John Calvin's doctrine of double predestination, which maintained human ignorance of the salvific mysteries of God. Wood, however, goes on to point out the unresolvable problem that nihilism and predestination posed for O'Connor: the fact that they both eliminate the essential ingredient necessary for belief in the first place, which is free will.

Although more than a few of her characters' prospects for salvation seem unlikely, O'Connor's development of her quasi-biblical characters goes to the heart of her belief in both grace and horrific wickedness in the mechanics of Christian salvation, as well as to O'Connor's belief in the devil. Always careful to avoid wooden, fundamentalist scenarios, O'Connor conceives of fictive conceits that defy facile interpretations. As she explains, again in "On Her Own Work":

> I don't want to equate The Misfit with the devil. I prefer to think that, however unlikely this may seem, the old lady's gesture, like the mustard-seed, will grow to be a great crow-filled tree in The Misfit's heart, and will be enough of a pain to him there to turn him into the prophet he was meant to become. But that's another story.

"Good Country People" *is* that "another story." O'Connor's two main characters, a Bible salesman and his intellectual but naïve customer, Hulga, both embrace "nothing" over faith and belief. These two characters' attempt to one-up each other by confessing their belief in "nothing," revealing both Heidegger's and Nietzsche's influence on O'Connor, as well as her own fascination with nihilism. But rather than conclude her story with a salvific "gesture" in the way she does at the end of "A Good Man Is Hard to Find," O'Connor chooses a *via negativa* strategy by creating a philosophical competition between her two prideful characters, which the Bible salesman wins in dramatic fashion by stealing Hulga's prosthetic leg after making out with her in a hayloft and then declaring, "I been believing in nothing every since I was born!" Hulga becomes no more than the Bible salesman's straw woman at this point, while the salesman reveals himself as the devilish atheist he is.

O'Connor found it much easier to believe in the devil than she did in God, for as she explains in the voice of The Misfit, "Jesus thrown everything off balance. It was the same case with him as with me except He hadn't committed any crime and they could prove I committed one because they had the papers on me." O'Connor essentially confesses in her fictional ventriloquism how much harder it is to possess faith than it is to believe in the literal evidence of the devil's work. She quotes Baudelaire on this matter in "On Her Own Work": "The devil's greatest wile is to convince us that he does not exist."

O'Connor succeeds with Miltonic verve and vision in writing about Satan. As her faithful muse, Satan, in the person of the Bible salesman, provides the fuel for her high-octane fictive "engine" on the one hand, while depriving her of any similar inspiration for beatific narratives on the other. She is in love with the Bible salesman's wiles and genius, as the haughty parting line testifies to in "Good Country People": "I haven't believed in God since the day I was born." At the center of her quest for belief lies Ivan Karamazov's famous adage, from Dostoyevsky's *The Brothers Karamazov*, that if God is dead, then "everything is permitted." The Misfit, who is also an impressive philosopher, exemplifies this atheistic syllogism in his homicidal rampages, asserting that criminals are only held accountable for their actions if the legal authorities have "the papers on them." O'Connor delights in both the wit and anarchy of The Misfit, relying on him for supplying her with infernal "material." There are, on the other hand, no comparable saintly characters in her fiction who inspire her with comparable theological bite.

O'Connor kept a prayer journal during her time as a student at the Iowa Writers Workshop from 1946 to 1947, which only came out as book in 2013 under the title *A Prayer Journal*. As a twenty-one- and twenty-two-year-old MFA student, O'Connor formulated many of the foundational ideas of her quintessentially human stories. The following passages shed a fascinating light on her genius for wrestling with themes of grace, faith, the devil, atheism, belief, and theodicy that would later manifest so "operatively" as allegorical stories in her first collection of short fiction, *A Good Man Is Hard to Find and Other Stories*:

> Learned people can analyze for me why I fear hell and their implication is that there is no hell. But I believe in hell. Hell seems a great deal more feasible to my weak mind than heaven. No doubt because hell is a more earthly-seeming thing. I can fancy the tortures of the damned but I cannot imagine the disembodied souls hanging in a crystal for all eternity praising God.
>
> Dear God, I cannot love Thee the way I want to. You are the slim crescent of a moon that I see and my self is the earth's shadow that keeps me from seeing all the moon.
>
> Dear Lord, please make me want You. It would be the greatest bliss. Not just to want You when I think about You but to want You all the time, to think about You all the time, to have the want driving in me, to have it like a cancer in me. It would kill me like a cancer and that would be the Fulfillment.
>
> The intellectual & artistic delights that God gives us are visions & like visions we pay for them; & the thirst for the vision doesn't necessarily carry with it a thirst for the attendant suffering. Looking back I have suffered, not my share, but enough to call it that but there's a terrible balance due. Dear God please send me Your Grace.

No one can be an atheist who does not know all things. Only God is an atheist. The devil is the greatest believer & he has his reasons.

There is nothing left to say of me.

In 1949, O'Connor was diagnosed with lupus, the same disease that had killed her father in 1941. It's only reasonable to assume that O'Connor feared that her father's fate awaited her also, which prompted her in turn to write about her own mortal concerns in her stories. It's easy to assume, therefore, that O'Connor identified intimately with the Grandmother in "A Good Man Is Hard to Find." Her accurate empathy with the Grandmother's dire circumstance inspired both her "anagogical gesture" of touching The Misfit, as well as her last words, "You're one of my babies." She also took obvious delight in her *via negativa* strategy of depicting two nihilists in "Good Country People" as archetypal examples of young misfits in the making.

In both of these stories, O'Connor employs what Søren Kierkegaard called "teleological suspensions of the ethical" in order to place her characters in life-and-death scenarios that lead, often brutally and in harrowing, picaresque conflicts to ultimate beatific outcomes. It is in her taut, poetic, violent suspensions of morality that she revs her "engine" of belief to profound epiphanies that ring with poetic economy. O'Connor's most paradigmatic title, "The Violent Bear It Away" (a quote from Matthew 11:12), serves throughout her fiction as a modus operandi for the terror that O'Connor deems necessary in her fiction for doing justice to the salvific tropes of the Christian story. They are, in this fictive sense, her own hard-won acts of faith as much as they are works of literary genius.

2023

The Sublime Irony of Nothing and the Divine Imagination

The most sublime act is to set another before you.
— William Blake

Nothing is the force / That renovates the World.
— Emily Dickinson

The legacy of sublimity in both secular and religious literature follows an arc that extends from the earliest Sumerian texts to contemporary literature. Both poetry and classical narratives—themselves usually written in verse—share a common hierophantic obsession with mining the fruits of uncertainty, mystery, alterity, nothingness, and the absurd. At the core of this lies the working paradox of something in nothing. "Saying nothing ... sometimes says the most," Emily Dickinson wrote to her friend Susan Gilbert in 1874; and then this gem in her poem (#1611, Franklin): "By homely gifts and hindered Words / the human heart is told / Of Nothing – / 'Nothing' is the force / That renovates the World –." Walt Whitman expressed a similar belief in "the force" of nothing in terms of his poetic praxis in canto 44 of "Song of Myself": "What is known I strip away." The reader of poems like this about the double nature of absence must—like the listener in Wallace Stevens's poem "The Snow Man"—behold "Nothing that is not there and the nothing that is." It is precisely this paradox that sounds so similar to the dual nature of light (which manifests both as a wave and as a particle), revealing an existential nexus between absence and presence, nothing and something.

* * *

Strangeness sustains the imagination in myriad classic texts in the face of nothing with events, facts, choices, reasons, acts, realizations, and outcomes that transcend the ordinary with mystifying weirdness—a fleeing youth at Jesus's arrest in Gethsemane, the shocking revelation of the Bible salesman's true identity in Flannery O'Connor's "Good Country People," a horrible commandment from God to Abraham to sacrifice his son, Isaac; the terrible realization by a young man in *Oedipus the King* that he's murdered his father unwittingly and then also unwittingly married his mother—to mention just a few.

A memorable literary synecdoche of human unknowing lies in James Wright's poem "October Ghosts," in which Wright announces his sublime ignorance to himself first, and then to his reader: "Now I know nothing, and I die alone." In admitting to knowing "nothing," Wright achieves a profound state of enlightenment that is synonymous with Socratic wisdom, allowing him to "die alone" in an heroic act of self-enlightenment. Unwittingly but archetypally, Wright describes nirvana in his conclusion to "The Journey" into "heart of the light."

This "light," as well as the poet's genius for line breaks, was on full display when he was dying of tongue cancer in Calvary Hospital in the Bronx. Donald Hall tells this story in his introduction to Wright's posthumous complete poems, *Above the River*: "At one point Jim started to write me a note, and paused after the third word. On his yellow scratch pad I watched him write, 'Don, I'm dying'—and then, after a tiny pause, as short as a line break—'to eat ice-cream from a tray.'"

* * *

The provenance of the other as a solitary divine entity resides in the earliest Hebrew scripture, where infinitesimal others emerge out of nothing in God's acts of creation. In choosing an unknowable God whose name is too holy to speak and who possesses a miraculously verbal power to transform "waste, void, and darkness" into natural wonders, including mankind, that are "good," the Israelites defined themselves as an anomalous people in the midst of a hostile array of neighbors devoted to anthropomorphic gods. In addition to being strange and different, Yahweh was terrifying, forbidding any graven image of Himself while demanding devotion to moral commandments that Moses had received in a mysterious mountaintop meeting in which Yahweh had revealed only His backside. The Yahwist author of most of the narratives in the Pentateuch, including the two creation stories, possessed a literary acumen for conveying what John Keats would define millennia later as "negative capability"—a preternatural human capacity to exist in "uncertainty, mystery, doubt without any irritable reaching after fact and fiction." William Blake put an element of this more succinctly in his Proverbs of Hell: "The most sublime act is to set another before you."

* * *

Nothing has served more fruitfully for literary inspiration throughout history as nothing itself, primarily because it is the seat of unknowing and creation itself and therefore infinitely beguiling. But from what irrational source did the Judaic insight into the generative void arise? The answer to this question is less "religious" than simply imaginative and supremely literary for its inscrutable oddness, which manifests in profoundly mysterious ways that endure in literature as sublime encounters with the other as Other—or, as Martin Buber would say, as *thou*. By avoiding any reification of their deity, the authors of the Pentateuch, along with the books of the prophets, Proverbs, Job, the Psalms, Song of Songs, Ecclesiastes, and the Christian Gospels, established unique theological conceits, particularly with regard to theodicy and their apophatic deity, that have served as foundational narratives for an enduring world literature.

In the cosmology of the Greeks, whose myth-makers perpetually "reinvented [their] own origins"—as Harold Bloom has noted in his book *Poetry and Repression* (an observation he borrowed from Giambattista Vico's *New Science*)—whereas the Judaic tradition featured a religious dialectic, alternating between what Søren Kierkegaard called God's "teleological suspension of the ethical" (as in Abraham's near sacrifice of Isaac), and "personal" and revelatory acts such as God's covenant with Abraham, and the delivery of the decalogue to Moses. Greek myth-makers had conceived of gods whose primary role was in maintaining the order of the universe, with no particular personal regard for human concerns. This notion of divine disinterest in human life and affairs realized its cultural apotheosis in the stoicism of Zeno and Marcus Aurelius. But juxtaposing Judaic revelation with Hellenistic mythology reveals an enigma: the same God who has, in Qoheleth's words in Ecclesiastes, "set eternity in the human heart; yet so no one can fathom what God has done from beginning to end" has also interacted with his prophets and people in intensely "personal" ways. Silence and revelation alternate in diachronic reprises throughout biblical history, from Job's terrible wait for a divine response to his inexplicable suffering, to Jonah's need for God to explain the reason behind his mission to Nineveh, to Jesus's last question to "Abba" before he died on the cross: "Father, Father, why have you forsaken me?"

* * *

"Nothing," in the form of silence, has played a profoundly ironic role in Western literature, especially in our post-biblical era in which the absence of divine utterance and revelation, particularly in the aftermath of the Holocaust, has left only echoes of Yahweh's voice. Heroic humor, absurdity, and nihilism have replaced what was once believed to be divine ventriloquism in Yahweh's prophetic agents. Prophecy evolved into literature that didn't always testify to the Deuteronomic code, evolving ultimately into profoundly existential fiction and poetry that questioned the canonical codes of scripture—texts that were too freethinking to be considered even apocryphal. What prophet could have prophesied *The Brothers Karamazov*, *Thus Spake Zarathustra*, *Heart of Darkness*, *Waiting for Godot*, *The Trial*, *The Fall*, *The Plague*, *The Waste Land*, *Fathers and Sons*, and *To the Lighthouse*? This shift from the mythopoetic age to the modern era seems inevitable in retrospect, as the theme and concept of theodicy increasingly captured the imaginations of philosophers and writers, inspiring them ultimately to write books like those cited above. The tropes of black humor and atheism in these texts belie any modern-day belief in the Deuteronomic code. Inherent in Judeo-Christian faith lies a divine absurdity that offers a paradoxical reason for believing in a divine Force that's greater than the self. In a formulation long misattributed to the third-century church father Tertullian, "Credo quia absurdum" ("I believe because it is absurd")—surely a prophecy about modernism, postmodernism, and post-postmodernism (which grows ominously closer to nothingness itself by the day).

* * *

Perhaps the most resonant admonition that has haunted the collective Western psyche over the past century and half is Ivan Karamazov's claim, in Fyodor Dostoyevsky's *The Brothers Karamazov*, that if there is no God, then "everything is permitted."

One example of a corrective that resounds deeply across the last century and a half is Christ's silence at the conclusion of the fifth chapter of *The Brothers Karamazov*. In a "parable" that Dostoyevsky calls "a poem," a duplicitous inquisitor in Seville, in the time of the Inquisition, promotes a counterfeit version of the Gospel. Ivan Karamazov, an agnostic at best, presents to his saintly brother, Alyosha, the Grand Inquisitor's central point that people need bread and miracles over freedom, if given a choice between a religion that promises miracles and bread and a religion that doesn't. The Grand Inquisitor contradicts Christ's call to forgo bread and miracles as necessary ingredients for faith, claiming that institutional Christianity needs them as necessary "signs" and rewards for "believing." The Grand Inquisitor's bastardized theology corroborates Karl Marx's claim that religion, specifically Christianity, is "the opiate of the masses." Alyosha, on the other hand, in true existential fashion, maintains that human freedom, onerous as it is, serves as a spiritual corrective to the Grand Inquisitor's misprision of Christ's criterion for true faith: a "religion" that excludes bread and miracles as necessary incentives for belief. The Grand Inquisitor in Ivan's telling responds to Jesus with this famously cynical reply:

> Thou wouldst go into the world, and art going with empty hands, with some promise of freedom which men in their simplicity and their natural unruliness cannot even understand, which they fear and dread—for nothing has ever been more insupportable for a man and a human society than freedom. But seest Thou these stones in this parched and barren wilderness? Turn them into

bread, and mankind will run after Thee like a flock of sheep, grateful and obedient, though for ever trembling, lest Thou withdraw Thy hand and deny them Thy bread.[1]

Alyosha's silence in response to his brother's "poem," a kiss on his lips, serves as a sounding board to the Grand Inquisitor's casuistry in the guise and garb of orthodoxy. Ivan immediately ridicules Alyosha, quipping, "That's plagiarism!" For Jesus also kisses the Grand Inquisitor at the end of his "poem." Alyosha's kiss, like Jesus's kiss, testifies to the power of his sublime act. Its silence speaks exponentially louder than words, intoning "nothing" as freedom's sacred rebuttal to the plethora of reassuring "somethings" of false religion. If Alyosha had spoken to Ivan, no doubt he would have echoed Søren Kierkegaard: "Where all are Christians, the situation is this: to call oneself a Christian is the means whereby one secures oneself against all sorts of inconveniences and discomforts.... And orthodoxy flourishes in the land, no heresy, no schism, orthodoxy everywhere, the orthodoxy that consists in playing the game of Christianity."[2] Although both Alyosha and Ivan see through the Grand Inquisitor's charade of "pushing" bread and miracles as lures for belief and devotion, it's Alyosha who maintains the difficult but true faith of "going without" in the face of nothing.

* * *

Writing around the same time as Dostoyevsky, Emily Dickinson embraced the same fertile void as the fictional Alyosha in several poems that approach the divine "nothing"—none more than #633 (Franklin):

> I saw no Way – The Heavens were stitched –
> I felt the Columns close –
> The Earth reversed her Hemispheres –
> I touched the Universe –
>
> And back it slid – and I alone –
> A Speck upon a Ball –
> Went out upon Circumference –
> Beyond the Dip of Bell –

---

1. Translated by Constance Garnett.
2. Translated by Walter Lowrie.

While Dickinson employs metaphorical imagery to express her venture to the outskirts of "Nothing," Franz Kafka remains grounded and literal in his description of Josef K.'s end in his novel *The Trial*; all his persecuted protagonist can feel at the end of his life is shame. K. stares into the void of his grave after being mortally wounded by his thuggish executioners. As his sight fails in his dying moment, he says to his killers, "Like a dog." Kafka then editorializes, "It seemed as though the shame was to outlive him."[3] It is precisely K.'s intransigent "shame" that haunts him, as if the fact of one's mere being predicates inevitable humiliation. Nothing Josef K. can point to other than his guilt over merely existing effects any exculpatory power in his mind capable of exonerating him. His seemingly irrational sentence echoes John Calvin's supralapsarian theology with a power that's even more disturbing for its absurd but deeply human appeal. Josef K. dies in the vacuum of "nothing" with only his awareness that his shame will "outlive him." So "nothing," besides its paradoxical function as a cauldron for creation, exists as a mirror for K.'s self-consciousness and shame. Such is its mimetic curse in K.'s last thought.

Unlike Dickinson, Josef K. eschews any lyrical temptation in his spare prose, implying that the subject of "nothing"—his inscrutable death sentence—is less a poetic or metaphorical subject than simply a literal one, which requires brutal honesty about the intrinsic self-consciousness of consciousness itself. Dickinson, a lapsed Congregationalist, largely resorted to poetry for her theological musings, as she does in #633, supplanting turgid theology and philosophy with exquisite poetry. Kafka avoids theology as a *via negativa* strategy for capturing his readers' imagination, with what Wallace Stevens called a "supreme fiction" whose narrative rings truer than the news.

It's not hard to imagine Alyosha kissing Josef K. as well, but more out of empathy for his spiritually honest resistance to any counterfeit assurance in divine intervention than for his agapeic love for him. Alyosha and K. have "nothing" in common. As does Job, who like both of them is left with the same hard reality of no prospect for bread or miracles to bolster his faith—only God's voice out of the whirlwind, reminding him of his paltry place as a human in the infinitely larger scheme of creation by

---

3. Translated by Breon Mitchell.

cataloging His miraculous efficacy as Creator in rhetorical questions about not only the provenance of creation but its utterly mystifying wonders. Conversely, with no such straining over revelation or divine reminding, Josef K. embraces his shame as a symptom of his human condition, with no supra-fictive conceits to provide divine solace. Such nothing is something, in its heroic testimony to one's human capacity for enduring—and even enjoying—life and its surreal adventures while it lasts.

* * *

The prerequisite for believing in the truth that shuns religious language, while adopting the idea of a transpersonal self that crosses over to "the other" with selfless sympathy and divine imagination, is no less than the absurd love known as *agape*, which, as James Wright declares at the end of his poem "Saint Judas"—"I held the man for nothing in my arms"—embraces the other for "nothing" with a passion that transcends sense, reason, and self-interest. It is precisely there, in that inscrutable realm of nothing, that truth needs only silence as its most effective expression. For this reason, in the extreme sense, Midrashic hermeneutics might accurately be summarized in one sentence: Scripture is the irresistibly absurd yet sacred story of Nothing that is Everything.

* * *

Nothing speaks more sublimely about nothing than the muse of nothing herself, who has inspired writers since *Gilgamesh* to write something about *it*. Nothing is something, in fact it's everything: the fertile void out of which the world was created and continues to evolve. It is the negative pole in the electrical polarity of creation. It is "the force," as Emily Dickinson wrote to her friend Susan Gilbert, "that renovates the world." It is the paradoxical absence of everything in the dialectic of existence—the inscrutable depository of infinite possibilities and "the new" that's perpetually vacuuming itself. It is, in Shakespeare's *King Lear*, Cordelia's truthful reply, "Nothing," to her father when he requests her declaration of love. Cordelia's "nothing" is everything in its safeguarding of its own genuineness. Lear's response to his favorite daughter, "Nothing can come of nothing," attests to his profound ignorance; for everything comes from Cordelia's "nothing," most notably her love's sacred condition of demurring from forced confession, which her feeble father is tragically blind to. Cordelia reveals nothing's subterfuge, which is that it conceals everything. It is that oceanic, personal address of the waves to each person who "has ears to hear," as Walt Whitman observed at the conclusion of his poem "Out of the Cradle Endlessly Rocking":

> ... the word up from the waves,
> The word of the sweetest song and all songs,
> That strong and delicious word which, creeping to
> my feet,
> (Or like some old crone rocking the cradle, swathed
> in sweet garments, bending aside,)
> The sea whisper'd me.

It is indeed eternity's lover.

* * *

I can think of no better way to conclude this essay than by citing several examples from both secular and religious texts that manifest the diachronic legacy of nothing with a universal appeal that erases any distinction between religious and secular genres. As conscious beings with the knowledge of death, how can we call literature that chronicles memorable human experience and history "meaningless," as Qoheleth, the author of Ecclesiastes, does below? Such a conceit points to the ultimate use of *via negativa*. But John Wilmot, Samuel Beckett, Thomas Gunn, Mark Wunderlich, Li Bai, and Mary Ruefle all add memorable commentary on this topic in the enduring poems that I have copied below—poems that add yet more "meaningless" memorable wisdom to the already overflowing canon of literature that has emanated from "nothing."

Upon Nothing

Nothing! thou elder brother even to Shade:
That hadst a being ere the world was made,
And well fixed, art alone of ending not afraid.

Ere Time and Place were, Time and Place were not,
When primitive Nothing Something straight begot;
Then all proceeded from the great united What.

Something, the general attribute of all,
Severed from thee, its sole original,
Into thy boundless self must undistinguished fall;

Yet Something did thy mighty power command,
And from fruitful Emptiness's hand
Snatched men, beasts, birds, fire, air, and land.

Matter the wicked'st offspring of thy race,
By Form assisted, flew from thy embrace,
And rebel Light obscured thy reverend dusky face.

With Form and Matter, Time and Place did join;
Body, thy foe, with these did leagues combine
To spoil thy peaceful realm, and ruin all thy line;

But turncoat Time assists the foe in vain,
And bribed by thee, destroys their short-lived reign,
And to thy hungry womb drives back thy slaves again.

Though mysteries are barred from laic eyes,
And the divine alone with warrant pries
Into thy bosom, where truth in private lies,

Yet this of thee the wise may truly say,
Thou from the virtuous nothing dost delay,
And to be part with thee the wicked wisely pray.

Great Negative, how vainly would the wise
Inquire, define, distinguish, teach, devise,
Didst thou not stand to point their blind philosophies!

Is, or Is Not, the two great ends of Fate,
And True or False, the subject of debate,
That perfect or destroy the vast designs of state—

When they have racked the politician's breast,
Within thy Bosom most securely rest,
And when reduced to thee, are least unsafe and best.

But Nothing, why does Something still permit
That sacred monarchs should at council sit
With persons highly thought at best for nothing fit,

While weighty Something modestly abstains
From princes' coffers, and from statemen's brains,
And Nothing there like stately Nothing reigns?

Nothing! who dwell'st with fools in grave disguise
For whom they reverend shapes and forms devise,
Lawn sleeves, and furs, and gowns, when they like thee look wise:

French truth, Dutch prowess, British policy,
Hibernian learning, Scotch civility,
Spaniards' dispatch, Danes' wit are mainly seen in thee.

The great man's gratitude to his best friend,
Kings' promises, whores' vows—towards thee may bend,
Flow swiftly into thee, and in thee ever end.

   (John Wilmot, Earl of Rochester)

*

From *Waiting for Godot*

ESTRAGON: What do you expect, you always wait till the last moment.

VLADIMIR: (musingly). The last moment ... (He meditates.) Hope deferred maketh the something sick, who said that?

ESTRAGON: Why don't you help me?

VLADIMIR: Sometimes I feel it coming all the same. Then I go all queer. (He takes off his hat, peers inside it, feels about inside it, shakes it, puts it on again.) How shall I say? Relieved and at the same time ... (he searches for the word) ... appalled. (With emphasis.) AP-PALLED. (He takes off his hat again, peers inside it.) Funny. (He knocks on the crown as though to dislodge a foreign body, peers into it again, puts it on again.) Nothing to be done. (Estragon with a supreme effort succeeds in pulling off his boot. He peers inside it, feels about inside it, turns it upside down, shakes it, looks on the ground to see if anything has fallen out, finds nothing, feels inside it again, staring sightlessly before him.) Well?

ESTRAGON: Nothing.

VLADIMIR: Show me.

ESTRAGON: There's nothing to show.

(Samuel Beckett)

*

The Annihilation of Nothing

Nothing remained: Nothing, the wanton name
That nightly I rehearsed till led away
To a dark sleep, or sleep that held one dream.

In this a huge contagious absence lay,
More space than space, over the cloud and slime,
Defined but by the encroachments of its sway.

Stripped to indifference at the turns of time,
Whose end I knew, I woke without desire,
And welcomed zero as a paradigm.

But now it breaks—images burst with fire
Into the quiet sphere where I have bided,
Showing the landscape holding yet entire:

The power that I envisaged, that presided
Ultimate in its abstract devastations,
Is merely change, the atoms it divided

Complete, in ignorance, new combinations.
Only an infinite finitude I see
In those peculiar lovely variations.

It is despair that nothing cannot be
Flares in the mind and leaves a smoky mark
Of dread.

       Look upward. Neither firm nor free,

Purposeless matter hovers in the dark.

  (Thom Gunn)

*

The God of Nothingness

My father fell from the boat.
His balance had been poor for some time.
He had gone out in the boat with his dog
hunting ducks in a marsh near Trempealeau, Wisconsin.
No one else was near
save the wiry farmer scraping the gutters in the cow barn
who was deaf in one ear from years of machines—
and he was half a mile away.
My father fell from the boat
and the water pulled up around him, filled
his waders and this drew him down.
He descended into water the color of weak coffee.
The dog went into the water too,
thinking perhaps this was a game.
I must correct myself—dogs do not think as we do—
they react, and the dog reacted by swimming
around my father's head. This is not a reassuring story

about a dog signaling for help by barking,
or, how by licking my father's face, encouraged him
to hold on. The dog eventually tired and went ashore
to sniff through the grass, enjoy his new freedom
from the attentions of his master,
indifferent to my father's plight.
The water was cold, I know that,
and my father has always chilled easily.
That he was cold is a certainty, though
I have never asked him about this event.
I do not know how he got out of the water.
I believe the farmer went looking for him
after my mother called in distress, and then drove
to the farm after my father did not return home.
My mother told me of this event in a hushed voice,
cupping her hand over the phone and interjecting
cheerful non sequiturs so as not to be overheard.
To admit my father's infirmity
would bring down the wrath of the God of Nothingness
who listens for a tremulous voice and comes rushing in
to sweep away the weak with icy, unloving breath.
But that god was called years before
during which time he planted a kernel in my father's brain
which grew, freezing his tongue,
robbing him of his equilibrium.
The god was there when he fell from the boat,
whispering from the warren of my father's brain,
and it was there when my mother, noting the time,
knew that something was amiss. This god is a cold god,
a hungry god, selfish and with poor sight.
This god has the head of a dog.

(Mark Wunderlich)

*

From Ecclesiastes, 1:1–11 (New International Version)

The words of the Teacher, son of David, king in Jerusalem:
"Meaningless! Meaningless!"
says the Teacher.
"Utterly meaningless!
Everything is meaningless."

What do people gain from all their labors
    at which they toil under the sun?
Generations come and generations go,
    but the earth remains forever.
The sun rises and the sun sets,
    and hurries back to where it rises.
The wind blows to the south
    and turns to the north;
round and round it goes,
    ever returning on its course.
All streams flow into the sea,
    yet the sea is never full.
To the place the streams come from,
    there they return again.
All things are wearisome,
    more than one can say.
The eye never has enough of seeing,
    nor the ear its fill of hearing.
What has been will be again,
    what has been done will be done again;
    there is nothing new under the sun.
Is there anything of which one can say,
    "Look! This is something new"?
It was here already, long ago;
    it was here before our time.
No one remembers the former generations,
    and even those yet to come
will not be remembered
    by those who follow them.

*

Zazen on Ching-t'ing Mountain

(Li Bai, translated by Sam Hamill)

The birds have vanished down the sky.
Now the last cloud drains away.

We sit together, the mountain and me,
until only the mountain remains.

*

From *A Little White Shadow*

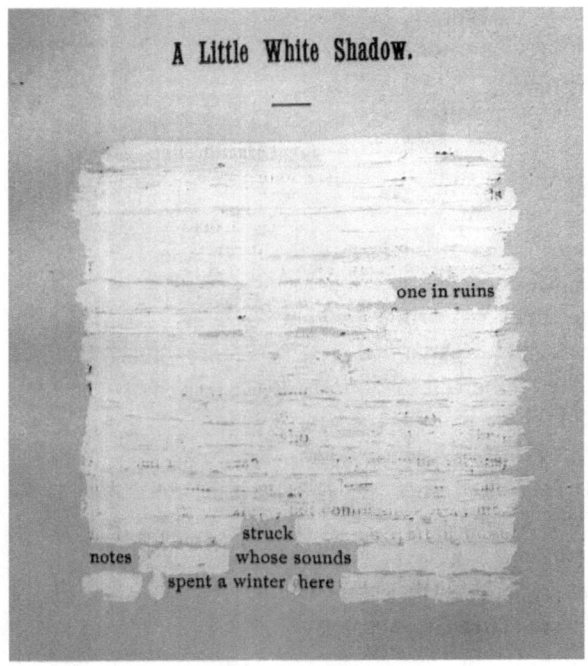

(Mary Ruefle)

2021

"Back to My Ohio": The Life and Poetry of James Wright

As both an exile and a witness to the poverty of his native Martins Ferry, Ohio, James Arlington Wright escaped the harsh fate of his parents and peers to become one of the leading poets of his generation. With deep affection for his hometown, Wright remained haunted throughout his career by the suffering of his townspeople, including his father, Dudley, an employee of the Hazel-Atlas Glass factory, and his mother, Jesse Lyons Wright, a laundress. Influenced initially by the narrative, iambic style and demotic subject matter of Edwin Arlington Robinson and Robert Frost, Wright turned to free verse and the more spare, imagistic strategies of the European Modernists and classical Chinese poets to develop the plain speech he called "the one tongue" he could write in, his native "Ohioian."

A deeply sensitive, intelligent poet, Wright risked sentimentality and naïveté, conjuring speakers who blurred the line between elegy and tragedy—the "famous men" and women on the streets and purlieus of Martins Ferry, Minneapolis, Chicago, and New York. He viewed the disenfranchised citizenry of his hometown as the blessed "non-elect," and himself as the scribe of their lawgiving. Going one step further than Walt Whitman in his social inclusiveness, Wright not only memorialized the otherwise anonymous lives of prostitutes, drunks, the unemployed and underpaid, suicides, the homeless, hapless family members, and his own supremely "lonely" self, but he bestowed beatitude on them as well, with no other authority than his own extravagant sympathy.

Before becoming a strong poet, however, Wright needed to scrutinize his untamed emotions and tendentious romanticism. His sympathy, for instance, for the criminal George Doty lacked moral and emotional checks in his first poem about him, "A Poem about George Doty in the Death House," from his first book, *The Green Wall*.

> But I mourn no soul but his,
> Not even the bums who die,
> Nor the homely girl whose cry
> Crumbled his pleading kiss.

In his second book, *Saint Judas*, Wright recognized his irrational grief and revised his mourning for Doty to sane antipathy, depicting him now with Dantesque revulsion in his poem "At the Grave of an Executed Murderer": "Wrinkles of winter ditch the rotted face / Of Doty, killer, imbecile, and thief: / Dirt of my flesh, defeated, underground." The anti-romantic pity, compassion, and hatred that emanate from this poem, which the critic Peter Stitt calls Wright's "first genuine poem," remained a hallmark of Wright's work, which would grow increasingly lyrical, ranging in style from tender elegies and pastoral lyrics to grievous apostrophes, political philippics, and fierce apologias to vernacular homages.

Born on December 13, 1927, in Martins Ferry, Wright attended his hometown public schools, graduating a year late from high school after a nervous breakdown his senior year. He would continue to suffer from bouts of depression throughout his life, as well as alcoholism, which his second wife, Annie, would help him overcome. He became especially close to his Latin teacher, Helen McNeely Sheriff, who introduced him to Catullus, Virgil, and Horace, poets who would remain lifelong influences. After spending two years (1946–47) in the army in Japan, he attended Kenyon College, where he studied with John Crowe Ransom, Charles Coffin, and Philip Timberlake, graduating cum laude and Phi Beta Kappa. After graduating from college in 1953 he married Liberty Kardules, also from Martins Ferry; with the help of a Fulbright fellowship grant they traveled to Vienna, where he spent a year translating Georg Trakl and Theodor Strom. In this same year,

Liberty gave birth to their first son, Franz Wright. In 1954, Wright enrolled in the PhD program at the University of Washington, where he studied with Theodore Roethke and Stanley Kunitz. His classmates included Carolyn Kizer, Richard Hugo, and David Wagoner. In 1956, while still a graduate student, he won the Yale Younger Poets Prize for his manuscript *The Green Wall*, which was published in 1957 with an introduction by the judge of the contest that year, W. H. Auden. Wright was hired at the University of Minnesota to teach English, where his colleagues included John Berryman, Allen Tate, and Sarah Youngblood, with whom he collaborated on translating the work of Rainer Maria Rilke. After completing his dissertation on the comic imagination of the young Charles Dickens in 1958 while on a Kenyon College fellowship, he received his doctorate in 1959. His second son, Marshall, was born in 1958. Wright's marriage failed over the next few years, and in 1962 he and Liberty were legally divorced. Wright remained in Minneapolis, teaching at the University of Minnesota, while Liberty moved to San Francisco with Franz and Marshall.

In 1958, Wright read a poem by Georg Trakl in Robert Bly's subversive new literary magazine, *The Fifties*, which showcased translations of several leading European Modernists. He was so moved by Trakl's poem, along with what Bly referred to as the magazine's "new imagination," that he wrote Bly a sixteen-page, single-spaced letter thanking him for sending him a copy of the first issue. He also digressed passionately about his need for such foreign influence in his own work, as in this passage where he laments American intellectuals' lack of responsiveness not only to the European Modernists, but to Walt Whitman as well:

> But back in America I have had an impossible time even trying to get anyone to admit that Whitman existed, to find anyone at all—*anyone at all*—who has even heard Trakl's name. So I used to get hideously drunk at parties of academic intellectuals, and after the point of no return I would stand and bellow Trakl, and Carossa, and Rilke, and Hölderin, because nobody knew what the hell I was saying, and because I only slightly *felt*, rather than *understood*, what in the name of God was crying in the miracles

of those images that were sane to the depths of their being and which yet followed no rules that anyone else had ever dreamed of, and in the tide-suck of that music that sounded like the sea burying its birds or a jellyfish crying out in pain.

Wright found a kindred spirit in Bly, who encouraged his Whitmanesque sympathies and newly adopted leaping style that incorporated the deep imagery and emotive imagination of Trakl. From 1958 to 1962, Wright frequently visited Robert Bly's farm in western Minnesota where he worked with him on translating Trakl, collaborated on a book of poems with William Duffy and Bly titled *The Lion's Tail and Eyes: Poems Written Out of Laziness and Silence*, contributed to *The Fifties*, and began writing poems that would appear in his next book, *The Branch Will Not Break*.

During these three years, Wright transformed his work from its former iambic style into a fresh free-verse expression that reflected the influences of the European and South American poets he had been reading: Georg Trakl, César Vallejo, Hermann Hesse, Juan Ramón Jiménez, and Pablo Neruda, as well as the classical Chinese poets Li Bai, Tu Fu, and Bai Juyi. Agonizing over how to go on writing after his early success with *The Green Wall* in 1957 and *Saint Judas* in 1959, Wright contemplated stopping writing altogether, searching in vain for a way to break away from the iambic line. In another 1958 letter to Bly, Wright opined:

> I mentioned having written a "Farewell to Poetry" even before I saw *The Fifties*.... The *new imagination* is so important, to all living human beings and not just the literati, that I am going to continue to search for it—and if I cannot find it in myself (though I believe I can), then I will identify and fight for it in others. And this is not mock-humility—I see blood in this matter, I really do.

In his next book, *The Branch Will Not Break*, published in 1963, Wright finally abandoned the iambic line, along with his American influences Edwin Arlington Robinson and Robert Frost, for his bold new experiment in free verse. His "new imagination" had discarded "iambic altogether" for highly modulated lines that avoided narrative in favor of a more purely lyrical expression. Gone were his discursive polemics, elegies, and reminiscences. With a newfound economy that wed natural objects to his speakers' emotions, Wright had discovered a way to lyricize his interior irritabilities, sympathies, and longings through imagery that simultaneously maintained his intense connection to his recurring subjects—the disenfranchised, and nature. The opening lines of "Goodbye to the Poetry of Calcium," the second poem in *The Branch Will Not Break*, announce his new lyrical voice most dramatically:

> Mother of roots, you have not seeded
> The tall ashes of loneliness
> For me. Therefore,
> Now I go.
> If I knew the name,
> Your name, all trellises of vineyards and old fire
> Would quicken to shake terribly my
> Earth, mother of spiraling searches, terrible
> Fable of calcium, girl.
> ...

Wright's switch to free verse also prompted him to simplify his syntax and become more creative with his line breaks, as in the following lines from his poem "A Blessing," where his enjambment in the penultimate line achieves the magic of both pathos and ecstasy: "Suddenly I realize / That if I step out of my body I would break / Into blossom." While his contemporary Spanish and German influences resonate throughout *The Branch Will Not Break*, strongly resembling many of his translations of Lorca, Jimenez, Vallejo, Hesse, Neruda, and Trakl, Wright's new style allowed him to write in a broader tonal register with colloquial freedom. Accomplished as Wright was as a formal poet in his first two books, he reveled in his new style that not only struck a new lyrical economy but unleashed vernacular testimonies as well, as in this memorable paean to his hometown:

Autumn Begins in Martins Ferry, Ohio

> In the Shreve High football stadium,
> I think of Polacks nursing long beers in Tiltonsville,

And gray faces of Negroes in the blast furnace at Benwood,
And the ruptured night watchman of Wheeling Steel,
Dreaming of heroes.

All the proud fathers are ashamed to go home.
Their women cluck like starved pullets,
Dying for love.

Therefore,
Their sons grow suicidally beautiful
At the beginning of October,
And gallop terribly against each other's bodies.

Despite abandoning the iambic line, Wright did not feel he had abandoned craft. He was now replacing formal verse with his own "meter-making arguments." This new style in his natural voice displayed sudden tonal shifts, broken emotional breath, an innate colloquial eloquence, clean grammar, deft verbal velocity and clarity, and thrilling enjambments. Annoyed by some critics' presumption that he had abandoned craft as well as form in his move to free verse, Wright wrote to Mark Strand in 1972 that "I have a secret with myself. I love the craft. The nihilists who damn delicacy and balance be damned. In a way, I flatter myself, but I think with good reason. Slithering technician, I know enough to know what craft is for."

In 1967, Wright married Edith Anne Crunk, the "Annie" who would become the subject of many of his later poems. The following year he published his fourth volume of poetry, *Shall We Gather at the River*, an intensely emotional collection that contained poems about the desperately poor and forgotten ("The Minneapolis Poem," "I Am a Sioux Brave, He Said in Minneapolis"), Wright's own extreme loneliness ("Before a Cashier's Window in a Department Store," "In Terror of Hospital Bills"), and his mythic muse, Jenny ("Speak," "To the Muse"). These poems combined Wright's most intensely personal and empathic expression with a plainspoken free-verse style.

Despite his established success, Wright continued to identify with the lost and disenfranchised. His affection for such troubled characters, as well as for family, former teachers, and friends from his hometown, outshone his love for attention and fame, although he remained intensely ambitious his entire career. The poems in *Shall We Gather at the River* expand Wright's Christlike vision of equating poverty, pain, loss, and longing with beatitude, beauty, and the impossibility of apprehending God's face. In a fashion not dissimilar to Solomon's futile search for his "gazelle" in the Song of Songs, he grieves for Jenny in his poem "Speak" as a way of yearning also for divine union.

> And Jenny, oh my Jenny
> Whom I love, rhyme be damned,
> Has broken her spare beauty
> In a whorehouse old.
> ...
> I have gone forward with
> Some, a few lonely some.
> They have fallen to death.
> I die with them.
> Lord, I have loved Thy cursed.
> The beauty of Thy house:
> Come down. Come down. Why dost
> Thou hide thy face?

* * *

After he was denied tenure by the University of Minnesota in 1964, Wright taught for a year at Macalester College in Saint Paul, Minnesota, before accepting a tenured position in 1966 at Hunter College in New York City, where he remained until his death in 1980.

In 1971, Wright published his *Collected Poems*, which won the Pulitzer Prize. He also published his translations of poems and prose by Hermann Hesse with his son Franz Wright in the same year, and received the Melville Cane Award from the Poetry Society of America. In 1973, following his father's death, Wright traveled extensively through England, France, Italy, and Austria. On a second Guggenheim fellowship in 1978, he returned again to France and Italy with his wife, Anne, to write. In 1973 he published his fifth collection of poems, *Two Citizens*, followed by *To a Blossoming Pear Tree* in 1978 and the posthumous *This Journey* in 1982.

In his last three books, Wright wrote increasingly about Venice, Verona, Fano, and Padua, while continuing to write about Ohio. He also began writing political poems ("Confession to J. Edgar Hoover" and "A Mad Fight Song for William S. Carpenter, 1966") in protest against the Vietnam War, as well as prose poems—particularly about Italy. Yet the more distant he grew from Martins Ferry as he taught in New York and traveled in Europe, the more fiercely he wrote about his Ohio roots. In "Ars Poetica: Some Recent Criticism," the first poem in *Two Citizens*—a book whose title emphasizes Wright's growing sense of himself and Annie as responsible literary witnesses—he chides his "Cambridge" readers with an Ohioan pride that extols his Aunt Agnes, "that slob / So fat and stupid," with a most ironic but effective affection:

> I gather my Aunt Agnes
> Into my veins.
> I could tell you,
> If you have read this far,
> That the nut house in Cambridge
> Where Agnes is dying
> Is no more Harvard
> Than you could ever be.
> And I want to gather you back to my Ohio.
> You could understand Aunt Agnes,
> Sick, her eyes blackened,
> Her one love dead.

So strong is Wright's anger by the end of this poem at "old position" intellectuals (Robert Bly's term for traditionalists) that he concludes with a Sylvia Plath-like invective, "Hell, I ain't got nothing. / Ah you bastards, // How I hate you." The solace he finds from his chronic homesickness comes ultimately from the memory of a little girl who speaks to him in a swimming pool that his father and uncle built in Martins Ferry. "When I rose from that water," he writes at the end of "The Old WPA Swimming Pool in Martins Ferry, Ohio," "A little girl who belonged to somebody else, / A face thin and haunted appeared / Over my left shoulder and whispered, Take care now, / Be patient and live."

In his patience during the last decade of his life, Wright juxtaposed the raw beauty of Ohio with the classical beauty of Italy. Sitting above the "sewer main" in Martins Ferry in his poem "Beautiful Ohio," he praises the fetid waterfall with stalwart hometown devotion. "I know what we call it / Most of the time. / But I have my own song for it, / And sometimes, even today, / I call it beauty." In Verona, he writes at the end of his prose poem, "The Secret of Light," "It is all right with me to know that my life is only one life. I feel like the light of the river Adige. // By this time, we are both an open secret." Alternating in his last three books between these disparate notions of beauty, Wright maintained a poetic dialectic that set the pathos of "beautiful Ohio" against the metaphysical beauty of the Adige's light—which revealed himself to himself as an "open secret." A poet of light and dark, tenderness and outrage, gatherings and loneliness, recrudescence and refinement, damnations and blessing, patriotism and protest, he had by now completely abandoned his semi-surrealistic style and deep imagery, and developed an elegantly descriptive plain speech that married luminous Italian and pastoral settings with metaphysical observations, as in these lines from "To a Blossoming Pear Tree": "Young tree, unburdened / By anything but your beautiful natural blossoms / And dew, the dark / Blood in my body drags me / Down with my brother."

In his introduction to Wright's *Selected Poems*, Robert Bly wrote, "Why are James Wright's poems so good? Besides his truth-telling, his grief, and his affections, he has a genius for language. His gift has something to do with interstices between words, the mysterious events that happen when simple words are placed next to one another." A natural comedian who loved to perform impersonations of Jonathan Winters, Wright had a gift for timing, verbal economy, clear language, complex ideas, native speech, risible asides, and oceanic feeling. He also knew how to harden his heart at just the right moment in order to safeguard against sentimentality, as in this masterful section of "Ars Poetica: Some Recent Criticism":

> Reader,
> We had a lovely language,
> We would not listen.

> I don't believe in your god.
> I don't believe my Aunt Agnes is a saint.
> I don't believe the little boys
> Who stoned the poor
> Son of a bitch goat
> Are charming Tom Sawyers.
>
> I don't believe in the goat either.

This was James Wright, defiant and compassionate, local and worldly, choosing the via negativa to point toward the unsayable, and then rejecting "the goat" to boot.

In December of 1979, Wright developed a sore throat that turned out to be cancer of the tongue. After attending a White House tribute to American poets and poetry in January of 1980, hosted by President Jimmy Carter and First Lady Rosalynn Carter, Wright turned his mind to completing his last collection of poems, but was soon forced to enter Mount Sinai Hospital in Manhattan. It was here that he decided to title his manuscript *This Journey*, requesting it be shown to Galway Kinnell, Robert Bly, Donald Hall, Robert Mezey, and Hayden Carruth for final review before its publication. Wright died on March 25 at Calvary Hospital, and was buried in Woodlawn Cemetery in the Bronx following his funeral service at Riverside Church in Manhattan, the same church in which he and Annie were married.

2010

Blurred Lines: Some Thoughts on Hybrid, Liminal, and Prose Poetry

In his poem "In the Evening Air," Theodor Roethke declares, "I'll make a broken music or I'll die." In this one line of blank verse, Roethke testifies memorably to the inherent lyricism of his mortal awareness, what he calls his "dark theme." The "broken music" Roethke makes resounds in his line breaks, which emanate breath catching and then resuming in organic interstices that echo the time and space in which his lungs breathe and his heart beats, and in which his "dark theme" cascades at the precipices of his line breaks as rhythmic yet "broken" responses to the void that lies beyond each of his lines. The evocative delusion that cries out in Roethke's credo is the phrase "or die"—since, as W. H. Auden also pointed out after making a similar claim about the mortal implications of failing to love in his poem "September 1, 1939," "we are going to die anyway." And yet this claim of eternal life, seen in both Roethke and Auden's poems, seems true enough in the lyric poet's timeless business of writing.

In a time when poets are experimenting with poetic forms in boldly unprecedented ways, often drawing a thin line, if any line at all, between verse and prose, one could be forgiven for wondering if poetry's river has flooded its banks. Poetry as a genre is boundless, and unlike prose is open to far more than just written expression. Anything that inspires or thrills—a beautiful dive, a balletic leap, a brilliant chess move—is considered poetic, defying categorization. Some of the best poetic lines have in fact appeared as prose, as evidenced by passages in such novels, memoirs, and essays as Herman Melville's Moby Dick, F. Scott Fitzgerald's *The Great Gatsby*, Vladimir Nabokov's *Speak, Memory*, Albert Camus's *Lyrical Essays*, James Joyce's *Ulysses*, Ralph Waldo Emerson's "The Poet" and "Nature," Eduardo Galeno's *Genesis*, Jorge Luis Borges' *Selected Prose*, the first chapters of Genesis, the Gospel of John, Franz Kafka's *Parables and Paradoxes*, William Faulkner's *The Sound and the Fury*, and Toni Morrison's *The Bluest Eye*, to mention only a very few that come immediately to mind. With regard to the poetic line specifically, its integrity as a "memorable unit of expression" (Cid Corman) relies more on the poet's bewitching expression than any specific definition, whether it's formal or not. A line of free verse can be just as memorable for its restraint and truth-telling as a formal line for its aural music, eliciting silence as much as sound between its words, as well as in its words—what Philip Levine called the unsayable in his poem "The Simple Truth"—truth that stays "unspoken" in "the back of your throat ... made of that dirt we call earth, the metal we call salt, / in a form we have no words for."

If a poet wishes to continue employing the line as "a memorable unit of expression," then his or her task becomes far more difficult in writing freely without the mnemonic help of prosody and rhyme. She must write powerfully enough to allow her content alone to etch itself in her reader's memory, no matter what shape or form it takes on the page. Lyrical truth-telling has resonated as powerfully in free verse as in formal verse throughout the centuries, and continues to do so, often appearing to poets as gift-like and even divine in its arrival from "elsewhere." The poet Ruth Stone maintained that her poems came to her from "across the universe." Samuel Taylor Coleridge credited a dream for "Kubla Khan," as did Rumi for his unslaked spontaneous inspiration. Coleridge's and Rumi's poems are formal, but there are just as many examples of poetry stripped bare of meter and rhyme whose expression pierces memory with vatic economy. Here, for instance, is Herbert Mason's powerful translation of eighteen lines about grief from *Gilgamesh*, which was written over 3,800 years ago:

> It is that inner atmosphere that has
> An unfamiliar gravity or none at all

Where words are flung out in the air but stay
Motionless without an answer,
Hovering about one's lips
Or arguing back to haunt
The memory with what one failed to say
Until one learns acceptance of the silence
Amidst the new debris
Or turns again to grief as the only source
Of privacy, alone with someone loved.
It could go on this way for years and years
And has for centuries,
For being human holds the special grief
Of privacy within the universe
That yearns and waits to be retouched
By someone who can take away.
The memory of death.

Or this poem by Ruth Stone:

The Wound

The shock comes slowly
as an afterthought.

First you hear the words
and they are like all other words,

ordinary, breathing out of lips,
moving toward you in a straight line.

Later they shatter
and rearrange themselves. They spell

something else hidden in the muscles
of the face, something the throat wanted to say.

Decoded, the message etches itself in acid
so every syllable becomes a sore.

The shock blooms into a carbuncle.
The body bends to accommodate it.

A special scarf has to be worn to conceal it.
It is now the size of a head.

The next time you look,
it has grown two eyes and a mouth.

It is difficult to know which to use.
Now you are seeing everything twice.

After a while it becomes an old friend.
It reminds you every day of how it came to be.

Robert Bly described the unteachable quality of resonant verbal compression in his dear friend James Wright's poetry as a "gift [that] has something to do with interstices between words, the mysterious events that happen when simple words are placed next to one another." By "interstices," Bly meant the silence that inheres in Wright's language and conjures "deep images" and feeling in such a way that breath, imagery, truth, meaning, and pathos combine to form an extraordinary verbal matrix of evocative expression that's memorable, in the way the best classical Chinese poets Wright admired do, especially Po Chui. The fact that James Wright started out as a formal poet, as did so many of his peers and teachers, should come as no surprise, as his mastery at composing evocative "interstices between [his] words" evolved, no doubt, from his uncanny ear for the deep silences between the metrical feet of formal verse. In his poem "Ars Poetica, Some Recent Criticism," which appeared in his book *Two Citizens* in 1972, Wright addresses the loss of what he calls the country's "beautiful language": "Reader, / We had a lovely language. / We would not listen." But as sardonic on the one hand as these lines appear in their criticism of formal verse he left behind, they also testify to the profound influence that formal verse had on Wright's free verse, specifically the well-placed interstices between his words.

* * *

Since MFA programs have proliferated so profusely around the country (there are now more than two hundred), the emphasis on teaching prosody, starting with the iambic line, has become almost passé. But it is clear just how influential early formal training was in instilling a verbal music in the aforementioned poets from one and two generations ago, even after they turned to free verse as their primary mode of expression. By contrast, the line in so much free-verse poetry today seems merely token and even moot—so much chopped-up prose—which begs the question: how many free-verse poems over the last half century would have worked better as prose or hybrid poems? How does the increasing dearth of verbal music-making redound on line-making? If budding poets in MFA programs aren't memorizing enduring poems from the past by such poets as Gerard Manley Hopkins, John Donne, William Shakespeare, Walt Whitman, Emily Dickinson, Thomas Wyatt, John Keats, Wallace Stevens, Elizabeth Bishop, Samuel Taylor Coleridge, George Herbert, Robert Lowell, William Wordsworth, Geoffrey Chaucer, John Berryman, William Carlos Williams, Thomas Traherne, Galway Kinnell, William Blake, James Wright, John Clare, Langston Hughes, Sylvia Plath, Marianne Moore, Gwendolyn Brooks, Allen Ginsberg, Ruth Stone, and Lucille Clifton, then what poetic foundation undergirds their own new music, whether formal or not?

* * *

It is nearly impossible to predict the fate of a particular poem or style within its particular epoch. Libraries are full of forgotten poems that were once considered important and even classic, so why make any aesthetic argument for one kind of poetry over another? For the purpose of this essay, I'm primarily interested in examining the historical function of the poetic line in the throes of free verse's current evolution on the ever-sharper cutting edge of "the new." Just what prosodic feature does poetry inherently possess that distinguishes it from prose? I think of the following quote by Sam Hamill as a cogent starting point, addressing the question of poetry's verbal legacy in light of the current rage to blur the poetic line—that is, to call into question the literary precepts that have defined poetry throughout the ages.

> Poetry transcends the nation-state. Poetry transcends government. It brings the traditional concept of power to its knees. I have always believed poetry to be an eternal conversation in which the ancient poets remain contemporary, a conversation inviting us into other languages and cultures even as poetry transcends language and culture, returning us again and again to primal rhythms and sounds.

In the irrepressible, ever-evolving, experimental process of "making new," many poets today are finding the traditional line inadequate for their urge for liminal and hybrid forms that obviate the line. Which raises the question: How can a poet write poetry without lines? Ride his or her bike not only without his hands but without his feet as well? Open almost any new book of poetry by a young poet today and observe the vast range of forms and shapes of the poems. The line between prose and poetry has blurred in poetry's current marketplace to the point where what used to be called lyrical essays are now appearing on the shelf as poetry. Claudia Rankine's Citizen is perhaps the most famous example. There are many other examples, and not just from the present day, as in this passage from Matthew Hittinger's essay "On the Transformative Power of Hybrid Forms," which appeared in the journal *Memorious*:

> As Virginia Woolf writes, "English is a mixed language, a rich language; a language unmatched for its sound and colour, for its power of imagery and suggestion...." And if the very words with which we work, our basic tools "of imagery and suggestion" are of a hybrid nature, and the "sound and color" of those words can and often do dictate form, then the forms themselves can and oftentimes must go hybrid. But what do I mean when I refer to hybrids, to hybrid forms, and to whom do we look for such forms? Where will we find such writing? In her book *Art Objects*, Jeanette Winterson writes: "We can only look for writers who know what tradition is, who understand modernism within that tradition, and who are committed to a fresh development of language and to new forms of writing.

Reginald Shepherd, the brilliant poet and essayist who died at the age of forty-five in 2008, addressed the profound "richness" of the

English language in a trenchant credo not long before he passed away. The literary *agon* he describes so eloquently here redounds prophetically on today's genre fluidity:

> My relationship to the Western literary canon (as if there were such a single and singular thing) has always been paradoxical: there is both no place already assigned to me and more of a possibility of creating a place for me than the world at large has offered. I have been oppressed by many things in my life, but not by literature, which for me has always represented potential and not closure. I would like to develop a poetic language capacious enough to accommodate all the things my previous books have tried to do, to span the multiple gaps between traditional and experimental poetry, personal poetry and political poetry: a poetic language, based in the lyric which I refuse to surrender or repudiate, which, holding in balance critique and creation, can be all of these poetries by turns or even all at once. This is undoubtedly an impossible ambition, but Allen Grossman has reminded us that all poems are attempts at poetry which remains an asymptote, never attained but always to be striven for. For me, there is no point in writing if not to attempt what one has not done and perhaps cannot do.

Shepherd's thoughts on his "relationship to the Western canon" provide a refreshing and poignant corrective to the increasingly tendentious craze to balkanize American poetics, especially given the "capacious" nature of literature and its tradition, echoing Whitman's opening paragraph in his 1855 preface to *Leaves of Grass*:

> America does not repel the past or what it has produced under its forms or amid other politics or the idea of castes or the old religions ... accepts the lesson with calmness ... is not so impatient as has been supposed that the slough still sticks to opinions and manners and literature while the life which served its requirements has passed into the new life of the new forms ... perceives that the corpse is slowly borne from the eating and sleeping rooms of the house ... perceives that it waits a little while in the door ... that it was fittest for its days ... that its action has descended to the stalwart and well-shaped heir who approaches ... and that he shall be fittest for his days.

Seventy years after Whitman published his first edition of *Leaves of Grass* in 1855, T. S. Eliot echoed Whitman's belief in tradition as an invaluable literary underpinning for any writer in his essay "Tradition and the Individual Talent":

> The existing order is complete before the new work arrives; for order to persist after the supervention of novelty, the whole existing order must be, if ever so slightly, altered; and so the relations, proportions, values of each work of art toward the whole are readjusted; and this is conformity between the old and the new. Whoever has approved this idea of order, of the form of European, of English literature will not find it preposterous that the past should be altered by the present as much as the present is directed by the past. And the poet who is aware of this will be aware of great difficulties and responsibilities.

Whitman's phrase "with calmness" presents perhaps the greatest challenge for today's poets in their struggle to discover "the life of the new forms" in the profusion of today's poetry publications. Neither Whitman nor Eliot could have predicted our current literary culture, in which so many volumes of poetry are published in hard copy and online every week that not even the Library of Congress can accommodate them. Amid such an unwieldy volume of new volumes, some that are brilliant and deserving of wider attention must go unread. The blessing of so much "daily" new poetry is therefore also a curse, for who can possibly keep up with all the "groundbreaking new work"?

Is it not surprising, then, that hybrid and liminal poetry has become an au courant "form" in a cultural zeitgeist that requires prodigious speed-reading, a kind of reading that poetry by its very lapidary nature resists? We now live in an unprecedented epoch, in which any responsible reviewer, critic, pundit, or *cognoscente* must confess to his or her ignorance of the hidden gems in the literary market's glut. If poets and critics felt acutely "aware of great difficulties and responsibilities" during Eliot's age, then they must feel the impossibility of reading responsibly now.

How blurry can the blurred line between verse and hybrid poetry become before it disappears altogether? In a 2003 Web del Sol roundtable discussion titled "Avant, Post Avant and Beyond," hosted by the poet Joan Houlihan, Kent Johnson attempted to answer this question with a trenchant peroration:

> Poetry is not so much about the two-dimensional issues of whether your unit of measure is feet or sentences, whether on the page you are thematically narrative or abstract, lyrical or non-syllogistic; it's about the four-dimensional challenges of how your self and non-self relate to poetry's total space, to how you are going to negotiate those ritualized modes of production and branding that are regarded—by Language, Post-Language, Pittsburgh UP, New Formalist, Cowboy, and Performance poets alike—as more or less natural and happily ancillary to the nature of the "poem proper."

To move poetic indeterminacy into the "practice of life," it is not enough to "torque" the linguistic sign, as the Language poets have believed; one must begin to torque the key cultural sign that fixes poetic practice in institutional frames of classification and control—the sign of authorship proper to which traditional and avant-garde wings in our poetry are identically beholden. The theater of poetry is still confined to its set stage; but there are certainly dimensions of poetic performance and possibility waiting to be unleashed beyond it. When that happens, one might predict that poetry will derive its mystery and force not so much from what it is "on the page" as from what it is *in the world*.

* * *

Since free verse has been the dominant form in American poetry over the past seventy years, beginning with the publication of Allen Ginsberg's *Howl* in 1955, and then the appearance of James Wright's *The Branch Will Not Break* in 1961, a majority of American poets have engaged in devising their own "meter-making arguments," leaving behind the prosody of received forms with an abandon that James Wright claimed in a letter to his friend Robert Bly was necessary for him to continue writing. "There is blood in it," he confessed. But now, nearly six decades later in 2019, poets are asking, what lies beyond the line? The innocuous phrase "poetic prose" fails to capture the vibrancy of the "new," as does also the phrase "lyrical essay." If the next line no longer serves as the primary answer to this question as the verbal "partner" that catches the meaning and music of its previous line in the drama of midair—verse poetry's stage—then what does? Perhaps free verse in today's mercurial literary zeitgeist has grown too token in its arbitrary line breaks—too much like the continuous line of prose whose periods disregard the physiological punctuation of breath or heartbeat—to answer this question. But what does answer it? Just as Whitman stressed the importance of literary tradition as integral to America's new poetry, in his self-acclaimed role as America's literary hierophant and visionary, he also gazed prophetically into the future, abjuring "poets to come" to compose "the main things" in a poem that reads as fresh today as it did in the late nineteenth century:

Poets to Come

POETS to come! orators, singers, musicians to come!
Not to-day is to justify me, and answer what I am for;
But you, a new brood, native, athletic, continental, greater than
    before known,
Arouse! Arouse—for you must justify me—you must answer.

I myself but write one or two indicative words for the future,
I but advance a moment, only to wheel and hurry back in the
    darkness.

I am a man who, sauntering along, without fully stopping, turns
    a casual look upon you, and then averts his face,
Leaving it to you to prove and define it,
Expecting the main things from you.

A century and a half after Whitman wrote this prophetic challenge, not only has the practice of line become obscured, but also the line between genres. In this present age of gender fluidity, environmental eschatology, and unprecedented connectivity, poets and critics are risking new definitions as never before in their wildly heterodox attempts "to prove and define it"—"the main things." But can the "main things" in any age include an almost complete rejection or obfuscation of the definitions of forms themselves, and by proxy, the tradition in which these forms were codified? Whitman himself blurred the poetic line radically in his own age, as the prophetic American harbinger that Emerson prophesied: that genius who would introduce groundbreaking "meter-making arguments." But one can only wonder what Whitman would have thought of Matthew Zapruder's blurb for James Tate's new and final book, *The Government Lake*, in which he praises Tate for avoiding distinguishing features of poetry altogether: "In his late narrative poetry, [Tate] was stripping away any of the accepted signifiers of free verse poetry, in order to see what remains when all things that usually tell us we are reading poetry are gone." But Tate is not the only poet finding new, radical, lineless "forms" that vacillate between hybrid and liminal expression. Others include Maggie Nelson (*The Argonauts*); Anne Carson (*Autobiography of Red*; *Glass, Irony and God*; *Float*; *Nox*); Brenda Miller (*Tell It Slant*; *An Earlier Life*); John D'Agata (*Halls of Fame*); Matthea Harvey (*If the Tabloids Are True What Are You?*); Elizabeth Powell (*Willy Loman's Reckless Daughter*); Eileen Myles (*Evolution*); Mary Ruefle (*My Private Property*); Bruce Smith's long poem "Lewisburg" in his new book, *Spill*; Claudia Rankine (*Citizen*); Ilya Kaminsky (*Deaf Republic*); and GennaRose Nethercott (*The Lumberjack's Dove*)—again, to mention only a few.

If poets have viewed the line and poetic forms over time as inexhaustible vessels for poetry, what exactly is compelling poets in the first half of the twenty-first century to forsake the line for liminal and hybrid expression? Is it an adherence to poetry's inherent compulsion to renew itself radically even in its most distinguishing features? An outright rejection of patriarchal forms and rules? An obedience to the muse's wild dialectic, culminating in a contradictory synthesis? Poetry's ultimate, predictable embrace of breaking even its own most-established laws? A prevalent but undeveloped belief among hybrid and prose poets that poetry conforms to Heisenberg's universal principle of uncertainty—namely, that like subatomic particles, poetry can exist in two places at once in form and content? An accommodating unstructured form for those poets who are disinclined to compose a music of brokenness?

As for the prose poem, hybrid poetry's antecedent, it has been reinvented, although not that significantly, as flash and micro fiction. Baudelaire would, I imagine, disparage the labels *hybrid* and *liminal* as overly academic alternatives to his paradoxical phrase. In an essay about the prose poem Peter Johnson, the founder and editor of the journal *The Prose Poem*, opined:

> When it comes to deciding on whether a work of short prose is a prose poem, a flash fiction, a micro-essay, or any other short genre you can think up, no one seems to care anymore. "Forget about genre," people say, "All that matters, is if the piece is any good." Well, of course, but these same people forget to mention that what's "good" is very subjective.... What makes a discussion of the prose-poem-as-genre even more confusing is that it has a long history of borrowing from other genres, and it often does this playfully.... The best we can do is to argue that the prose poem exhibits certain characteristics, and even those characteristics are determined by the literary background and tastes of the person reading the prose poem. Any approach to it as a genre must necessarily be eclectic. When pressed, my go-to description of prose poetry is Michael Benedikt's. He writes that prose poetry "is a genre of poetry, self-consciously written in prose, and characterized by the intense use of virtually all the devices of poetry, which includes the intense use of devices of verse," except for the line break.

* * *

Two anecdotes about two senior poets who have recently passed away help illustrate the line's mercurial state and the extent of just how open the open forms became in the last half of the last century, with little or no adherence to traditional forms or prosody. The first involves Russell Edson, who, at a gathering of MFA students at New England College during an MFA residency in 2006, made the claim that prose poetry was more poetry than prose. A well-known verse poet in the audience took issue with Edson, arguing that only verse poetry, "by definition," was poetry and that prose poetry was essentially a misnomer. After several minutes of listening to the verse poet's vehement defense of poetry as a genre whose distinguishing feature was the line, Edson replied deferentially with a wry smile, "As long as a poem, no matter its form, contains 'poetry mind,' I think it's a poem."

The second anecdote involves Philip Levine, who was asked by a man in the audience at the Brattleboro Literary Festival following his reading, "Could you please tell me why you call your poems *poems*, because they seem more like prose to me?" Levine responded curtly, "I have my tricks" and left it at that. However, in a 2008 interview with Sally Dawidoff in *Poets and Writers*, he explained his "tricks" in the context of his poem "A Theory of Prosody":

> That poem, "A Theory of Prosody," was about the cat line, that narrow line. And people would say, "Why do you write in that line?" And I would say, "Well, *The New Yorker* pays by the line!" But that had nothing to do with it. What it had to do with was my total entrancement with Yeats's trimeter line and an effort to convert some of that energy that he could get in long passages into free verse. I wanted to write something that moved with the beauty and force of "Easter 1916": I thought, "You can't write a form more beautiful than this. This is so gorgeous." And when you want it to be epigrammatic, you can hold the lines up and make the rhymes consistent, when you want it narrative you can let it overflow—it's just such a supple, wonderful form. I had tried to do it in rhyme, in metrical poems, earlier, but now I was trying to do it in free verse. I just loved doing it, when I could do it right. You know, which certainly wasn't always."

Levine's ambivalence toward form and prose, which he confesses to in the same interview, is typical of a lot of poets who, for one reason or another, can't always explain why they prefer poetic prose over formal verse:

> So I started writing something, and I wrote a little piece about a Dutch doctor that I knew and loved. And it was the first good prose poem I ever wrote. And then I wrote a couple more, and they weren't any good (I published them, but they stunk). And then about six or seven years ago, I wrote a bunch, and I didn't do anything with them. And then one day a friend asked me if I had

any prose poems—he wanted to publish them—and I went back and looked at those poems, and I could see that each one had a kind of germ in it, and so I began rewriting them, and then I got the idea for more, still more.... And they were great fun to write, but I'm going to go back to verse now.

Despite the freedom that many poets like Philip Levine feel to switch back and forth between the prose poem and verse poetry, they also find themselves embroiled in the perennial argument about whether prose poetry is a legitimate poetic form. The poet Charles Coe captures both the humor and rancor of this endless academic debate in a risible observation he posted on Facebook about the poetic validity of the prose poem: "How many butter knife fights over the years in faculty lounges between guys in jackets with elbow patches arguing about what makes a prose poem?"

In the innovative American tradition of eschewing tradition, American poets, for better or worse, continue to experiment with forms and the line, as if they both contained endless malleable possibilities within the ever-elastic entity of poetry itself, supplanting keener formal sounds, as well as memorable free verse, with language that's increasingly amorphous, erased, theoretical, obscure, elusive, synchronic, and prosaic.

* * *

The lure of blurred lines in today's poetic climate reflects not only an iconoclastic urge to find new forms beyond the traditional ones—the line beyond the lines in poetry—but a form that also reflects the blend between genders—new hybrid and liminal forms following discontent with the old order. A form that accurately reflects the blur and ambiguity of trans as both verbal and physical reifications of natural but heretofore *verboten* human expression. But how far can such iconoclasm go without challenging the tenets of language itself, and risking vagueness to the point of irreconcilable contradiction? This seems a moot question for many experimental poets, including the hybrid poets mentioned above, so bold is their exploration. Breaking the broken line by making it continuous and still calling it poetry seems hardly a violation at all, since for many hybrid poets, hybrid and liminal expression weds poetry with prose in a way that makes overdue sense, as less of a question of form and rules than an effective (if iconoclastic) way of writing. The weight of tradition weighs hardly at all on more and more poets. Yet the question remains, if for no other reasons than organic and mnemonic ones: Does poetry lose its salt without the line? As the most restless genre, poetry has thrived from generation to generation since its earliest days by virtue of reinventing itself. Experimentation sustains its restive spirit.

In the midst of the rage over blurred lines, in which formal poets are offering a persuasive defense of the line as an essential component of poetry, lies the question: Do they even need to do this?

In a recent defense of the formal line, Marilyn Nelson—who writes in both formal and free verse—explained at the Brattleboro Literary Festival that she had written her poem "A Wreath for Emmitt Till" as an ambitious crown of sonnets in order to fix the tragic legacy of Emmitt Till "to memory"—her implication being that carefully wrought, rhyming, metrical lines best served her purpose in memorializing Till.

She joins other such accomplished contemporary new formalists as Marilyn Hacker, Richard Kenney, Stanley Plumly, Richard Wilbur, Dana Gioia, Stephen Sandy, Gjertrud Schnakenberg, Mark Jarman, Rodney Jones, Carol Frost, Andrew Hudgins, James Merrill, Carl Phillips, Maxine Kumin, Natasha Trethewey, J. Allen Rosser, T. R. Hummer, Wyatt Prunty, James Kimbrel, David Bottoms, Jay Wright, Sydney Lea, and Alfred Corn in feeling this way about the ancient lure of the metrical line.

* * *

As poetry continues to chart new territory in its quest for vital forms and expression in the twenty-first century, while at the same time continuing its tradition as that genre "that sounds better and means more" (Charles Wright), poets must face the refining heat of critical inquiry "with calmness" as they pursue their near-impossible task of making new paradoxical sense—not just for the usual iconoclastic reasons, but for musical reasons as well—the kind that Theodore

Roethke aspired to in his either/or credo in "In the Evening Air": "I'll make a broken music or I'll die."

In *99 Poets/1999: An International Poetics Symposium*, the expatriate Syrian poet Adonis charged all poets with this prophetic caveat:

> To save itself, poetry will need to progressively espouse the unknown eternal truths and refuse again and again to be regimented from the outside by any kind of ideology, system, or institution.... Poetry will have to advance by exploring regions the invader cannot reach.... The traditional view of the poem cannot survive, it will have to be transformed in its very structure. Just as the traditional concept of poetry has already broadened to exceed the limits of traditional forms of speech, so, in order to resist the utilitarian goals which nearly strangled it this century, in order to escape ideology, the structure of poetic language will have to open itself to more movement, and move always toward a concept of the total poem.[1]

More than two decades after Adonis wrote this eloquent call to his fellow poets to "espouse eternal truths" anew, American poets have taken up his challenge with startling boldness, in ways that hark back to Modernist poets' receptivity to Ezra Pound's exhortation to "break the back of the goddamn iamb." In light of hybrid poets' willingness to break the line altogether, one wonders what's left to break, and whether breaking forms continually is consistent with the goal of moving toward "a concept of the total poem." One must have faith in poetry itself.

2019

---

1. Translated by Pierre Joris.

Lone Strikers: Some Thoughts on the Legacy of Poetry in Vermont

> He knew a path that wanted walking;
> He knew a spring that wanted drinking;
> A thought that wanted further thinking;
> A love that wanted re-renewing.
> Nor was this just a way of talking
> To save him the expense of doing.
>
> — from "A Lone Striker" by Robert Frost

What makes Vermont such an appealing state to writers? According to Timothy Consedine, the regional economist for the U.S. Bureau of Labor Statistics' New England Information Office, a disproportionate number of authors live in Vermont relative to other states in the country, ranking it within "the top five states in terms of concentration of jobs within this category." Poets tend to hide in the open in Vermont without much worry of being recognized or harassed, which makes most of them feel right at home. In 2010, when I interviewed Galway Kinnell, I asked him why he had moved to Sheffield, Vermont, from New York in 1962; he responded: "The silence."

When my predecessor as Vermont poet laureate, Sydney Lea, and I ventured to edit an anthology of contemporary Vermont poets in 2015 titled *Roads Taken: Contemporary Vermont Poetry*, we included the work of more than ninety poets who had lived in Vermont for at least five years and published one or more books of poetry with a commercial press. But then we discovered twelve more poets who met our criteria a year later, prompting us to put out a second edition. And in the third edition (2022), published like the first two by Green Writers Press, the number had grown to 142. The poets range from unknown aspiring poets to such world-famous treasures as Robert Frost, Louise Glück, Robert Penn Warren, Ellen Bryant Voigt, Hayden Carruth, Galway Kinnell, and Ruth Stone.

According to the *Washington Post*, Vermont has the second-greatest number of working writers per capita among all the states. Why have so many poets gravitated to Vermont over the past century? The simple, easy, Yankee answer would be: It's in the water. Which really is as good an answer as any other, since the actual answer is as mysterious as Vermont's landscape itself. Yet one must be cautious about romanticizing Vermont too freely as such a special "poetic" state, for myriad great poets have written memorably in far less pastoral places.

So, pastoral beauty can be ruled out as a prerequisite for either poetic inspiration or the writing of strong poetry. Vermonters have to be careful, therefore, not to tout their state as superior in any way to other states despite its obvious splendor, lest they indulge in any unwarranted boosterism; for as all poets who are worthy of their muses' blessings understand implicitly, inspiration is supremely democratic, interior, surprising, and catholic, countervailing against any geographic or political hubris that only betrays a counterfeit muse.

But the question about Vermont's plethora of both prestigious and aspiring poets persists. Why so many? If it's not Vermont's inspirational landscape that's responsible for them and their remarkable poetry, then what is it? The answer is deceptive and perhaps a bit disappointing, especially to Vermonters. It's not that Vermont is so "poetic" per se as that it is both beautiful *and* hardscrabble, both stunning *and* austere, especially in the winter months. Vermont farmers, as predisposed to masochism as they are to ecstasy in their successes against the elements, live by the Yankee aphorism "Take what you want and pay for it." Its poets must abide by this also, for it is Vermont's essential calculus.

One cannot appreciate Vermont's poetry without first appreciating Vermonters' most salient character traits, namely their self-reliance, their perseverance, their mental toughness, their ingenuity, their creativity, their courage, and perhaps most famously, their contrariness. Although Vermont has existed as a state since 1791, it wasn't until 1928 that President Calvin Coolidge coined the phrase "brave little state" as a moniker lauding Vermont's intrepid heritage, particularly the Green Mountain Boys' surprising victories over British and Hessian troops during the Revolutionary War, the early settlers' relentless clearing of old-growth forests (more than 80 percent of the state's original woodlands) for grazing and farming, the prodigious construction of thousands of miles of stone walls, and the state's first legislators' attempt, under the leadership of Governor Thomas Chittenden, to declare Vermont a sovereign republic rather than join the union as the fourteenth state. So it is no surprise that several of Vermont's poets would rise to the occasion of capturing the dramas of their fellow Vermonters' fiercely independent, larger-than-life enterprises, as well as the empyreal beauty of Vermont's landscape. But it would take a while—more than a century after statehood, in fact—before a truly great poet would emerge with the gift to memorialize Vermont's "bravery" in poems destined to outlast their own epoch.

This poet was, of course, Robert Frost, who divined the reality of Vermont's hardships, ecstasies, griefs, loves, and terrain in poems that have become ingrained in New Englanders' collective psyche, as well as that of readers around the world. Vermont claimed Frost as its first poet laureate in 1961, despite the fact that he had also lived much of his life in New Hampshire and titled his 1923 Pulitzer Prize–winning book *New Hampshire*. In the long title poem, specifically its conclusion, he seems to state implicitly, and rather coyly, that despite preferring the plain life as a New Hampshire farmer, he'd rather live in Vermont than New Hampshire, at least for the inspirational view of Vermont's neighboring state across the Connecticut River. His first choice is vocational, his second, aesthetic. But there's his catch. As a poet he finds the task of writing about New Hampshire from his poet's seat in Vermont even more arduous as well as less lucrative than farming in New Hampshire, where he'd be paid by local patrons rather than by "a publisher in New York City." His hard-won solace emanates from his "lone striking" in Vermont as a poet:

> Well, if I have to choose one or the other,
> I choose to be a plain New Hampshire farmer
> With an income in cash of, say, a thousand
> (From, say, a publisher in New York City).
> It's restful to arrive at a decision,
> And restful just to think about New Hampshire.
> At present I am living in Vermont.

How fortunate indeed for Vermont that, after his mostly failed ventures as a farmer in the Granite State, Frost chose to make his home in the Green Mountain State, in Shaftsbury and Ripton, although several generations of poets throughout northern New England have stood on his shoulders to gaze anew at the landscapes he immortalized. But like Frost, poets who call Vermont their home have struck out on their own and "made new" in brave, big ways that belie the merely physical size of their state.

2020

What Do You Think?: Some Thoughts on Reading and Teaching Poetry

In memory of Thomas Lux

It is remarkable, the character of the pleasure we derive from the best books. They impress us with the conviction that one nature wrote and the same reads. We read the verses of one of the great English poets, of Chaucer, of Marvell, of Dryden, with the most modern joy,—with a pleasure, I mean, which is in great part caused by the abstraction of all time from their verses. There is some awe mixed with the joy of our surprise, when this poet, who lived in some past world, two or three hundred years ago, says that which lies close to my own soul, that which I also had well-nigh thought and said. But for the evidence thence afforded to the philosophical doctrine of the identity of all minds, we should suppose some pre-established harmony, some foresight of souls that were to be, and some preparation of stores for their future wants, like the fact observed in insects, who lay up food before death for the young grub they shall never see.

— Ralph Waldo Emerson, from "The American Scholar"

Literature holds meaning not as a content that can be abstracted and summarized, but as experience.... It is a participatory arena. Through the process of reading we slip out of our customary time orientation, marked by distractedness and superficiality, into the realm of duration... We hold in our hands a way to cut against the momentum of the times. We can resist the skimming tendency and delve; we can restore, if only for a time, the vanishing assumption of coherence. The beauty of the vertical engagement is that it does not have to argue for itself. It is self-contained, a fulfillment.

— Sven Birkerts, from *The Gutenberg Elegies*

When it comes to poetry, the particular "fulfillment" that Sven Birkerts alludes to in his quote above as the emotional and intellectual reward of reading tends to resonate more memorably in poetry than in fiction and nonfiction for its distilled language, and what W. H. Auden called its "memorable speech." The rare success of a memorable poem's verbal magic lies in its execution of mnemonic pleasure, new meaning, and oral music. When a poet writes a poem that rises to all three of these challenges, often largely unconsciously since the unconscious exists so often as the muse's hideout, she feels she can't take credit for what she's written. "I did not write it!" Ruth Stone often proclaimed to me near the end of her life when I asked her about why and when she had written a particular poem. While it is ultimately impossible to explain the compositional mystery behind a memorable poem, the one thing that an enduring poem displays is the happy marriage of emotion to the psyche in lapidary expression that balances the literal with the connotative. Not that this doesn't also occur in successful fiction, but such verbal economy has always defined the power of poetry for its efficacy in beguiling its reader both immediately and lastingly.

In 2017, only a small minority of Americans, 11.7 percent according the National Endowment of the Arts, read poetry. But why? It's no secret that most Americans don't have time to read poetry, especially poetry that isn't immediately accessible. And since the multifarious, often dense, figurative language of poetry intimidates most novice readers and nonreaders of poetry, poetry tends to sit on the back shelves of bookstores and libraries. Most American college students find little "use" for it as a promising vocational subject and tend consequently to believe that there are more important fields of study leading to gainful employment. This was my experience observing and teaching myriad undergraduates at a prestigious northeastern college for twenty-two years. Over the past fifteen years, this same attitude among the architects of higher education has led to a national curriculum of required courses dubbed STEM (science, technology, engineering, and math), which is less wholistic than the original STEAM curriculum (which includes art in the acronym). Omitting the A takes the steam out of the pedagogical vision for young American students.

In America's largely utilitarian culture, poetry tends to be viewed as a subjective literary art without any one instruction manual. Its verbal beauty appeals selectively and in often unwitting ways as essential, "memorable speech" first rather as an aesthetic art, as one witnesses, for instance, in so many citizens' admiration and even reverence for the language in that most seminal prose poem, the Declaration of Independence. But how to extrapolate from and extend beyond such institutional poetic appeal of a public poem like that to more everyday subjects? How to instill poetry into America's psyche as common, transformative language that even the government would celebrate, as, say, Brazil did by putting the picture of the poet Carlos Drummond de Andrade along with one of his poems on its fifty-cruzado banknotes? Poetry must be demythologized as a runic literary art in America if it is ever to reach a national audience in the way Andrade's poetry has in Brazil if it is to be valued as timeless language that functions, as Andrade wrote as a credo, "to awaken men and make children sleep."

In thinking about the primary conceit of this essay, I asked myself: If one had to pick an American poem has served for over a hundred years now since its publication in 1923 as an enduring riddle for understanding both the difficulty and immediate appeal of poetry, what would it be? There are many options, of course, but if I had to choose just one, I think it would be William Carlos Williams's poem "The Red Wheelbarrow," which descends so tightly:

> so much depends
> upon
>
> a red wheel
> barrow

glazed with rain
water

beside the white
chickens

When one searches for a correct interpretation of this poem's single enigmatic assertion, no sensible explanation comes immediately to mind. No sane reader could be blamed for thinking that this poem exposes an aborted assessment of something that needs further explanation. So why then give it any further thought? Williams, unlike Andrade in his credo, leaves his reader in the dark in his best-known poem's famous ellipsis. Even after close consideration, the poem reads more as an unfinished poetic puzzle than anything else. What exactly was Williams thinking when he wrote it, besides saying something incoherent about, of all things, a red wheelbarrow?

That's a more than fair question. One might assume from this poem that Williams preferred a nonsensical proclamation about an unspecified subject's need for a red wheelbarrow over and against any need to make sense of it. The poem's vagueness and seemingly purposeful disregard for poetry's "bad name" among many novice readers of poetry has no doubt contributed to poetry's reputation as being gratuitously esoteric, difficult, and inaccessible. Surely Williams anticipated his American readers' response to his little poem's seeming nonsense, but wrote it anyway. However, if one suspected while reading "The Red Wheelbarrow" for the first time in 1923, at the height of modernism, that more was going on than mere obfuscation, then she would have been correct in suspecting Williams's intention for this poem to be more of a hint at something that was "so much"—something, in fact, that he felt was ineffable, even in poetry. He took a bold poetic risk in trusting his reader to intuit his hint. He had recently read Ezra Pound's definition of an image as "an intellectual and emotional complex in an instant of time" and seemed, in his writing of "The Red Wheelbarrow," to be viewing his composition of the poem almost as an assignment for illustrating Pound's criterion for "the image."

When readers and students of poetry grasp this implicit definition of an image in Williams's poetic illustration of it, purposefully incomplete as it is without any explanation of what "so much" actually *is*, then they grasp the verbal efficacy of the word *image*, as well as the simultaneous psychic and emotional results it elicits. Williams purposefully omitted any explanation of just why the red wheelbarrow is the source of "so much" because he felt the image alone of the "red wheelbarrow" sufficed to imply his vague hyperbole, and also because he didn't want to compromise the painterly image of the wheelbarrow with any obvious literal reference or footnote. However, it's precisely this omission of an explanation of the wheelbarrow's figurative capacity that has ironically catapulted the poem into the worldwide fame it enjoys. So succinct and simple as "an intellectual and emotional complex in an instant of time" is William's poetic demonstration of how an image can trigger the reader's imagination that it has become a memorable epigram, not just for poets but readers of poetry throughout the country.

This is the poem's omitted footnote: Williams, a family doctor, wrote "The Red Wheelbarrow" on a prescription pad while tending to a boy dying of tuberculosis. During his vigil, he gazed out the window of the second-story tenement where the boy lived and saw a red wheelbarrow wet with rainwater beside some white chickens. The reader is, of course, ignorant of this when reading the poem for the first time, yet he or she doesn't need it to understand the electric power of the poem's imagery to enjoy it. It triggers other scenes and emotions in the reader as well as just the literal image itself.

A fascinating follow-up assignment after reading this poem is to ask students what exactly depends on this image, with the caveat that there is no right or wrong answer but rather simply something one feels is important in relation to a vital emotion or thought that this image evokes. When poetry isn't taught in this pedagogically open way, especially in students' early curricular stages, they are robbed of one of poetry's most exciting attributes, namely, its verbal power to transport them from the literal to the imaginative, from the mundane to the transcendent with language that doesn't even make conventional sense.

So, how to overcome students' initial off-putting experiences with poetry, as well as devise a comprehensive poetry curriculum for teachers of grades one through twelve? A contemporary language arts curriculum must include poetry as a subject that celebrates and affirms the imagination; it might include reading from such books as *Wishes, Lies, and Dreams* and *Rose, Where Did You Get That Red?* by Kenneth Koch, *Writing Down the Bones* by Natalie Goldberg, and *Poems and Stories for Extremely Intelligent Children of All Ages* by Harold Bloom if young minds at their formative stages of cognitive development are to develop a keen sense of poetry's vital aesthetics.

The strong American tradition of building a better mousetrap has led to a tendentiously utilitarian, capitalistic culture in which the arts, and poetry in particular, have ranked low in importance on both the cultural and industrial scales. Walt Whitman wrote, "The proof of a poet is that his country absorbs him as affectionately as he absorbs it." Perhaps American poets have failed to be affectionate enough toward their country, writing more as critical witnesses, as Allen Ginsberg famously did in his hallmark poem, "America," than as affectionate bards. But they have also felt largely ignored and excluded by politicians and pedagogues alike, which has had the adverse effect of causing them to become ingrown and rarified, unlike poets in Latin America, Russia, Japan, and Europe, where they are celebrated as gurus and national celebrities. Sit next to a Russian on a bus and most likely he or she, if asked, will recite entire passages from *Eugene Onegin*. In his recent collection *The Republic of Poetry*, Martín Espada concludes his title poem with this stanza, which he claims is precisely what happened to him the last time he visited Chile:

> In the republic of poetry,
> the guard at the airport
> will not allow you to leave the country
> until you declaim a poem for her
> and she says, Ah! Beautiful!

As Walt Whitman's work demonstrates, poetry doesn't have to be difficult or abstruse or academic, although when it does embody these qualities successfully, as in T. S. Eliot's "The Waste Land," it's often groundbreaking, epiphanic, and memorable.

Poetry has exploded in America over the past fifty years, largely due to the internet and the publication of thousands of new books of poetry and literary journals each year. And yet poetry remains largely a secret discipline for many aspiring poets. In an essay I wrote for Plume a few years ago titled "Can Poetry Save America?" I attempted to define poetry in this way:

> Poetry is a transformative language with the capacity to issue passports to its readers for entering transcendent realms of awareness where the mind broadens and affections deepen; where strange associations make striking new sense; where unlike things coalesce in figurative magic; where minuscule details turn into immense particulars; where "language means more and sounds better," as Charles Wright has claimed so succinctly; where language ends and silence begins; where the sayable defers profoundly to the unsayable.

After writing this, I realized that my attempt to capture the mercurial nature of poetry in any ultimately definitive way was futile. So, what to say when a high school or college student asks me or any poet to define poetry? Perhaps this: "I can't say, but I know it when I hear, see, and feel it for reasons I can't, nor would want to, describe to you, except in my own personal way. Here's an example: William Carlos William's poem 'The Red Wheelbarrow.' What do you think?"—the implication in my question being that one can't begin to define poetry without reading and rereading it. And then answering, "It's a magical bird that changes color and appearance in flight as it wings its way into your mind and heart."

2024

Acknowledgments

I am grateful to the editors of the following publications, where these essays first appeared:

Academy Of American Poets: "Silence Amidst the Crowd: Philip Levine's 'The Simple Truth' and 'Call It Music'"

Associated Writing Programs Chronicle: "The Nature of Voice"

Cortland Review: "Like a Book at Evening Beautiful but Untrue, Like a Book on Rising Beautiful and True"; "Getting It Right" (originally published as "The Trouble with Poetry"); "That Odor, That Other: On Louise Glück's 'Mock Orange' and Beyond"; "The Tradition of Resistance and Independence in American Poetry" (originally published as "Resistance and Independence in Contemporary American Poetry"); "A Tribute to the Current"

Green Mountains Review: "The Teasing Corners of Oblivion: On the Career and Poetry of Ruth Stone"

Green Writers Press: "Getting It Right" appeared in *Vermont Poets and Their Craft* (edited by Neil Shepard and Tamra Higgins, 2019)

Harvard Review: "He Who Remembers His Shoes: Charles Simic"; "Sad Friend"

The Literary Encyclopedia: "'Back to My Ohio': The Life and Poetry of James Wright" (originally published as "James Wright")

Marick Press: "Silence Amidst the Crowd: Philip Levine's 'The Simple Truth' and 'Call It Music'" appeared in *Sad Friends, Drowned Lovers, Stapled Songs* (edited by Chard deNiord, 2011)

New England Review: "The Place Where You Lie: James Wright's 'To the Muse'"

Plume: "Blurred Lines: Some Thoughts on Hybrid, Liminal, and Prose Poetry"; "'But They Have Dwindled': Wordsworth's 'Resolution and Independence' as a Modern-Day Cautionary Tale"; "Can Poetry Save America?"; "The Other"; "The Poetic 'Engine' in Flannery O'Connor's Fiction"; "What Do You Think?: Some Thoughts on Reading and Teaching Poetry"; "The Sublime Irony of Nothing and the Divine

Imagination"; "Suspense, Suspension, and the Sublime in the Poetry of Robert Frost"

Poetry International: "For Each Ecstatic Moment: Impossibility, Unknowing, and the Lyric"

Times Argus: "Swimming in the Drowned River of Contemporary American Poetry"

Valley News: "On Poetry: Looking Out from a Poem's Second-Story Window"

Vermont Magazine: "Lone Strikers"

I am deeply grateful to Michael Fleming and Katy Evans-Bush for their invaluable editorial acumen, assistance, and advice on these essays, and finally but not least, many thanks to Marc Vincenz of MadHat Press, for believing in this book.

Works Cited

Adonis (Ali Ahmad Sa'id Esber). *The Pages of Day and Night.* Translated by Samuel Hazo. Marlboro, VT: Marlboro Press; Evanston, IL: Northwestern University Press, 2001.

Alpaugh, David. "The New Math of Poetry." *Journal of Higher Education* (February 10, 2010).

Beckett, Samuel. *Waiting for Godot: A Tragicomedy in Two Acts.* Translated by the author. New York: Grove Press, 1954.

Birkerts, Sven. *The Gutenberg Elegies: The Fate of Reading in an Electronic Age.* London: Faber & Faber, 1994.

Bishop, Elizabeth. *The Complete Poems, 1927–1979.* New York: Farrar, Straus & Giroux, 1979.

———. *One Art: Letters.* Edited by Robert Giroux. New York: Farrar, Straus & Giroux, 1995.

Blake, William. *The Marriage of Heaven and Hell.* In *Blake: Complete Writings.* Edited by Geoffrey Keynes. London: Oxford University Press, 1966.

Bloom, Harold. *Poetry and Repression.* New Haven, CT: Yale University Press, 1976.

Buber, Martin. *I and Thou.* Translated by Ronald Gregor Smith. New York: Scribner, 1958.

Coleridge, Samuel Taylor. *Biographia Literaria.* Edited by Adam Roberts. Edinburgh, UK: Edinburgh University Press, 2014.

Dawidoff, Sally. "An Interview with Poet Philip Levine." *Poets and Writers,* March 10, 2008. https://www.pw.org/content/interview_poet_philip_levine.

deNiord, Chard. *Sad Friends, Drowned Lovers, Stapled Songs: Conversations and Reflections on 20th Century American Poets.* Grosse Pointe Park, MI: Marick Press, 2011.

deNiord, Chard, and Sydney Lea, eds. *Roads Taken: Contemporary Vermont Poetry.* 1st edition, 3rd edition. Brattleboro, VT: Green Writers Press, 2015, 2022.

Des Pres, Terrence. *Praises and Dispraises: Poetry and Politics, the 20th Century.* New York: Viking, 1988.

Dickinson, Emily. *The Poems of Emily Dickinson.* Reading Edition. Edited by R. W. Franklin. Cambridge, MA: Belknap Press, 2005.

———. *The Letters of Emily Dickinson.* Edited by Cristanne Miller and Domhnall Mitchell. Cambridge, MA: Harvard University Press, 2024.

Dostoyevsky, Fyodor. *The Brothers Karamazov.* Translated by Constance Garnett. London: Heinemann, 1912.

Eliot, T. S. *Selected Essays, 1917–1932.* New York: HarperCollins, 2014.

Emerson, Ralph Waldo. *Essays and Lectures.* Edited by Joel Porte. New York: Library of America, 1983.

Espada, Martín. *The Republic of Poetry.* New York: W. W. Norton, 2006.

Fitzgerald, F. Scott. *The Great Gatsby.* New York: Scribner, 1925.

Frost, Robert. *The Poetry of Robert Frost: The Collected Poems, Complete and Unabridged.* New York: Henry Holt, 1979.

———. *Selected Letters of Robert Frost.* Edited by Lawrence Thompson. New York: Holt, Rinehart & Winston, 1964.

Gilgamesh: A Verse Narrative. Translated by Herbert Mason. Boston: Houghton Mifflin, 1970.

Gioia, Dana. *Can Poetry Matter?: Essays on Poetry and American Culture.* Anniversary Edition. Minneapolis, MN: Graywolf Press, 2002.

Ginsberg, Allen. *Collected Poems, 1947–1980.* New York: HarperCollins, 1984.

Glück, Louise. *The First Four Books of Poems.* New York: Ecco Press, 1995.

Graver, Bruce. *Rome and the Romantics.* Oxford, UK: Oxford Academic, 2012.

Gunn, Thom. *Selected Poems.* New York: Farrar, Straus & Giroux, 2009.

Hall, Donald. *Poetry and Ambition.* Ann Arbor, MI: University of Michigan Press, 1988.

Hamill, Sam. Quoted in "Sam Hamill: Poetry, Politics, and Zen." *Vox Populi* (website), 2017. https://voxpopulisphere.com/2017/09/03/sam-hamill-poetry-politics-and-zen/.

Herbert, Zbigniew. *Selected Poems*. Translated by Bogdana and John Carpenter. Oxford, UK: Oxford University Press, 1977.

Hikmet, Nazim. *Poems of Nazim Hikmet*. Translated by Randy Blasing and Mutlu Konuk. New York: Persea Books, 1994.

Hittinger, Matthew. "On the Transformative Power of Hybrid Forms." *Memorious* 7 (2007).

Ingraham, Christopher. "Poetry Is Going Extinct, Government Data Show." *Washington Post*, April 24, 2015.

Jarrell, Randall. *No Other Book: Selected Essays*. Edited and with an Introduction by Brad Leithauser. New York: Perennial, 2000.

———. *The Complete Poems*. New York: Farrar, Straus & Giroux, 1969.

Johnson, Kent. Quoted in "Avant, Post-Avant, and Beyond: An email-assisted roundtable discussion hosted by Joan Houlihan." *Perihelion* (website), 2006. http://www.webdelsol.com/Perihelion/p-roundtable3.htm.

Johnson, Peter. "The Prose Poem and the Problem of Genre." *Plume* 94 (June 2019). https://plumepoetry.com/the-prose-poem-and-the-problem-of-genre/.

Johnson, Samuel. *The History of Rasselas, Prince of Abissinia*. Mineola, NY: Dover, 2005.

Kafka, Franz. *The Trial: A New Translation Based on the Restored Text*. Translated by Breon Mitchell. New York: Schocken Books, 1998.

Keats, John. *Selected Poems and Letters*. Edited by Douglas Bush. Boston: Houghton Mifflin, 1952.

Kierkegaard, Søren. *Attack upon Christendom*. Translated by Walter Lowrie. Princeton, NJ: Princeton University Press, 1968.

———. Fear and Trembling. In *A Kierkegaard Anthology*. Edited by Robert Bretall. Princeton, NJ: Princeton University Press, 1973.

Lawrence, D. H. *Tortoises*. New York: Thomas Seltzer, 1921.

Levertov, Denise. *O Taste and See*. New York: New Directions, 1964.

Levine, Philip. *Breath: Poems*. New York: Penguin Random House, 2006.

———. *The Simple Truth: Poems*. New York: Knopf, 1994.

Li Bai (Li Po). "Zazen on Ching-t'ing Mountain." In *Crossing the Yellow River: Three Hundred Poems from the Chinese*. Translated by Sam Hamill. Rochester, NY: BOA Editions, 2000.

Lorca, Federico García. *Theory and Play of the Duende*. Translated by A. S. Kline. Sackville, NB: Hardscrabble Press, 2022.

Lowell, Robert. *Life Studies*. New York: Farrar, Straus & Giroux, 1959.

Márquez, Gabriel García. "The Handsomest Drowned Man in the World." In *Collected Stories*. Translated by Gregory Rabassa and J. S. Bernstein. London: Jonathan Cape, 1991.

Merwin, W. S. *Migration: New and Selected Poems*. Port Townsend, WA: Copper Canyon Press, 2005.

Miłosz, Czeslaw. *The Collected Poems 1931–1987*. Translated by Czeslaw Miłosz. New York: Ecco Press, 1988.

Nussbaum, Martha. *The Fragility of Goodness: Luck and Ethics in Greek Tragedy and Philosophy*. Cambridge, UK: Cambridge University Press, 1986.

O'Connor, Flannery. *The Complete Stories of Flannery O'Connor*. New York: Farrar, Straus & Giroux, 1971.

———. *A Prayer Journal*. Edited by W. A. Sessions. New York: Macmillan, 2013.

Ovid. *The Erotic Poems*. Translated by Peter Green. London: Penguin Classics, 1983.

Pasternak, Boris. "It Is Not Seemly to be Famous..." Translated by Lydia Pasternak Slater. In *RuVerses: Russian Poetry in Translations* (website), n.d. https://ruverses.com/boris-pasternak/to-be-famous/4698/.

Petrarch, Francis. *The Canzoniere, or Rerum vulgarium fragmenta*. Edited and translated by Mark Musa. Bloomington, IN: Indiana University Press, 1999.

Pound, Ezra. *ABC of Reading*. Reading, UK: Cox & Wyman, 1934.

———. *The Pisan Cantos*. Edited by Richard Sieburth. New York, New Directions, 2003.

Rilke, Rainer Maria. *The Selected Poetry of Rainer Maria Rilke*. Translated by Stephen Mitchell. New York: Random House, 1982.

Roethke, Theodore. *Collected Poems*. New York: Anchor, 1974.

Ruefle, Mary. *A Little White Shadow*. Seattle, WA: Wave Books, 2006.

Rumi, Jalal al-Din. "Language." Translated by Fatemeh Keshavarz. *On Being* (website), 2024. https://onbeing.org/poetry/language/.

Santos, Sherod. *Greek Lyric Poetry: A New Translation*. New York: W. W. Norton, 2005.

Simic, Charles. *Dime-Store Alchemy: The Art of Joseph Cornell*. New York: New York Review Books Classics, 2011.

———. *New and Selected Poems: 1962–2012*. New York: Ecco Press, 2013.

Shelley, Percy Bysshe. "The Defence of Poetry." In *Criticism: The Major Texts*. Edited by W. J. Bate. New York: Harcourt Brace Jovanovich, 1970.

Shepherd, Reginald. *Contemporary Authors*. Republished in "Reginald Shepherd, 1963–2008." Poetry Foundation (website), 2024. https://www.poetryfoundation.org/poets/reginald-shepherd.

Stafford, William. *The Answers Are Inside the Mountains: Meditations on the Writing Life*. Edited by Paul Merchant and Vincent Wixon. Ann Arbor, MI: University of Michigan Press, 2003.

Stevens, Wallace. *The Auroras of Autumn*. New York: Alfred A. Knopf, 1950.

Stitt, Peter. *James Wright: The Heart of the Light (Under Discussion)*. Edited by Peter Stitt and Frank Graziano. Ann Arbor, MI: University of Michigan Press, 1990.

Stone, Ruth. *What Love Comes To: New & Selected Poems*. Port Townsend, WA: Copper Canyon Press, 2010.

Strand, Mark. *Elegy for My Father, Robert Strand 1908–1968*. Iowa City, IA: Pillar Guri Press, 1973.

Szybist, Mary. "Mary Szybist Accepts the 2013 National Book Award in Poetry." National Book Award speech (video), 2013. https://vimeo.com/80287662.

Trilling, Lionel. "A Speech on Robert Frost: A Cultural Episode." *Partisan Review* 26 (Summer 1959): 445–52.

Vico, Giambattista. *The New Science of Giambattista Vico: Unabridged Translation of the Third Edition (1744) with the addition of "Practic of the New Science."* Translated by Thomas Goddard Bergin and Max Harold Fisch. Ithaca, NY: Cornell University Press, 1984.

Weil, Simone. *Gravity and Grace.* Translated by Emma Craufurd. New York: Routledge & Kegan Paul, 1963.

Whitman, Walt. *The Complete Poems.* New York: Penguin, 2005.

———. *Specimen Days.* Edited by Max Cavitch. New York: Oxford University Press, 2023.

Williams, William Carlos. *The Collected Poems. Vol. 1, 1909–1939.* Edited by A. Walton Litz and Christopher MacGowan. New York: New Directions, 1986.

Wilmot, John. *The Complete Poems of John Wilmot, Earl of Rochester.* Edited by David M. Vieth. New Haven, CT: Yale University Press, 2002.

Wilson, Edmund. *Literary Essays and Reviews of the 1930s and 40s.* Edited by Lewis M. Dabney. New York: Library of America, 2007.

Wood, Ralph. *Flannery O'Connor and the Christ Haunted South.* Grand Rapids, MI: William B. Eerdmans, 2004.

Wright, James. *Above the River: The Complete Poems.* New York: Noonday Press, 1990.

———. *Selected Poems.* Edited by Robert Bly and Anne Wright. New York: Farrar, Straus & Giroux; Middletown, CT: Wesleyan University Press, 2005.

———. *A Wild Perfection: The Selected Letters of James Wright.* Edited by Anne Wright and Saundra Rose Maley, with Jonathan Blunk. New York: Farrar, Straus & Giroux, 2005.

Wunderlich, Mark. *God of Nothingness: Poems*. Minneapolis, MN: Graywolf Press, 2021.

Yeats, W. B. *Collected Poems*. London: Macmillan, 1979.

About the Author

Chard deNiord is the author of nine books of poetry: *Westminster West* (Tupelo Press, 2025), *Bestiary*, with the artist Brian Cohen (Bridge Press, 2023), *In My Unknowing* (University of Pittsburgh Press, 2020), *Interstate* (University of Pittsburgh Press, 2019), *The Double Truth* (University of Pittsburgh Press, 2011), *Speaking in Turn with Tony Sanders* (Gnomon Press, 2011), *Night Mowing* (University of Pittsburgh Press, 2005), *Sharp Golden Thorn* (Marsh Hawk Press, 2002), *Asleep in the Fire* (University of Alabama Press, 1990), as well as three books of interviews with eminent American poets: *Sad Friends, Drowned Lovers, Stapled Songs* (Marick Press, 2011), *I Would Lie to You if I Could* (University of Pittsburgh Press, 2018), and *Learning to Be Everyone and No One* (University of Alabama Press, 2025).

He cofounded the Ruth Stone Foundation with Bianca Stone and her husband, Ben Pease, in 2010, and then served as a trustee of the Ruth Stone Trust and board member of the Ruth Stone Foundation from 2010 to 2021.

In 2001, along with Jacqueline Gens and Gerald Stern, he cofounded the MFA Program in Poetry at New England College, which he then codirected with Jacqueline Gens until 2008. He retired in the spring of 2020 from teaching English and Creative Writing at Providence College, where he is now Professor Emeritus.

He is currently the essay editor at *Plume*, an online poetry magazine, and he serves as a board member of the Sundog Poetry Center in Vermont; he's also the poetry director of the Bookstock Poetry Festival in Woodstock, Vermont. From 2015 to 2019 he served as Vermont's Poet Laureate.

With his wife, the artist and ceramist Liz Hawkes deNiord, he lives in Westminster West, Vermont, where he gardens, writes, and poses for his wife's abstract paintings.

www.ingramcontent.com/pod-product-compliance
Lightning Source LLC
Chambersburg PA
CBHW020050170426
43199CB00009B/233